Jesus of Nazareth

KING OF THE JEWS

VOLUME 1

JESUS OF NAZARETH

WHAT IF THE GREATEST MAN WHO EVER LIVED,
LIVED FOREVER?

STEPHEN HOUSER

A Novel by Stephen Houser

Copyright © 2018 by Stephen Houser

Lionel A Blanchard, Publisher

All rights reserved. No part of this publication may be reproduced, stored in a retrieval system, or transmitted, in any form or by any means, electronic, mechanical, photocopying, recording, or otherwise, without the prior written permission of the author.

This is a work of fiction. Names, characters, places, and incidents either are the product of the author's imagination or are used fictitiously.

Any resemblance to actual persons, living or dead, events, or locales is entirely coincidental.

First Printing

Ltd. Ed. Hardcover ISBN: 978-0-9972984-4-4

Hardcover ISBN: 978-09972984-5-1

Softcover ISBN: 978-0-9972984-6-8

Cover Art and Design by Vincent Chong

Printed in the United States of America

*Dedicated to the God-man in my life,
William G. Houser, my father*

CHAPTER ONE

The dead man looked at him, blue eyes staring. The boy looked back. *You can't be here* was all he could think. The eyes gazed at him, distant and melancholy. *No*, the boy wanted to cry out. *You're dead! You're dead!*

He sat up in his bed and looked around the dark room. No one was there. It was just a dream, a sad and tragic dream. The master was indeed dead, killed, and buried. He knew that because he had seen it all himself. Jesus wasn't there, and he wasn't ever coming back.

He glanced out the open window. The sky was black. It was midnight, or later. Why wasn't his brother awake? James was the oldest and should have been up by now. He got up and crossed the room to his brother's bed. He wanted to shake James a good one, but that would wake up everyone in the house.

People said they looked alike, James and John, the sons of Zebedee. They both had black curly hair, square faces, and hooded brown eyes. They did look alike, along with just about every other Hebrew male in Israel. Except for Jesus. He had pale skin, long, wavy auburn hair, freckles on his nose, and, of course, those blue eyes. Everyone knew that his handsome face and blue eyes had come from his famous ancestor King David.

John reached down and touched his brother's shoulder. James was wearing a robe and had a plain wool blanket pulled up to his chin. He looked like he was sleeping the sleep of the innocent. John shook his head. Enjoy that, brother, he thought, for after tonight you and I will be wanted for sedition, theft, and maybe murder. How many broken commandments was that? Two for sure. He wasn't sure about sedition.

John reached down and grasped his brother's shoulder. He shook it. James sat up and held the tip of a fish gutting knife at John's throat. John didn't breathe. Slowly his brother recognized him and lowered the knife. James pulled his blanket down and stood up. He slipped into his leather sandals and brushed off his white wool robe, the color of the Hebrew tribe of Zebulon. James walked silently through the dark house, pushed aside the heavy blanket hung in front of the outside door, then waved John out and followed him.

Houses were crammed along the narrow Jerusalem street, simple one-room wood-and-plaster dwellings whitewashed to deflect the heat of the sun. This neighborhood housed the impoverished and the almost impoverished. Yet there was also an occasional two- or three-level limestone house stuck like a thumb in the eye of this poor neighborhood because the land was cheap. The rich tore down the old houses and built mansions with vine-covered arbors for shade and sanctuary. In Jerusalem's hot dry climate, the poor named such green parcels Paradise. Off limits Paradise.

John had heard Jesus promise one of the criminals crucified next to him that they would be together in Paradise that very day. The real Paradise. Some Jews believed that after a person died there was only the void. Other more hopeful Hebrews thought that one's dead body would be raised by Jehovah at the end of time to live in a new Jerusalem. However, John didn't know *anyone* who believed that when the breath of life left your body it went straightaway to live with God. John shook his head. How had that worked out for Jesus?

The street was dark and quiet. James and John were the only ones out and about.

"What woke you up?" James asked his brother.

"I dreamed the master was looking at me."

"That can't happen. His body is bound in linen and myrrh."

"I said it was a dream," John said, defending himself. "Anything can happen in a dream."

The brothers walked on in silence wondering about the significance of John's dream. Jesus was dead. And gone. John had witnessed the Roman centurion thrust his sword up behind Jesus' ribcage and pierce his heart. The master's body had not even twitched.

He had watched as a friend of Jesus named Joseph of Arimathea and his son had lowered Jesus from the cross and carried him to a waiting wagon. Mary, Jesus' mother, followed it, along with another young woman named Mary Magdalene. John had walked beside them feeling miserable and alone.

All of the other disciples, including his brother James, had rushed into hiding afraid of Pontius Pilatus, the military commander of Judea. They were sure he would be scouring Jerusalem for Jesus' followers, now enemies of the Emperor Tiberius. What a laugh, John thought. Enemies of the emperor. That Roman *zaqencock* had holed himself up in his summer palace on Capri with a spate of young boys and had left the running the empire to others.

Before the disciples became quivering masses of jelly following Jesus' arrest, they had donned straight faces and warned John that the emperor's Praetorian Guards were prowling the city looking for pretty young Hebrew boys to ship off to the ancient pedophile. John didn't like being teased about that. There were some things worse than being crucified.

"Where are you going?" he asked his brother, following him through deserted Jerusalem in the middle of the night.

"We are meeting the master's two brothers," James replied. "They have money to bribe the guards at the tomb."

So plan A was actually an attempted bribe. Plan B was stealing Jesus' body and running for their lives.

Though believers, Jesus' brothers, James and Jude, had not been at his crucifixion either, had not seen him suffer, had not seen him die broken-hearted. "My God, my God," Jesus had cried in his anguish. "Why have you forsaken me?"

Jesus' dead body had been laid on a limestone slab inside Nicodemus' personal tomb, the same man who had now anted up a fortune to have his body spirited away from it. John had looked at the ruin of Jesus' flesh. Ribbons of skin and muscle hung from his chest and shoulders, ripped loose by Roman whiplashes. His back was completely flayed, only clotted blood and shredded muscle remained.

His hands and feet had gaping holes where they had been ripped off the nails, black pools filled with splintered bones and clotted blood. Even Jesus' face had been ruthlessly abused, bashed and bruised by clubs and brass knuckles, and a plaited crown of thorn branches had been crushed down over his head by soldiers who mocked him, saying, "Hail, Jesus of Nazareth, King of the Jews!"

John had watched the women clean and wrap Jesus' body. Oddly, no one had closed the master's eyes. He bent over and looked into them. At first it felt like they were looking back. But no, they were devoid of the master's spark and humor. Now they were just two orbs of blue emptied of light. John reached down and closed them. The lids were soft and yielding.

Mary told John to kiss Jesus goodbye. The master's body was wrapped tight in linen strips smeared with an unguent of myrrh. She held a small embroidered cloth she had made. When everyone had said their farewells she would place it over Jesus' face. John kissed Jesus' cool cheek and Mary Magdalene did as well. Then Mary, Jesus' mother, kissed both of his cheeks, looked at his face for a long moment, then slowly and gently laid the funeral cloth over his face.

Weeping, she turned and left the tomb. Mary Magdalene followed her. John departed last, glancing at the wrapped body on the limestone slab as he left. He knew that it was truly Jesus' cadaver, but how could he believe it? How could Jesus of all men be dead? Hadn't he said that God was his father and that he himself was divine? The same yesterday, today, and forever. He had said those exact words. Yet he was none of those things. He was a poor murdered fool. Captured and exposed. Crucified, dead, and buried.

A Roman centurion and two soldiers arrived. The officer inspected the tomb and lifted the cloth off of Jesus' face. He was the Centurion Longinus, son of Pomponius, and he had presided over Jesus' crucifixion. Longinus dealt with death every day. He's seen too many dead bodies to think or care where anyone went after death. He just knew that they didn't come back.

He replaced the cloth and ordered the two soldiers to roll the great round stone outside the tomb down its track to block the entrance. They did, whereupon the centurion pasted warm wax where the stone touched the channel and impressed the seal of his own ring into it, certifying that he had observed a very dead Jesus of Nazareth inside, and closed the tomb.

John followed the two Marys to the house where they were staying. They wept and moaned, keening in the dark for the man they had laid to rest. John did not cry, but he knew in his sorrowful heart that he would never recover from loving and losing Jesus of Nazareth.

John had planned to return to Galilee the next day, but his brother James told him that some of Jesus' disciples wanted to remove the master's body from Nicodemus' tomb and hide it where it could not be found. John was shocked. They wanted to steal Jesus' body? James told him that the Lord's remains not only had to be made safe from desecration by vengeful enemies, but also protected from fanatical scavenging by grieving followers wishing to take some remnant of his clothing or corpse.

"Besides us," John asked, "who else is going to the tomb?"

"Two friends and a man with a donkey and wagon to carry the body."

"Which friends?"

"Disciples. Judas, and—"

"Judas?" John hissed. "I thought he was dead!"

"Far from it. He may have triggered the events that led to Jesus' capture, but he never moved a finger without the master's permission."

"I don't believe it."

"You don't have to believe it, but Judas is coming with us."

John grimaced and kicked the cobblestone road. Judas was a betrayer, a turncoat, the very devil who'd led the Romans to the Garden of Gethsemane where the teacher was praying. He had disappeared afterwards, only to be spotted later hanging from a tree in the Valley of Gehenna where Jerusalemites burned their garbage. It was a fitting place for trash such as he, but if Judas was coming to the tomb now then the rumors of his death had just been hopeful exaggerations.

"First he betrays our master and now he's going to betray the Romans," John whined.

"He's going to *double-cross* the Romans," James corrected him harshly. "Do you know the difference?"

"Don't know and don't care," John said. "I never want to see him again."

James shook his head, but didn't bother to protest. Truth be told, he didn't really want Judas around either. None of the disciples liked him. Jesus had welcomed him, even though he was a Sicarii, a member of the Jewish terrorists who kidnapped and murdered Roman soldiers and officials. Go figure.

"Tell me at least that the big clown has not been invited," John said, resuming the conversation.

"Simon is the other sword."

"That stupid jackass?"

"We may need big and strong tonight."

"Well, good luck to us all then," John said sarcastically. "Let's hope he can do better than lop ears off."

James grinned, but made sure his brother didn't see it. They walked on, skulking through the winding alleys of the inner city, dodging Roman sentries and hiding in the shadows. At last James stopped and knocked softly on the door of a large two-story limestone house. John knew the place. A tall and heavy silver-haired man opened the door a crack, recognized James, and motioned for them to enter. He led the brothers up a set of wooden stairs anchored against the inside wall of his house and stepped through an open doorway into the upper story.

Both James and John stopped and gazed at the room, the place where only three nights earlier they had shared a last supper with Jesus. There were several round olivewood tables with dining couches next to them. Sitting together on one of them were Jesus' brothers James and Jude. Both men were short and dark, the sons of Joseph's desire and Mary's body. They wore sky-blue wool robes identifying them as Judeans.

"How do you fare?" Jude asked them, rising and offering each brother a kiss on the cheek. He was no more than twenty, blessed with the perfect oval face of his mother Mary and colored dark like his swarthy black-haired father. His younger brother James looked more like Joseph with chiseled good looks, possessing an agile mind and a clever tongue. Jude handed a small leather bag to James who took it and shoved it into a secret pocket inside his robe. It was gold from Nicodemus to be offered to the Roman guards for Jesus' body. Gold or blood, it would be their choice.

"Where are the others?" he asked Jude.

"Simon and Judas have hired a driver with a wagon and donkey and are waiting in the garden by the tomb."

"Is Simon clear on the fact that he is not to draw his sword except to save our lives?"

Jude nodded.

"I told him to leave it in his sheath unless you cry out for help."

John looked around the room.

"Everything is still here from Passover," he said wistfully. Memories of that final supper tugged at his heart.

"It seems impossibly long ago," James, Jesus' brother, commented to John. "Even *your* baby face has aged in the days and nights since then."

Tears welled up in John's eyes.

"He let me recline next to him at dinner. He said I was his favorite."

His brother James ruffled his black curls with his hand.

"You are *all* of our favorites," he said, tenderly.

"Where will you take the body," Jude asked, "assuming that you gain possession of it?"

"Well, we can't go far with it, at least not tonight," James answered. "We were thinking maybe Nicodemus' house for now, or that of Joseph of Arimathea."

"Why not just bury him," James, Jesus' brother asked, "in an anonymous grave that only the disciples know about? Cleopas, the owner of the olive grove at Gethsemane, was a follower of Jesus. I'm sure you could get his permission to bury the master there."

It made sense. The man had loved Jesus. He could provide a place where Jesus could be secretly buried and very few would ever know that he was hidden there. Jude looked at the three men in the upper room.

"Gethsemane then?" he asked.

Each of them nodded. The olive grove was close and it was safe. Jesus' interment could be concealed. The owner of the house brought a tray with a silver pitcher of wine and silver cups for each of them. He was old, but he had loved Jesus, too. Each disciple took a cup.

Their host poured red wine mixed with water into all of them. John remembered Jesus' words as he held the Passover cup. "This is my blood poured out for you. When you drink it remember me." John hadn't understood then what Jesus meant. But he knew now. He had seen Jesus' blood poured out and he would never drink wine again without remembering his crucified Lord.

"We have to go," James told Jesus' brothers. He embraced each of them. "Pray that we see each other again."

"I am sure that we will," Jude told him. "May the Lord bless and keep you until that day."

Jesus' brothers left. James and John left as well. James led his brother further through the ancient neighborhoods of old Jerusalem, descending past the ruins of David's palace and down the narrowest, darkest alleys of the old city heading for the Jaffa Gate and the tombs outside the city.

Roman soldiers were posted at the gate. James and John walked past them. "Don't bother to come back," one of the soldiers called after them. The rest of the soldiers laughed.

"Anti-social asses," another soldier shouted at them.

James and John kept walking. That insult was as old as the Roman presence in Israel. Calling Jews asses was scurrilous homage to the rumor that donkeys were sacrificed in the Temple. James and John went on, ignoring the pagan occupiers who themselves slit bulls' throats and divined bird guts. They were so much more mature than Jews, John thought, and grinned.

The night skies were overcast. There were no stars to see, no moon to guide their footsteps as the brothers headed for the forested hills looming ahead. The hillsides were dotted with carved tombs sealed tight by large stone wheels that were only rolled back to admit the newly dead.

Judas and Simon stepped out of the shadows. Simon put his hand on John's shoulder and a finger to his lips. Silence. John shook Simon's hand away. What did the dope think he was going to do, shout out greetings and salutations? James kissed Judas' cheek, then Simon's. John stayed away from both of them. If that offended them, they didn't show it.

Simon was not tall, but was barrel-chested and loud, both traits making him seem bigger than he really was. He had shaggy brown hair that he never washed, unless one counted the times he jumped into the Sea of Galilee to pull in a fish net. He wore a white robe of the tribe of Zebulon. Judas had an undyed wool robe and a red vest for the tribe of Rueben. He was the only disciple who was not a fisherman.

Ironically, stories had circulated that as a baby he had been locked in a chest and thrown into the Sea of Galilee after his mother had been told by a fortune-telling sibyl that he would grow up and murder his father. Truth be told, he looked the part. He wore his black hair short and slicked it back with olive oil. He had a gaunt mean face, a narrow moustache, and a pointed beard on his chin which made his face appear long and sinister. Though he was only in his mid-thirties, white hairs sprouted on his chin that he covered with black wax. The net effect of Judas' features rendered him creepy and unpleasant to look at, which was very likely the effect he wanted to achieve.

Even Jesus had once commented that Judas looked like one of the mysterious Nizari. "The knife-wielding Persian assassins," Judas had asked? He then flashed his own twisted Sicarii blade.

"No, the hash-eating Nizari," Jesus answered, looking at him. "Might mellow you out a little. For that matter, *I* can help reduce your intensity, too. Hand me your knife," he told Judas. Judas did. Jesus tossed it into a sheep waterhole by the side of the road. Startled, Judas frowned. He fished his knife out of the muddy water, stuck it in his sash, and stalked off.

"Don't think that mellowed him out," one of the disciples commented.

"No," Jesus agreed, "but flipping his blade into the pond mellowed me out." He chuckled.

"Ever worried that it might wind up in your back?" someone asked.

"No," Jesus answered. "My pinning will be from the front." The conversation died at that point. No one wanted to know what the master meant.

Judas looked at James.

"So, what's the plan?"

"After we get the Lord's body we will take it to the Garden of Gethsemane and bury it in secret."

Judas thought about that a moment, then nodded his head.

"That's good," he said. "Who is going to deal with the guards at the tomb?"

"No violence if we can avoid it. We brought a fortune in gold to buy possession of the master's body."

Judas' eyes narrowed.

"How much of a fortune?"

"Enough aureus for the Roman guards to retire on a rich man's estate, and ten times that amount for the centurion."

Judas scowled.

"Do you really think you need to offer that much?"

James didn't answer. Judas' avarice was legendary. As was his thievery. He had been the treasurer for Jesus and the Twelve until funds kept coming up short. Jesus didn't comment on it, but James, John's brother, had confronted Judas in private and from that point on he had carried the group's money.

"I have the gold and I will act as spokesman," James told Simon and Judas. "If the negotiations falter I will step aside and one of you may take over. Tender any offer you see fit, kill the guards if you must, but remember,"—James jabbed his forefinger at them as he spoke—"our only goal tonight is to take Jesus' body away."

Judas nodded, but didn't speak.

Simon pulled out his short sword.

"One way or another issues will be resolved," he said.

"Then your swordsmanship will have to be better than last time," John sneered.

"Huh?" Simon grunted. "What are you talking about?"

"Your foray in Gethsemane?" John reminded him. "You managed to cut some poor soldier's ear off and that was about all you accomplished, remember?"

"Shut up, runt," Simon snapped. "If Jesus hadn't stopped me I'd have gone wild."

"And at least cut off the man's *other* ear," John offered.

Simon started towards him. James held out his hand and Simon stopped.

"Enough," he said. "It's time to approach the guards. John, come with me. Your age will disarm their suspicions."

"How are we supposed to know if you are successful?" Simon asked.

"I will come and tell you. Stay by the wagon until I return."

"*If* you return," Judas said under his breath.

James walked toward Jesus' tomb. It was cut into the rocky shoulder of a hill with a six-foot-high round stone slab blocking the entrance. Three Roman soldiers sat around a small fire. They stood up when James and John approached. They were wearing armored steel breastplates, helmets, and thick leather skirts. Despite being prepared to fight, they did not reach for their spears, nor did they pull out their swords.

John noted that all three of the soldiers were older. They sported several days' growth of white whiskers; silver and white locks stuck out below their helmets. Roman soldiers served a single term of twenty years. These three looked like they should have retired long ago.

"Who goes there?" one of the guards called out in Latin.

"Two brothers," James answered in Greek, "sent to you by Fortuna."

At that two guards pulled out their swords. They seemed on edge and jumpy. The other soldier, husky and tall, was sure of himself.

His helmet plume bespoke his rank as a centurion. He responded in Greek, but had recognized his Hebrew accent.

"So, what tricks are you boys up to?" he asked in a friendly manner.

"No tricks, sir," James replied. "We have come to offer you gold in exchange for the body of the man in the tomb."

"The body of the criminal we are guarding?" the centurion asked.

"He was more than just a criminal, my lord," James answered, "or an officer of your rank would not be here keeping an eye on his body."

The centurion stood a bit straighter as though acknowledging the man's declaration of his seniority and importance.

"Perhaps. Pontius Pilatus believes the same radicals who proclaimed him the Jewish messiah while he lived, may try to steal his body and claim that he rose from the dead. We're here to make sure no one gets any ideas about proclaiming the dead man a god."

"You mean like the Romans did with Augustus?" John piped up.

The centurion glared at the boy. Was he mocking the Roman Senate's proclamation of Augustus Caesar as a god after his death? Or was he just citing a parallel? It didn't matter. A kid was a kid. Whatever he said was just shit.

"We done when dawn breaks today," the centurion said, "the third day after his burial.

Jesus of Nazareth is damned to Tartarus no matter who people thought he was."

Tartarus was the dark and shadowy place where Romans believed shades of the deceased were confined forever.

"Not the Elysian fields?" John asked, alluding to the Paradise reserved for Latin royalty and heroes.

"Not for a fuck-face Jew," the Roman answered. "Now what are you proposing?" It was time to find out whether these two young men really had any money.

"We can offer one gold aureus to each of the soldiers with you," James answered, "and ten gold aureus to you."

The centurion tried not to reveal his astonishment. One Roman gold aureus was the value of about 200 Roman silver denarii, the entire twenty-year salary of a Roman officer. He was being offered ten lifetime incomes for turning an unseeing eye at the removal of Jesus of Nazareth's cadaver only hours before he was going to pull his detail and leave anyway. No one would know. Not for at least a year anyway, when his body had decayed and relatives entered the tomb to place his bare bones in a limestone burial box.

"Let me see the money."

James withdrew the bag of gold from inside his robe and handed it to the Roman officer. The centurion opened the bag and took out one of the gold aureus. He studied it for a long moment as if pondering the almost unlimited buying power of the remaining aureus in the bag. He flipped the coin in the air towards one of the soldiers on duty with him. The guard caught it and hid it in a small pocket inside his leather skirt. Longinus tossed another aureus to the other soldier and then closed the pouch, putting it in a pocket inside the folds of his own leather skirt. He extended his hand to James. Without a word they shook.

"Roll the stone back," Longinus ordered the soldiers.

"We have a wagon and donkey nearby with two more men to help," James said. "May I send the boy to fetch them?" The centurion locked eyes with him. "You may. But if anything or anyone materializes other than what you've just described, every one of you is dead."

James nodded, and told John to go and fetch the others. John took off at a run while Longinus walked over to the round slab that blocked the tomb entrance. The other soldiers joined him. The stone wheel was set in a channel engineered so precisely that the two Roman guards were able to easily roll the slab up to the beginning of the track, opening the tomb.

John arrived with Simon and Judas, accompanied by the driver and his wagon. The Romans looked at Jesus' disciples. They looked back. No one spoke. The centurion and his soldiers walked back to their fire. Simon reached into the wagon and took out several torches, thick green tree branches with tips wrapped in wads of oiled wool. He handed one to each disciple, and with the permission of the centurion, they lit them at the fire. James entered the tomb first. Judas and Simon followed him. John went in last, not so sure that the crusty old Roman officer now in possession of a fortune in gold wouldn't just push the stone back down the track and seal them in.

The disciples surrounded the stone bier that bore the body of Jesus. James handed his torch to John, reached down, and pulled away the face cloth. Jesus' skin was dark, covered with cuts, bruises, and punctures. His features were swollen and distorted. Truthfully, only his copper hair bespoke the fact that it was indeed Jesus.

James turned to Judas.

"Cut through the wrappings."

Judas used his knife to cut through the winding cloths. Simon and John removed them, piling up yards and yards of the linen strips heavy and greasy from the sweetly perfumed myrrh. Jesus lay naked except for a modest loincloth. His chest was sliced to pieces by whips and swords, his hands and feet were marked with nail holes, and though his corpse had been washed reverently, his skin was torn and ripped in so many ways that virtually none of it remained attached to his body.

Witnessing Jesus' injuries, both James and John began to weep. Judas stood back scowling, hiding thoughts that he would share with no man. Overcome, Simon dropped to his knees and grasped one of Jesus' hands. He kissed it and then just held it sobbing, great tears falling onto the cold ruin of a hand that had once blessed children and healed the sick.

John remembered holding onto Jesus' hand as they walked along the shore of Galilee waiting for Simon and the rest of the disciples to return from a night of fishing. When their boats appeared at first light, Simon called out that they hadn't caught a single fish. Jesus looked down at John and winked.

Then he pointed to a nearby spot in the lake and called back, "Try there!" Simon did and the boat's nets instantly filled to overflowing. Jesus looked down at John again and laughed, his blue eyes twinkling. John's heart almost burst with happiness at that moment, thinking in quite a heretical way that if Jesus really was the Son of God, he was sure a lot more fun than Jehovah.

His brother James turned to him now.

"John, there is a shroud in the wagon. Fetch it, please."

John ran to get it. Odd that he should still be treated as the errand boy when he—and only he—had not abandoned Jesus in the hour of his trials. He supposed it was the curse of being the youngest. But whether it was acknowledged or not, he was also the bravest.

John lifted the shroud out of the wagon and took it back to the tomb. Neither the
centurion nor his soldiers paid any attention. James wrapped the shroud around the corpse. He, Simon, and Judas lifted the body and carried it to the wagon. The centurion approached them.

"Let me see his face," Longinus commanded.

James turned and looked at the centurion.

"Why?" he dared ask.

"I would see his face one more time."

James nodded and lifted the funeral cloth from Jesus' face. Though the Lord's countenance was utterly mutilated, his features were untroubled. However terribly Jesus had suffered, he had died at peace.

Longinus gazed at Jesus' face. Then he pulled open the shroud to reveal Jesus' chest and carved the letter "L" on its pale flesh with his knife.

"You may leave," he told James and walked away. James stared at the "L," then pulled the shroud closed again and placed the funeral cloth back over Jesus' face. He told the waggoneer to head for the Garden of Gethsemane at the base of the Mount of Olives. The man knew the place. He yanked the donkey's muzzle and the beast began to pull. The disciples walked beside the wagon while Longinus' legionnaires rolled the stone wheel down its track and blocked the entrance to the empty tomb.

The sun was edging above the top of the Temple behind the city walls when the disciples reached Gethsemane. Cleopas was already there laboring in his olive grove. He was a small bony man worn down by labor and age, but in spite of his infirmities he dug a grave for the master in a remote corner of the garden.

The disciples carried Jesus' body to the spot and laid it down beside the muddy hole. The sun rose in the sky and lighted up the grove. James removed the cloth from the master's face one last time so that those who had loved Jesus might have one final glance. James left his face exposed as they began to lower him into the grave.

Suddenly Jesus' eyes opened, he took in a great breath, then spoke loudly and forcefully, "Stay thy hands, I am alive!"

CHAPTER TWO

No one moved. It was as though their senses had been blown away. The Lord Jesus was alive! But how could that be? They laid him on the ground beside the pit that had almost been his final resting place, but Jesus spoke no more. He had closed his eyes and his lungs rose and fell deeply and with regularity. He was asleep. But there was no doubt that he was alive.

James and John stared at each other. Then suddenly John burst out laughing.

"Hallelujah!" he cried.

Then suddenly all of the men were praising God and laughing and hugging each other. The most impossible event ever had just occurred before their eyes. Jesus had returned from beyond the grave. He had been stone cold dead, yet now his face was pink and though covered with cuts and gouges it was already beginning to heal. The lacerations had closed. The punctures had filled with blood and water. His followers did not know how long they danced and sang, but it was Cleopas who finally interrupted.

"You must hide him! The Roman guards you bribed may keep silent, but anyone who sets their eyes on Jesus will know that it is him. He has to be taken somewhere where he can heal and decide what he will do next."

The disciples fell silent. Jesus belonged back in Galilee, but that was four or five days away by wagon, too long and too visible to pilgrims returning to their homes after Passover.

"What about Lazarus' house?" Judas spoke up. "Bethany is less than an hour from here." Bethany was the home of one of Jesus' best friends and without a doubt his most generous and hospitable follower, Lazarus. He was young and handsome, rich and genteel, taking care of both of his younger sisters, Mary and Martha, until that day they picked eligible suitors.

Lazarus himself was tall and slim, handsome with a square face and brown eyes so dark they looked black. He wore his curly dark hair full, but trimmed. Unlike his sisters he had no desire to be married. The women he knew and enjoyed were available for a night of pleasure without the commitment of a lifelong relationship. Plus, unlike anyone's wife, they went away in the morning.

Both of his sisters were in their twenties, and though beautiful and gifted with bountiful dowries, they had no suitors. Most men wanted women at least ten years younger to provide children. Jesus' own mother had only been twelve when betrothed to Joseph and she gave birth to Jesus when she had just turned thirteen. Lazarus hadn't given up on his sisters' prospects, but he wasn't thinking about that now. He was in mourning.

This day Lazarus wasn't thinking of such things. He was in deep mourning and inconsolable. Jesus was dead, and though he had once called Lazarus out of the grave, he would not be able to do that for himself. Lazarus had not gone to the crucifixion, nor had he been present at Jesus' burial. He was rich, but he was not brave. He had been hiding away alone in his darkened home ever since he'd received word that Jesus had been found guilty of treason against the Roman Empire and sentenced to be crucified.

Lazarus had been devastated. He had truly believed that Jesus was the long-awaited messiah, a mesmerizing teacher who held people in thrall like a god, spinning ingenious parables with impossible standards. (Love your neighbor as much as yourself still made Lazarus shake his head.) He had healed. He had forgiven. He had loved God and man. But now he was dead. Had been dead for three days. Who Jesus truly was would never be answered. What he could have been would never be realized.

Lazarus' thoughts were interrupted by one of his sisters' attendants, Michal, who addressed him from outside the scarlet drapes that separated his private chambers from the rest of the house.

"Master," she said, "some of Jesus' followers are at the door. They told me that you alone may hear the urgent tidings they bear."

Lazarus frowned.

"Is one of them Simon?"

"Yes."

"Tell them to go away."

"James and John are here as well. Also, Judas."

Lazarus sat upright and got out of bed. He was still wearing his sleeping apparel, a light white woolen robe, simple and warm. He pulled open the drapes and greeted the servant. She wore a long, cream-colored silk robe embroidered with dragons and phoenixes that Lazarus had given her after one of his trips to Cathay. Her feet were bare lovely creatures that she kept as soft as baby skin. She had an almond-shaped face with full lips, narrow brown eyes, and uncut long hair that she kept wrapped up in a bun on top of her head. Michal was a girl from a poor family, but here she lived almost as an equal to the sisters she served, Mary and Martha.

"Are you sure that one of the men was Judas?" Lazarus asked.

"One and the same."

Lazarus scowled. It couldn't be Judas. That man was dead, hung by his own hand. There was evil magic afoot if Judas had somehow reappeared. And horse's ass magic if Simon was here. Lazarus walked quickly to the front door and opened it. Several of Jesus' disciples were indeed waiting there as well as a man with a donkey-drawn wagon.

"Peace," Lazarus said to the men. He saw James and John, Simon, and—damn it to hell—there was Judas, too. That made him angry, but he kept his temper in check for now.

"May the Lord bless you and your household," James responded.

Thank God, Lazarus thought. If James was speaking first it meant that neither that idiot Simon nor the son of perdition Judas had managed to seize control of Jesus' group of disciples.

"Come in," Lazarus offered. "Mary and Martha are away taking solace with friends in Sebaste after the sad events of the last few days. Rest awhile with me and take some refreshment."

"We will, gladly," James responded. "But first would you look into the wagon and see what we have brought with us?" James grinned like an idiot. Been hanging around Simon too long, Lazarus thought. He walked up to the wagon and looked inside. His jaw dropped and he pulled back in disbelief. He steadied himself, gripped the side of the wagon, and looked again.

"You stole his body?" he cried in disbelief.

James grinned again.

"Look carefully, Lazarus, son of Cyrus."

Lazarus looked down at the face of the crucified Lord. It was Jesus. He'd recognized him the first time he had looked, but what he had not seen was that Jesus was no longer a dead man. His face was flushed, his chest rose and fell. Shockingly, his long hair was turning completely white. Yet beyond all hope or expectation he had returned from the grave. Lazarus shook his head and stared. James touched him gently on the shoulder.

"May we accept your invitation to come in?" he asked. "You have seen that the master is alive, but there are others who should not."

"Yes, yes, of course," Lazarus stuttered. "Bring him into the house."

As tall as Jesus was, he was trim, and the disciples easily lifted him out of the wagon and carried him inside the house. They passed through a large tiled entry adorned with tall painted pots from Corinth decorated with painted scenes taken from myths. John saw naked breasts and open legs on nude women. He had trouble taking his eyes off them. So that is art, he thought.

Lazarus led them to his private chambers in the east wing of his mansion. There was a bedframe of gold, a mattress of goose down, and embroidered wool blankets woven in the faraway Seven Kingdoms of Indus. There was a large polished brass mirror set on a vanity table, and throughout the room were cushioned divans and wooden chairs brought from Egypt and carved with Nile beasts and birds then inlaid with blue lapis and orange carnelian. There were iron tripods holding alabaster bowls filled with olive oil to provide light at night, and colorful Turkic hand-knotted carpets on the floors. Lazarus' bedroom was stunning. The disciples had never seen anything like it. Without hesitation Lazarus yielded it to Jesus.

They laid him on the bed and Lazarus assigned two of his male servants to wash Jesus and dress him in a new robe. Lazarus led everyone else out of the room.

James spoke to his brother John.

"I am going to pay the waggoneer and send him on his way. Why don't you ride down to Jerusalem with him and invite Jesus' mother to come here?" James lowered his voice. "Tell no one else."

"Can I tell Mary that Jesus is alive?"

"No. Tell her only that disciples of her son beg her appearance at Lazarus' house."

"Do you know where she is staying?"

Jesus' mother had continued to live in the small rural village of Nazareth after Joseph's death. She had journeyed to Jerusalem to share Passover with her cousin Elizabeth and was still staying with her.

"Why don't you pay the wagon driver to take me there *and* to bring Mary and me back?" John suggested.

"Good idea. Come with me. I'll make the arrangements."

James paid the driver and gave him directions to where Mary was staying in the city. He reminded his brother to watch out for soldiers and to avoid any suspicious-looking men who might well be spies for the Temple authorities.

"Do you really think that High Priest Caiaphas is really worried about us?" John asked his brother. "As far as he's concerned Jesus is dead and gone."

"He's probably still thanking his Kabbalah numbers for that," James responded, "but it doesn't hurt to be cautious. There are other fanatics out and about besides Caiaphas."

"Wouldn't be Israel if there weren't."

James grinned and patted John on the shoulder.

"Go with God, little brother."

The wagon trip along the Bethany-Jerusalem road was quite pleasant. The sun was warm and the sky clear, and it was always better to ride than walk though John rarely had been afforded that opportunity. Fishermen had boats and nets, not wagons and donkeys. Jerusalem became visible in the distance and John savored the view of the vast marble and gold Temple inside the city walls.

He remembered one of Jesus' last public acts, a truly surprising one that got him into a lot of trouble with a whole lot of people. In an uncharacteristic show of anger, Jesus had lashed a whip over the heads of the money changers in the great Temple courtyard and overturned their tables. Everyone knew that the changers were cheats, taking Roman and Greek coins from pilgrims and charging them an unfair rate of exchange for Temple money to buy animals for sacrifice. Furious, Jesus had swept through the plaza like a typhoon at sea.

The Pharisees were stunned and then outraged. Who had given him the authority to do what he had just done? Actually, any decent man should have done what he had done, but Jesus answered them with a strangely puzzling rebuttal.

"Destroy this temple and in three days I will raise it up."

Everyone was horrified, thinking that Jesus was referring to the Temple towering above them, a structure so high and mighty that the Jews believed it could never be destroyed. What the hell was this country rabbi babbling about? It turned out that Jesus was referring to another temple of God. Who knew?

"You need to walk from this point," the waggoneer told John. He had entered the city through the Golden Gate, circled the Temple mount, and stopped next to a narrow alley. "I'll wait here for you and your guest."

John climbed out and headed down the alley. It jogged here and there, but he was mindful not to miss the small house with the purple door. It had been painted that way to honor Jesus when his followers had lined the streets from Bethany all the way to the Temple, crying out a royal welcome to Jesus who was riding into Jerusalem on a donkey as had the kings of old.

The people had cried out as he passed, "Hosanna to the son of David! Blessed is he that cometh in the name of the Lord! Hosanna in the highest!" They further honored Jesus by covering the cobblestone roads with their vests and outer tunics and tossing palm branches down as well so that Jesus' donkey might not touch the road even once while carrying his royal rider.

John found the house and knocked softly. No one opened it. He knocked again louder. The door opened slowly and a hunchbacked old woman looked up at him. How humiliating, John thought, to be so old and bent that even young boys towered over you.

"Yes?" she asked, her voice surprisingly full and sweet.

"Ma'am, my name is John, son of Zebedee, one of Jesus' disciples. I am looking for his mother. I was told she was here."

The old woman swung the door all the way open, and John saw Mary sitting inside the house.

"Hello, John," she said, rising and approaching him with her arms open. John went to her and held her tight. Mary was a small, middle-aged woman, with soft brown hair and blue eyes. She wore a dark blue dress with a white sash over her shoulder and a light blue scarf over her head. While her countenance was not as striking as her son, Jesus, she was still a beautiful woman, enough so to turn male heads whenever she chose to be out and about.

She and Jesus looked very much alike, descendants of the ruddy, red-haired, famously handsome King David. Jesus never talked about such things, but the disciples did, often joking behind his back that if they had his face they'd abandon fishing and chase comely females for the rest of their earthly lives.

"Dear boy, why are you here?" Mary asked, holding onto John's hands. Of all Jesus' proclaimed friends and supporters, only this lad had been brave enough to stand by her below the cross of her crucified son.

"I have come from Lazarus' house," he told her. "Several of the disciples have gathered there, and they are requesting that you join them."

Mary frowned.

"Join them?" she hissed. "If I ever see any of those cowards again, I will spit in their faces."

That didn't sound promising. John knew though that she really had to come. He would have to somehow delicately hint at the reason the disciples were gathered at Lazarus' house.

"Jesus is alive," he told her. "The disciples brought him from the tomb to Lazarus' house."

Mary put her hands to her face in shock and cried out, "No!"

John stood unnerved.

Mary looked at him as sternly as she ever had.

"I will ask you this only once, John, son of Zebedee," she said, her voice flat and menacing. "Did you see with your own eyes that my son is alive?"

"I swear on Jehovah's holy name that not only have I seen Jesus, I heard him proclaim, 'I am alive!'"

Mary shook her head and burst into tears. John led her by the hand up the alley to the waiting wagon and helped her climb in. They sat next to each other on a bundle of blankets. The wagon driver left the city and headed back up the Jerusalem–Bethany road. Mary wept softly and did not speak. Ever since John had known her, it had always seemed that she preferred to ponder her worries and joys instead of talking about them.

Jesus was actually very much the same. Though he was a winsome public speaker sharing stories, morals, and predictions that were both enlightening and beguiling, he only rarely engaged in private conversation with his own disciples. When he did he revealed a gentle, speculative side, displaying an intellectual curiosity and a willingness to ponder great questions, even asking out loud what was God up to? Did he ever talk like that with his mother? John didn't know, but there was no doubt in his mind that whatever it took he would make it a point to be watching and listening when Jesus and Mary were reunited.

— ⚜ —

Jesus slowly awakened. He was lying in bed, bathed and perfumed and covered in warm Hindustan blankets, light but warm. His head was propped with pillows and his arms were at his sides. Lazarus was sitting in a chair watching him.

Jesus gazed at his friend's face.

"How can you be here?" he asked. "Did you manage to die again?"

"Ha!" Lazarus exclaimed, then jumped up and went over to Jesus.

"I like how you've done the tomb," Jesus commented. "Nicodemus have any objections?"

Lazarus grinned.

"You're pretty funny for a dead guy."

"Actually, *ex*-dead guy if I'm not mistaken."

Lazarus leaned down and kissed Jesus on both cheeks.

"By God, you are really back, no question about it. How did you do it?"

"Later, *por favor*," Jesus answered slowly, borrowing a phrase from Lazarus' two Spanish servants who had repeated it over and over while they had cleansed his body, Jesus being the first man they'd ever washed who'd spent his last few days being dead.

"May I bring you something to drink?" Lazarus offered, "or to eat?"

"I'm thirsty, and I don't want any of that cheap sour stuff poured on the sponge while I was on the cross." He looked at Lazarus. "Speaking of which, I wouldn't recommend that experience to anyone."

"Do you want to talk about it?"

Jesus shook his head.

"Later."

"I'll get you some wine," Lazarus said.

"Mostly water."

"Sure. Bite of bread with it?"

"Just wine, thank you."

Lazarus leaned down again and kissed Jesus' forehead.

"I thought we'd lost you," he said softly.

Jesus smiled, and closed his eyes. In moments he was asleep again. Lazarus studied the wounds on Jesus' face. They were healing at an unreal pace. Dark scabs had appeared inside the puncture wounds, and most of the slashes, cuts, and abrasions had mostly healed with white scars and patches appearing where bloody marks and torn skin had been only hours earlier. His hair had now turned completely white—evidence of his death or of his resurrection? *Where have you been, my friend,* Lazarus wondered? *Where have you been?*

In his own four-day journey beyond death Lazarus had felt alert the whole time. Imagining himself a traveler into the cosmos he had flown far above Earth and beheld its majesty. It was round like a ball, and not flat like unleavened bread. He flew higher, passing a fiery red planet, another surrounded by rainbow rings, and yet another with a huge red eye staring at him. Ever higher he flew through clouds of stars, balls of fire suspended in endless black space.

He wondered if Jesus had journeyed in a like manner after his death, his mortal corpse left behind and his spirit unleashed. He and Jesus were the only two men who had ever traversed the scenery of the afterlife only to discover that it led right back here. Maybe he should write a book about his experiences, Lazarus thought. Then he laughed and shook his head. He was too rich to waste time doing that.

Had Jesus gone to God? Had he seen heaven's streets of gold and the Almighty himself seated upon his diamond throne? Had he heard the angel choirs sing their hallelujahs to the King of the Universe and witness the fiery brilliance of the archangels stationed around his throne? Or had he perhaps just had a little chat with the prophet Isaiah? Why not, telling the old codger that he could have gone a little easier on the brutal punishments foretold for the messiah. Had Isaiah apologized or just shrugged it off? If he had seen Jesus' face straight out from the cross Isaiah would have apologized.

Lazarus beckoned to his personal attendant, Miguel, and asked him to prepare wine for Jesus, one-third grape and two-thirds water. Miguel nodded. He was a well-built young Jew from Santiago de Compostela, a Galician village perched on the western tip of Spain. He had dark skin, a large nose which gave his young face character, wavy brown hair, and a perpetually amused expression. Years earlier he had made a pilgrimage from Spain to Jerusalem to sacrifice in the Temple. He discovered a climate that was comfortably familiar—and though there were Romans here just like Spain—there were a lot more Jews than Latins and he liked that.

Miguel knew the man Lazarus was caring for. Jesus had been a frequent and welcome guest in this house. Miguel liked his gentleness and his sense of humor. He also envied his size and presence though neither had saved him from the cross. Jehovah must have liked him as well, or he wouldn't be alive now. Miguel shook his head at the wonder of it all, and then went to fetch the wine Lazarus had ordered for his special guest.

In the kitchen he opened a skin of Lazarus' favorite Italian red wine and poured some into a beautifully chased silver goblet. Then he fetched cool water from one of the fresh water storage jars buried in the earth outside and filled the goblet. He took the cup to his master's bed chambers. Jesus was still asleep. Miguel set the goblet on a small table next to the bed.

He looked at Jesus' face. Miguel had never hurt a living thing in his life. He knew that this man hadn't either. So why had he been tortured and murdered by the Romans? The official story was that he told the Jews he was the messiah. Every Hebrew knew that the messiah would overthrow the Romans, so it was a pretty serious claim. The Jewish religious officials had taken the admission seriously and so had the Romans. Hence the cross, and Pilate's cruel but telling sign over Jesus' head, **JESUS OF NAZARETH, KING OF THE JEWS.**

Miguel and his friends had exhausted themselves in endless discussions about the real reason for Jesus' execution. Herod, the head house servant to Caiaphas, the high priest of the Temple, repeated conversations he'd witnessed in the past where his master had paid for Roman influence with gold syphoned off the Temple treasure, and describing how on more than one occasion he'd been ordered to carry a chest of gold to the governor's residence.

Such a delivery had taken place only a few days before Jesus had been arrested. It was impossible not to make a connection. Jesus was a thorn in the side of the Pharisees, the religious party of rednecks, farmers, and fishermen. The other political circle made up of wealthy Sadducees had turned against Jesus to a man after he had overturned their changing tables in the Temple courtyard. Injustice was swift and complete. Pilatus was bribed and Jesus was crucified.

Miguel took one last look at Jesus. He retreated at last and went about his chores agitated that he could not tell Herod and his other friends about the secret activities here at Lazarus' house. He'd have to wait until Jesus had been taken somewhere else or captured by Romans or Jews. Whatever happened, it was going to be the story of a lifetime.

CHAPTER THREE

MARY STOOD BESIDE LAZARUS LOOKING at her son. Jesus was still sleeping in his host's majestically-sized bed, fitted with a carved cedar headboard from Lebanon that depicted the Hebrews crossing the Red Sea. The story of my life, Lazarus loved telling his guests. Rags to riches. Which was anything but true. His father Cyrus had been a very successful importer of fabrics from all over the world and he had left his trade and his considerable wealth to Lazarus, his apprentice as a child and partner as an adult. The actual truth was riches to amazing riches, but what did that really matter? Anyone who'd ever been invited into Lazarus' bedroom hadn't been there to discuss the headboard.

Mary stood silently and watched the healthy, pain-free respiration of her son. His face was peaceful, his newly whitened shocks of hair cleaned and combed. The cuts and abrasions on his face were fading and his skin was pale and whole. Mary reached out and took one of Jesus' scarred hands in her own.

"Son," she whispered.

Instantly Jesus' eyes opened. He looked at his mother's face then pulled her hand to his lips and kissed it. Mary tried to smile, but happy tears came to her eyes instead. She leaned down and kissed Jesus' cheek.

"You came back," she said.

"Yes," Jesus answered, and kissed her hand again. "I missed your cooking."

Mary snorted, surprised, and then laughed out loud. Lazarus did as well. He knew that Mary hadn't cooked an edible dish in her entire life. Jesus had been one of the skinniest men he had ever met on first acquaintance, and it had taken countless dinner invitations serving who knew how many roast lambs to put some meat on Jesus' frame.

Lazarus noticed that Jesus' bones had somehow survived intact despite the Roman juggernaut of whippings, beatings, and piercings he had been subjected to. That brutal savagery had ground Jesus' body into a flayed and bloody corpus, but somehow his bones had been spared. It was an odd oversight by the Roman beasts, but one that would allow Jesus to get back on his feet fairly quickly. Which was critical. In days, or perhaps even in hours, Jesus would have to flee for his life.

Neither the Roman nor the Jewish authorities apparently had any idea yet that Jesus had been removed from his tomb, but sooner or later they would be informed and like Greek furies they would explode in a frenzy of fear and hatred trying to find him. Whenever that moment came Jesus had to be far, far away.

Lazarus left Mary and Jesus to their conversation while he sought out his estate manager Alejandro to begin planning Jesus' escape.

"Does anything hurt?" Mary asked Jesus.

"No," he answered. "Nothing hurts, and everything seems to be healing except the nail holes in my hands," Jesus held them both up, "and in my feet." He slid one of them out from under the blankets. The holes were dark and apparently permanent.

"They are the symbols of your suffering," Mary told him, "the icons of your sacrifice. Wear them proudly is what your father Joseph would have told you. Remember that time he embedded that ax in his thigh?"

Jesus grimaced remembering. His dad had borne the terrible injury with stoic bravery and told everyone that he was changing his name to Tepish, Hebrew for idiot. His thigh had healed rapidly, God's name be blessed, without even leaving a scar.

"Did you ever tell Joseph that you were the one who healed him?" Mary asked.

"Are you serious?" Jesus replied, his expression incredulous. "The only miracle he ever wanted to talk about was changing water into wine, and that was only because he was trying to get me to do it at home."

Mary smiled.

"Your father knew you were special even when you were only a little boy. He just didn't know how to handle it."

Jesus shrugged.

"Nor do most other people, including me."

Mary's face grew serious.

"Not for my lack of trying, son."

"I know, Mom. You did your best. It was a tall order to get me to accept that somehow, someway, I was God's long-promised messiah. Even now I don't know what Jehovah really expected. My ministry ended abruptly, and I was put to death. And why? For telling people that God was love? Apparently, not even he liked hearing that."

"Shush," Mary snapped. "God brought you back from the grave itself. He has validated your work and has a future planned for you. You do not yet know the ultimate meaning that he has invested in your life and death, but you will. Everyone will."

Jesus stared at his mother's face. It was careworn. The events of the last days had etched deep lines on her face.

"Why did you come to Golgotha?" he asked.

"Nothing could have kept me away."

"I asked you not to come."

"And you really expected me to listen to you? Did you think that I would leave you to suffer alone without being at your side, the one who birthed you and raised you knowing all the while that suffering and death were God's final intentions for you?"

Mary had always believed that the Archangel Gabriel had appeared to her when she was but a young maiden. Not a dream. Not a vision. The real angel. She told Jesus that Gabriel had revealed to her that she would bear God's son who would be the messiah, the savior of Jews everywhere. But Jesus hadn't seen an archangel and *he'd* never received a message about God's plans.

To this day, he could not authenticate that he was really and truly the messiah. Perhaps he should view his resurrection as proof. Yet he'd raised Lazarus, and that didn't make *him* the messiah. Maybe the quest for legitimacy was like a hunt for treasure. It could never be proved valid and true until the treasure was actually found. Whatever the treasure was.

"So what are you going to do, son?" Mary asked.

"I am going to propose marriage to Mary Magdalene, and if she'll have me we'll leave Judea." Mary glared at Jesus. Jesus stared back at her. "You can go, too, if that's what you're wondering."

"That's *not* what I am wondering," Mary answered upset. "When did you come up with this, this *tryst* as the objective for the rest of your life?"

"It wasn't an overnight decision," Jesus replied defensively. "I always wanted a family like we had. After Dad died I knew my place was to provide for you and everyone at home, and it was only when Jude and James were old enough to carry on the trade that I began my preaching. Lots of families came to hear my words, and sometime during those years I decided that I wanted a wife. Mary Magdalene, if she'd say yes. And I wanted a family, too. However, death put an end to those dreams. Or so I thought. When I woke today and realized that I had somehow been returned to life, I instantly thought of Mary and of having a family once again."

"So, God brought you back to give me grandchildren?" Mary mocked.

"Why not?" Jesus replied. He grinned and pretended to rock a baby in his arms.

He held it out to Mary.

Mary's stone face cracked and she smiled.

Lazarus tucked his head in the bedroom entrance.

"May I come in?" he asked.

"Of course," Mary answered.

"There are several folks in the house who would like to come and visit Jesus."

"I'm accepting no visits from grave robbers," Jesus said.

Lazarus grinned.

"How about fast-talking, Roman-bribing hooligans?"

"Those folks I'll see."

Lazarus left to fetch the disciples who had brought Jesus. They wanted to see the risen Lord with their own eyes and hear his voice with their own ears. Lazarus had assured them that Jesus was recovering nicely, which, of course, made them want to see him all the more.

Mary looked at Jesus.

"Will you promise me that you will talk to me again about these family dreams?"

"Yes, but you're not going to change my mind. I've earned this, Mom, and I am going to do what I want to do."

"Let's just talk one more time later, and that will be it."

Jesus doubted that, but he kept silent. Mary bent down and kissed him on the forehead.

"I love you," she said.

"I love you more," he told her.

John came bursting through the doorway and stopped at the edge of the bed. Simon, Judas, and the others crowded in behind him.

"It *is* you!" John cried tossing off his sandals and crawling onto the bed. He sat down beside Jesus. "What hurts?"

"Nothing hurts, you rascal," Jesus answered.

John laid down next to him and wrapped his arms around Jesus' chest. He hugged him hard.

"Bet that hurt, huh?"

"Actually, no."

"What?" John responded. "Let me see your chest."

Jesus obliged his young friend by opening the top of his robe. There were thick, white scars on his shoulders from the whiplashes administered by Roman soldiers before his crucifixion and a huge mass of scar tissue in the center of his chest left by the coup de grace that had killed him. John looked at Jesus' face. Unlike his shoulders and chest, it was smooth and unmarked as if it had never been subjected to the soldiers' whips and brass knuckles. But John remembered how damaged and brutalized it had looked when Jesus had been taken down from the cross. The change was nothing short of miraculous.

"You look young again," John said in awe. "Except for your hair."

"How did I look before?" Jesus asked.

"Cut up, worn down, old."

"Old?"

"Yes. And dead. We all cried our eyes out when we saw you."

"Even big old Simon?"

"He blubbered worst of all."

"I did not!" Simon objected.

"Oh, yes, you did," Judas corrected him. "I saw you. We all saw you."

Simon bit his lip and refrained from continuing his objections.

"Why did you take me from the tomb?" Jesus asked. "And for that matter, how did you manage it?"

"We were afraid that the authorities would leave your body unprotected from your enemies *and* your followers. Now, of course, they'll wish they had just destroyed it. Nicodemus provided gold to bribe the Roman soldiers guarding your tomb. Their orders were to prevent anyone from stealing your body until the third day after your crucifixion so no one could say that you had risen from the dead. They were good at guarding. Resisting bribes, not so good."

"So did any of you believe that I would come to life again?"

"I did," Mary said. "I knew you would return."

"I did until I saw your body laid out in the tomb," John said honestly. "You were more dead than any dead man I'd ever seen left in the streets or put into the ground. And your body wasn't just dead, it was ruined, destroyed. The only thing on you that wasn't wrecked were your eyes. Those, by the way, refused to stay closed."

Jesus looked at John, a bit of mischief in his eyes.

"Maybe I was watching you," he said.

John's eyes went wide and he shot a quick look at James. His brother looked equally unsettled. He remembered quite distinctly the night John told him that Jesus was watching him.

"Really?" John asked, panicked.

"I'll never say," Jesus said. "But it does seem to me that I told all of you that if I was killed I'd rise on the third day."

Everyone nodded, but only Simon responded.

"We thought you were talking about the Temple."

"I was," Jesus responded. He touched his chest. "This temple."

No one spoke this time. This small group of men were the closest followers Jesus had, yet none of them truly believed that he would rise from the grave. To tell the truth, Jesus himself had spoken those words not really knowing if God would honor his prophecy. Factoring his own doubts into the equation then, only his mother had truly believed that he would rise from the grave. There was an uncomfortable silence in the room. Lazarus finally broke it.

"What are you going to do now?" he asked.

Jesus glanced at Mary who was staring straight at him.

"Leave Jerusalem," he answered.

"What?" Judas cried upset. "Every Jew who can carry a sword will rally around you now. You can take back our land from the Romans."

"I know your heart, Judas, but I will not remain here. My kingdom has never been of this world."

"You will really leave Judea?" Lazarus asked.

"Yes," Jesus replied, "but not forever. Men change, leaders change, even enemies change. I will go into exile anticipating the day when I will be able to return, a day when my words and my presence will no longer make those who misunderstand desire to silence me."

"I'll be pretty old by the time that happens," John declared, sitting up and challenging Jesus. "You will be, too," he said.

"You may be right, John." Jesus scanned the room full of people he loved. "Anyone who chooses to go with me is welcome."

No one spoke.

With that Jesus held up his scarred hands and blessed them.

Then he was gone from their sight.

Two travelers on the road from Jerusalem to Emmaus were taken aback by the sheer physical size of the man on the road ahead of them. He was walking slowly, favoring his feet. As they drew near he turned and looked at them. He had long white hair thick as wool and penetrating blue eyes. The travelers greeted him and fell in step beside him.

"Were you in Jerusalem for Passover?" the stranger asked them.

"I live in Jerusalem," Rueben answered. "My name is Rueben, son of Alpheus, and this is Jacob, the son of my brother, Nehemiah. I am accompanying my nephew back home to Emmaus. He came to Jerusalem to see Jesus of Nazareth, and together we saw him enter the city. People cried 'Hosanna to the son of David,' and laid their cloaks and palm branches on the road for his donkey to tread on. Do you know the man of whom I speak?"

"Many people thought he was the messiah, didn't they?"

"Yes, they did," Rueben said. "But he was crucified by the Romans. He was a hero, but he was not the redeemer."

"So your beliefs were in vain?"

Both travelers nodded. How could one believe in a dead messiah? Jesus pressed them on their knowledge and faith.

"Yet did not Jesus live the life and accept the burdens required of Jehovah's anointed one? Born of David's line he healed the ill, raised up the destitute, and took upon himself the fury of the Temple *and* the violence of the empire, so that the people of Judea could rise above their captivity and live in freedom."

"There is no question that he did all of those things," Rueben responded. "He was stricken, smitten, and afflicted, just as the Scriptures prophesied, accepting death on the cross rather than recant his belief that God is love. But the fact is he died, and, no matter who he was, he *is* no more."

The white-haired man nodded and walked on slowly.

"What is your consideration," he asked, "of King David's prophetic words that God would not allow the messiah to decay in the grave, nor depart for the land of the dead?"

Rueben's face suddenly looked animated.

"That is a much debated psalm right now, let me tell you. Some of Jesus' followers believe that he will rise from the dead this very day."

"Yet you are walking *away* from Jerusalem?"

"My faith is weak," Rueben said and looked downcast. "I won't deny it. If I were half a man, I would turn around and go straight to his tomb waiting to see him burst back out to life."

The three men walked on together silently. The sun was setting and the village of Emmaus was visible on the horizon.

"We are only a short way from my brother's house," Rueben spoke up. "Will you break bread with us this evening?"

"Thank you. It would be an honor."

Rueben introduced the traveler to his brother Nehemiah and to his household. Nehemiah's oldest daughter Naomi bid the three travelers to sit, then with a cloth and a basin of water she knelt to wash the dust of the road from their feet. She was a petite girl with a pretty face and long auburn hair secured in a bun on top of her.

She placed a basin under the stranger's feet first and poured water over them with a clay pitcher. Holding her tears back she carefully washed and dried the piercings in his feet. Seated next to him, Rueben and his nephew were astonished at the man's terribly scarred feet. How had he come by such horrible injuries? Naomi then washed Rueben's feet and Jacob's. No one spoke. It was as if some great weight hovered over them. Perhaps bread and wine at dinner would lift their spirits.

The large wooden table in the kitchen was set for the four men. Nehemiah's wife Sarah served them, a soft-spoken brunette with brown eyes, wearing a cream-colored robe and a blue scarf over her hair. She and her daughter stood respectfully away as the men sat to eat.

"Would you offer the blessing for this food?" Nehemiah asked the guest.

He nodded, lifted up a loaf of bread, and looked towards the heavens. He uttered words of thanksgiving and broke the bread, his actions suddenly revealing him to be none other than Jesus of Nazareth whom they had witnessed ride into Jerusalem. Fear and awe struck everyone.

Rueben lifted his hands and cried out, "Blessed is he that cometh in the name of the Lord!"

Jesus stood, blessed everyone, then was gone from their sight.

Many of the disciples who had fled Jerusalem after Jesus' crucifixion were gathered in Galilee. They were in hiding, fearful of Roman reprisals against them. None of these young men had ever feared a thing in their lives, but dread seized them now. Only a handful of small clay lamps were lit inside the house where they had gathered, and these diminutive flames scarcely illuminated the room where they were sitting, sharing a cold meal of baked fish and bread.

Suddenly a figure appeared in the shadowy room. Tall and majestic, it was undeniably Jesus himself. The men cried out and cowered.

"Peace be with you," Jesus said, his voice kind and comforting. The disciples knew it was Jesus, but they were afraid to speak.

"Can't you see that it is me?" he asked. "Look at my hands." He held them out for them to see the now permanent nail holes. "It is me in the flesh, risen from the grave."

Jesus' disciples stared at his wounds and his white hair, but he was free of other injuries, his face unmarked and beautiful. How could such a thing be?

Jesus smiled and shook his head.

"You are thinking I am an apparition. I assure you, it is me, your friend and teacher. Do you have something I could eat?"

Instantly a plate with bread and fish was handed to him. Jesus ate it all, nourishing the body that had abstained from food since the Passover supper he had shared with these very same men three days ago. His disciples responded at last, coming forward to kiss his cheeks and touch the holes in his hands.

"Forgive us, Lord," Andrew spoke up. "We did not think that we would ever see you again."

"Because you did not believe what I said when I was still with you," Jesus reminded him. "I had to fulfill all the things written by Moses, and the Prophets, and the Psalmists, before my work was done. I told you that I would suffer and die and rise again on the third day. Why didn't you believe?" No one answered, though more than one man thought that Jesus had not been quite so clear about these things before he died.

Jesus bid the men sit and eat their food while he spoke to them about how the Scriptures had foretold his ministry, his death, and his resurrection. And, though he had been executed by fearful men and faithless priests, God had brought him back to life to show everyone that his words of love could not be killed and buried. Just as surely as he had exited the tomb, he assured them his message of God's grace would traverse the world.

Jesus ended his teachings and blessed his friends.

Then he was gone from their sight.

— ⚜ —

Jesus walked the dark highway back to Jerusalem. It was odd to think that he didn't have to walk if he chose not to. Since his resurrection he had found that he could merely visualize a house, or a town, or a place, and he'd instantly find himself there. Other than the gift of healing, this was the only manifestation of divine power that God had ever granted him.

Such transporting was not new. There were many tales in the Scriptures where Jehovah, or his angels, had literally appeared to or disappeared from human company. Jehovah vanished in the midst of a meal with Abraham. An angel engaging Jacob in a strange and wondrous wresting match suddenly disappeared after blessing him. A fiery chariot driven by angels materialized out of the heavens and then disappeared bearing Elijah to Paradise. The Archangel Gabriel speaking to his own mother Mary and vanishing after his stunning words to her.

Why God should bless him with this gift now was actually obvious to him. He was going to be pursued by his enemies the moment they learned of his resurrection. Probably to the ends of the earth. Maybe for the rest of his life. For a moment Jesus contemplated how such hounding would affect Mary Magdalene's desire to be with him.

She had been part of a small group of women that had followed him for the entirety of his mission. Only on rare occasions had she spoken to him, but she was so pretty that he often lost track of what she was saying, just staring at her. It would have been easy to fall in love with Mary Magdalene and have the children he coveted. Babies to hold, boys to wrestle with, girls to teach how to be the equal of any man.

Mary Magdalene was bright, verbal, and loyal. Would she, however, be willing to leave the safety of her home and her friends and plunge herself into a life of danger as his wife? If the Temple authorities caught up with him here in Judea, there'd be no trial. Their assassins would simply slit his throat, stick a knife in his chest, or slice his head off. That would pretty much end his dream of having kids and watching them grow up.

If he escaped, who knew what length the Jews or Romans would go to find and kill him. And these dangers were imminent. Even if his empty tomb had not yet been discovered, many of his followers were now telling anyone who would listen that they had seen Jesus with their own eyes. He was alive. He had spoken to them. He had eaten with them. He had shown them his scarred hands and blessed them.

Jesus tried to pick up his pace, but his damaged feet ached painfully, and Lazarus' frou-frou silk robe wasn't much warmth against the cold night air. There were no other travelers on the road and Jesus walked off to the side to relieve himself. Simon had once done so alongside Jesus. The awestruck fisherman couldn't help but comment that Jesus had produced at least twice the amount of urine he had. Simon shook his head and told Jesus that he pissed like a race horse. Jesus never figured out exactly what that meant, but he decided after a while that it was some kind of manly compliment. He cinched up his loincloth now, pulled the Persian shirt close, and walked on.

Jesus entered Jerusalem and went to the cemetery where Nicodemus' tomb, *his* tomb, was located. On an anxious whim, he decided to see whether or not the stone had been rolled back and the interior of the charnel house revealed. He walked through the gardens by the tomb as the first light of dawn began to appear. Shapes and shadows turned into trees and shrubs as he approached the burial place. He paused where the garden gave way to open ground, revealing the rock face from which the tomb had been hewn.

There was no longer a Roman detail guarding the tomb, but the stone slab still blocked the opening. No one, at least no one in authority, had yet tried to verify that the body of the crucified Nazarene was missing. There was a figure huddled up and leaning against the stone, however. It was a woman, and Jesus knew who it was. He walked up, knelt on one knee, and touched her shoulder.

The woman did not raise her head, but spoke softly. Her voice was devoid of passion or hope. It was the voice of a person who had lost everything that she had held dear.

"If I am not supposed to be here, I understand," she said. "Just a few more moments, sir, and I promise I will leave."

Jesus reached out and put his hand on her scarf-covered head.

"Mary," he said softly.

She turned and looked directly into Jesus' eyes, then gasped and covered her mouth with her hands.

"Master!" she cried, bursting into tears.

Jesus stood up.

Mary did also and stared at Jesus.

"I knew you would return," she said.

Jesus nodded.

"God is honorable and keeps his word, even unto the end of the world."

Mary looked at Jesus' face, then suddenly stepped forward and hugged him hard.

"I am so glad you're back," she whispered.

"I am staying at Lazarus' house. Come with me."

"I am staying with your mother in Jerusalem."

"She is already at Lazarus' house."

"Has she seen you?"

"She was almost the first to do so. I have been traveling through the night bidding farewell to my disciples."

Mary's hazel eyes narrowed a little.

"Am I the last to know?"

Jesus smiled.

"Perhaps."

"How did you know I would be here?"

"Honestly, I didn't know. I came back to see if the tomb had been opened. And here you were. Thank you for believing. Your faith is great."

Mary put her head down. Jesus reached out his hand to her chin and raised it again.

"We must go now. Sooner or later, the Romans will march back here to scotch the rumors that I have been resurrected."

"Won't those bastards be surprised?"

Jesus' eyebrows shot up.

"Who have you been hanging around?"

"Fishermen," Mary answered. "A bunch of them. For three years."

Jesus shook his head. Mary reached out and took his hand. He looked down at their clasped hands and then at her face.

"Better get used to it," she told him. "I'm not letting go of you again."

Jesus smiled tenderly. He couldn't think of a single objection.

CHAPTER FOUR

Lazarus stood at his desk while his servants led Jesus and Mary Magdalene into the room he occupied for his business affairs. He and Jesus wore white linen evening robes and leather sandals. Mary wore a long blue gown, but had slipped her jeweled sandals off. She was not very tall, but she had a nice, womanly shape, fine hips, and full breasts, which she did not flaunt, an olive complexion, hazel eyes, and lustrous black hair, which was usually put up and covered with a scarf, like now.

Mary was also bright with a quick tongue, though she was never mean. Lazarus had watched her grow up during the years she had followed Jesus. He liked her a lot. So, evidently, did Jesus. Lazarus went over and gave her a hug. She hugged him back.

"Hello, little girl," he said. It was all he had ever called her. She had been a little bony thing when he first saw her tarrying at the edge of the crowds.

"And how are you, my friend?" he asked, giving Jesus a kiss on the cheek. "Yesterday at this hour you were dead."

"'Twas indeed the case," Jesus responded affably. "Feeling alive today though. And when I went to check on the tomb, I found a wonderful person who'd gone to see if it had opened up and spit me out."

"Like Jonah," Lazarus remarked.

"Exactly like Jonah," Jesus affirmed. "Everyone figured him drowned and dead. But in my situation an angel believed me when I said I'd wash up on Jerusalem's shore." He gently took Mary's hand and looked into her eyes. "Thank you for that."

Lazarus didn't say anything. He regretfully belonged to the 99.99 percent of Jesus' followers who hadn't believed for a moment that the crucified rabbi would come forth from the grave. Which was shameful in that Jesus was the same man who had brought *him* back to life. Not that Jesus had expected any reciprocity. Lazarus was mortal. Jesus obviously was in a different category. But what category? Demi-god? Son of God? It was another one of those curious gray areas about Jesus.

When asked if he was the Son of God, Jesus always replied that anyone who accepted his teachings was a Son of God. No one really knew what he meant by that, and many reacted exactly like his disciple Simon who muttered, "Clear as mud." Lazarus would have been happy to believe in Jesus' divinity if he had taught it plainly or preached it outright. But he hadn't. Jesus hinted at it to confuse the Pharisees, but the trouble was that he confused his disciples, too. And that was not the only time. Many of Jesus' believers were puzzled by his apparent contradictions, his puzzling abstractions, his seemingly simplistic parables with morals as complicated as Gordian knots.

Add to that his tendency to slice and dice everything Jewish, rooting through laws and traditions looking for the core truths and throwing out what he didn't like. Jesus sorted through all of it, keeping the wheat, and winnowing the absolute shit out of the chaff. Can't cook on the Sabbath because it's work? Nonsense. Can't have relations with your wife because her period makes her unclean? Ridiculous. Can't talk to your Samaritan neighbors because they are Jews who intermarried? Not Scriptural.

On and on, Jesus had plowed through the sense and nonsense of Jewish traditions and produced his own compilation of core teachings about God, good works, sharing, sickness, love, forgiveness, life, and death. Lazarus shook his head just thinking about it all. Someone really should write Jesus' words down.

"Have either of you eaten?" Lazarus asked.

Mary Magdalene shook her head.

"I did," Jesus said, "but I wouldn't say no to some bread and a cup of wine."

"How about a late supper for the three of us?" Lazarus offered. "All of your big boys have eaten and drunk and are snoring away on the roof. Claimed to a man that they stayed awake all last night hauling your body around." Lazarus winked. "Come with me and we'll dine in the garden."

He led the way out of the back entrance of his house into a walled garden where torches lit the retreat to a genteel, dusk-like ambiance. Two house servants appeared, and Lazarus instructed them to bring wine, bread, goat cheese, olives, and fresh green herbs. Off they went, anxious as always to please their kind lord.

One was a thirty-something Egyptian galley slave who had been purchased and set free by Lazarus. The other was a young African man who'd been driven out of his homeland for declaring himself homosexual. Exhausted and starving, Lazarus had found him begging outside a city gate and had taken him into his house.

Both of these servants were bonded to their employer as only rescued men could be. It was rather like how Lazarus felt about Jesus who had walked four days to Bethany after receiving a message sent by his sisters saying that he was fatally ill. Jesus arrived after he had died and raised him from the dead that very moment.

Mary sat on a wooden chair with a cushion. Jesus reclined on a long couch. Lazarus pulled up another chair facing both of them. It was cool out, but pleasant, the warmth of the day's sun slowly yielding to the night. After a while, Lazarus would have iron braziers lit.

Right now, he had a lot of questions for Jesus and who knew when he would have him under his roof again. Lazarus was hoping for a long night of conversation with his friend.

"So, what are your plans, Rabbi, if it is not too early to ask?"

"I think I am going to get married," Jesus replied. He glanced over at Mary who looked back at him without embarrassment.

"Oh, my," Lazarus exclaimed. "The greatest calling in all of Jehovah's creation. One also to which I have never been summoned. However, I will honor your bond and do whatever I can to bless your union."

"Will you babysit?" Mary asked.

Lazarus looked at her. Then he laughed hard.

"Too much pontificating?" he asked.

"Babysitters should be seen and not heard," she said and smiled wickedly.

"Just like good wives," he shot back.

"Where did you get that idea?" she asked.

"Somewhere in Scripture," he answered, "expressly commanded by one sexist male bigot or another." Lazarus turned to Jesus. "Lord, do you know of any prohibitions in the Holy Writ concerning female speech in the context of married life?"

"No," he replied slowly, "but I don't know all of the writings."

Both Mary and Lazarus stared at Jesus, surprised at his admission.

"What?" Jesus asked.

"I presumed you had all of them memorized," Lazarus answered.

"Including all the begats and the thou shalt nots?" Jesus questioned.

Lazarus grinned.

"Only synagogues possess complete Torahs," Jesus went on. "It was a rare privilege that the rabbi in Nazareth allowed me to study it, and even then he limited me to the sections that he felt were the most important: the Creation, patriarchs, kings, psalms, and anything that could be said to foretell the coming of the messiah."

"So, how many verses do you actually know?"

"You mean by heart?"

"Yes."

"I would say less than a hundred."

Lazarus looked surprised again.

"May I remind you, Lazarus, son of Cyrus," Jesus said a bit curtly, "my authority comes not from the words of men, but by heaven above."

"Which means exactly what?" Lazarus dared ask.

"I speak as I am moved by the spirit of the Most High."

"But isn't that the presumption we have for all of the writers of the Scriptures?"

"Yes," Jesus agreed. "They all believed that whatever came into their heads was from Jehovah. The problem comes when we try to figure out when they actually *did* experience inspiration and permission to speak for the Divine."

"And how do you know that *you* are moved by the Holy Spirit?" Lazarus asked.

"You'll just have to take my word for it."

While Lazarus, a liberal and opinionated student of the Bible, usually enjoyed the wide ranging and surprisingly unfettered views Jesus had on who wrote what and whether he was inspired or not, this answer seemed rather flippant. But then, Jesus laughed with such delight that both Lazarus and Mary joined in.

"So what's the real answer?" Lazarus asked.

"Oh, that's the real answer," Jesus said. "It just sounded pretty funny when I heard myself say it."

"Master," Lazarus said, "there is another question on my mind, but I need to ask if you are willing to allow me to engage you with a strictly personal inquiry."

"Speak," Jesus answered.

"Where did your spirit sojourn during the days your body lay in the tomb?"

Jesus gazed at his friend. An odd question, yet one posed by the only other man who had ever experienced an earthly death and resurrection. Lazarus deserved an answer, but how could he describe the phantasmagorical dreams, nightmares, or alternate realities that he had experienced those three days?

"May I ask you something first, brother?" Jesus replied. "What did *you* experience in the days you were departed from your flesh? Somehow I suspect that you weren't dining with the prophets or listening to angel choirs."

Lazarus smiled.

"I believed all of my life that when I died I would be interred in my tomb to dance with the worms until the end of time, at which point I would be restored to life and behold God with my own eyes. I was wrong. When I died, or should I say when my body died, I remained fully awake, able to see and hear everything even while being whisked away to places where I experienced great exultation and overwhelming fear."

Jesus looked intrigued. Mary hugged her knees close with her arms wrapped around them and stared at Lazarus with rapt attention.

"Whatever I was, or whatever I had become, I rose above Earth and passed through the firmament hurtling at an unnatural speed, like a comet flying through the sky. I raced past the moon and saw that it was a big pale rock and nothing more. I discovered that the stars were not shining jewels, but fiery bodies too hot to approach. The sun itself was the greatest of all the stars sending heat and light to pierce the dark of night and bring day to Earth.

"Beyond Earth there were more planets, and beyond those even more, suns and stars in such numbers I couldn't count them. I felt like I was traveling through neighborhoods where only God himself had trod. Then I heard your voice calling to me, 'Lazarus, come forth!' and I came speeding back thinking he's never going to believe where I've been!"

"Yet you never said a word when you awakened," Jesus commented, "nor any time since then."

"No, I didn't," Lazarus admitted. "When I opened my eyes and saw you, I knew that I was safely back in Bethany and my little part of the world. My travels seemed nothing more than fanciful imaginings."

Jesus shook his head.

"On the contrary, I believe that your experiences were quite real. You were given the privilege of viewing the heavens and the earth as seen by God himself."

"Why me?"

"Kabbalah scholars would say that Jehovah plans to require much of you in the time ahead. Obedience. Even sacrifice."

Lazarus sat silently. Then he called to his servant, Benjamin, a teenage boy quietly standing near.

"Yes, sir?" the lad asked coming to his side. He was a Samaritan boy, a half-breed Jew disdained by his peers, but welcomed into Lazarus' employ for the guileless child that he was. The dark-skinned, green-eyed boy waited for his master's commands.

"Go check on the wine I ordered, son. And quickly, please. I am in need of a calming medication." He winked and Benjamin was gone.

Lazarus looked at Jesus.

"I know you'll have some wine. You've never said no before."

Jesus nodded and laughed.

"The Pharisees called me a winebibber, remember?"

Lazarus chuckled.

"And I don't recall you denying it. It really pissed off old Caiaphas when he heard about your partying."

"How do you know that?"

"Gossip brought home by Miguel, one of my most trusted servants. He's networked all over Jerusalem and the things he's learned could topple the high priest, the Roman prefect, and even King Antipas."

"Whenever the golden age of Israel was," Jesus remarked glumly, "we're down to the tin age by now."

Lazarus looked over at Mary Magdalene.

"What about you, little girl? Going to have some wine with the grown-ups?"

"Be nice," Mary answered. "And don't mix so much water in mine."

Lazarus stared at the petite beauty.

"Pardon me, my lady. I underestimated you. Would you like some meat to go with that wine?"

Mary grinned.

"Of course, dear host. You are so clever and charming."

"Only for you, sweet Mary, and it's too late to do me any good as someone else seems to have caught your eye."

Mary laughed and Jesus blushed. Lazarus waved Benjamin and Miguel over as they entered with trays of food and drink. He pointed at the side table next to his chair. Miguel set down a large silver platter bearing a silver pitcher of chilled wine, another of cold water, and three golden goblets. Benjamin set his platter on a nearby table. It held three gold plates filled with a variety of dried fruits and nuts, cold lamb and venison, olives, herbs, crackers, and bread rolls.

"Serve everyone, dear boy," Lazarus told Benjamin, "and I'll prepare the wine." Benjamin filled plates for the guests as Lazarus poured the wine. For Jesus, one-third grape and two-thirds water; for Mary, two-thirds wine and one-third water; and just wine, no water, for himself. He passed them out and lifted his goblet in a toast to his friends.

"What could I possibly propose that would honor the momentous event of this day?" Lazarus looked into Jesus' eyes and held his cup toward him. "Welcome back from those who love you." Then he held his goblet in Mary's direction. "Happy prayers for your future, may it be filled with matrimony and progeny." Then he looked again at Jesus and offered praise to the risen Lord. "Hosanna to the son of David. Blessed is he who comes in the name of the Lord. Hosanna in the highest."

Everyone drank, and Lazarus spoke again. "Lest he think that I have forgotten, let it be noted that I have not yet heard the record of the days and nights Jesus spent flown from his body. Was your afterlife a scenic passage through the cosmos as was mine, or did you pass deeper into the heart of all things real and behold the mysteries of God?"

Jesus smiled, and then revealed his secrets.

CHAPTER FIVE

Jesus was not sure he could adequately convey the disturbing content of his after-death experiences, be they visions, dreams, or reality. He would try, but he had no idea whether Lazarus or Mary would be able to comprehend the disturbing events that he had witnessed beyond the grave.

"After I died, I sprang from my body like a lightning bolt and did not look back. It was as though I was leaving a house where I had lived with no plans to return. I must tell you that whatever consciousness I possessed it was not linked to a corporeal shape. I could see and feel everything, but I myself was nothing.

"At the speed of the light of the sun I traveled through the sky beyond Earth, flying past planets and stars unknown to my mind or imagination." Jesus looked at Lazarus. "You might think, and correctly so, that I partook of the same heavenly phenomena as you. But I sped on past the heavenly bodies you spied until I actually found myself on another world standing outside a great walled city, watching a man carrying his cross to the place of execution.

"It was Israel, and yet somehow it was not, and the city was clearly Jerusalem, and yet oddly not. The man was guarded by soldiers and a great crowd of onlookers followed behind him. The man looked at me. He had the saddest face I had ever seen. It was hurt and bleeding. His naked body had been whipped, stabbed, and cut.

"The man collapsed under his cross and lay on the road. A centurion knelt and looked at him. He stood back up and said, 'He's dead.' The officer drew his sword and plunged it into the fallen man's back. The man did not move. I was overwhelmed with pity and crushed by the knowledge that the dead man would have given anything to finish his sacrifice on the cross. Not only was it a strange and distressing experience, what did it mean? That man couldn't be me. I had not faltered on the way to my crucifixion. I had endured to the very end.

"I was transported to yet another Israel and another Jerusalem, and this time I beheld a man praying in a garden like Gethsemane. A man led soldiers to that private place. One man drew his sword. The soldiers pulled out their swords and proceeded to massacre everyone. One soldier thrust his javelin all the way through the man who had gone to Gethsemane to pray. He died, alone and heartbroken.

"Such sad and heartbreaking visions continued one after another, man after man, victim after victim, all murdered by torture, abuse, or assassination before ever mounting the cross. Some men gave testimony that they were the messiah. Others that they were not the messiah. Some men even rebuked the idea of a suffering servant and declared themselves the militant sons of the Almighty. In the end, however, it didn't matter what any of these men were or thought they were. They all died.

"In the very last of these maddening episodes, I found myself at Golgotha, but not hanging on the cross. I was standing in the crowd below yet another man's cross. He was scourged, bloody, and dying. He asked for something to drink. A soldier put a sponge full of vinegar to his lips. The crucified one drank despite the cruelty of the gesture.

"Afterwards, he looked at the mountains beyond the city and cried out in utter despair, 'My God, my God, why hast thou forsaken me?' There was no answer, but over the next few minutes the sky darkened, covering the land in a blackness so intense that it was almost impossible to see. Then the man on the cross looked directly at me and said the very words from Scripture that you did Lazarus.

"'Hosanna to the son of David. Blessed is he who comes in the name of the Lord. Hosanna in the highest.'

The dying man gazed down at the crowd that had gathered to see him suffer, then lifted his eyes to the dark mountains once again, crying out to Jehovah who stayed his hand and watched him die.

"'It is finished,' he said. 'Father, into thy hands I commend my spirit.'

"Great bolts of lightning struck the bald rock of Golgotha lighting the man's cross with a brilliance that equaled the light of day. Then the dying man on the cross spoke directly to me one last time.

"'Brother, your hour has been fulfilled. You finished the work that God gave you to do. Now the Father will clothe you with the power and glory that he has held for you before your world even was.'

"At that moment I opened my eyes and beheld that my disciples had removed me from the tomb and were lowering me into an earthen grave. I breathed a great breath and cried out, 'Stay thy hands, I am alive!'"

Mary held her goblet and looked at Jesus. Lazarus drank down the contents of his cup quickly and beckoned Miguel to fill it again.

"Too strange to comprehend?" Jesus asked. "To nightmarish to embrace?"

"I am speechless," Lazarus conceded.

"I am struck by the failures and deaths of the many messiahs," Mary said. "What was the point of that?"

"I can no more fathom what I saw than you," Jesus said. "The multitude of men carrying the burden of being the messiah, some giving up, some despising the role, most dying before being crucified, and only one, only one out of all the suffering men I witnessed was able to make the sacrifice and complete his mission."

And he talked to you," Mary said, "as though he had waited specifically to bless you for finishing your task. I think the man on the cross was Jehovah himself, sharing the suffering and pain of his son and glorifying his work and person."

Jesus looked stunned.

"What are you saying?" he asked, barely able to speak.

"He was you," Mary told Jesus. "At the end of your life, in the very moment that you died, Jehovah finally offered you the truth: You are human and you are God. Your preaching, your healings, your resurrection all point to the truth—you can be none other than God incarnate in human flesh. You are the long-awaited messiah. No one else. You."

With that Mary clasped her hands and fell to her knees. Lazarus, overwhelmed, dropped to his knees next to Mary. Jesus stood and touched them, encouraging them to stand up which they would not do.

"Master!" Miguel cried bursting into the garden. Lazarus looked up.

"There are Roman soldiers at the front door demanding that you surrender the body of Jesus."

"What?" Lazarus cried, jumping to his feet. Mary stood and clung to Jesus' hand. "You bid them wait at the threshold?"

"Yes. I said I'd fetch you."

"Where are Jesus' disciples?"

"They're asleep on the roof."

"Take Jesus and Mary out the garden gate and make haste for where Jesus' mother is staying in Jerusalem." Lazarus' face was fraught with anxiety. "I will stall the soldiers while you get a start. Fly!"

Jesus and Mary were dumbfounded. Lazarus threw open the gate.

"Go!" he commanded.

Miguel reached for Mary's hand and led her out of the garden. Jesus stared at Lazarus in silent disbelief, then hurried after Mary.

Miguel took Jesus and Mary to a road that descended straight down the mountain toward Jerusalem. Jesus was sure the Romans had discovered the empty tomb at last and were now hunting him. But who had told them to go to Lazarus' house?

Lazarus opened the front door to his home and stepped out to meet the Roman soldiers. He immediately recognized Longinus, one of the senior centurions stationed in Jerusalem. He had been introduced to him by the governor Pontius Pilatus himself, and the centurion had often come by Lazarus' house for wine and gossip and to get away from the rest of the Roman soldiers.

"Longinus," Lazarus said, extending his hand.

Longinus shook it.

"I apologize for arousing you and your household at this hour," the centurion said, "but the prefect has been pestered by rumors that a criminal named Jesus whom I executed last Friday has had his body removed from the tomb where he was laid."

Longinus stood rigid, wearing a steel breastplate, plaited leather belt and skirt, his sword, and leather boots laced up his calves. Interestingly, though the long-serving Roman officer was Spanish, with dark skin and curly black hair, he could have passed for a Jew. Lazarus imagined that he took a lot of grief for that from the other officers in the garrison.

"Weren't there soldiers posted at his tomb?" Lazarus asked. "And the great stone rolled in front of its entrance?"

Longinus nodded.

"I was in charge of that guard and dismissed it at dawn this morning. Evidently that was premature. It was rumored that the man would rise in three days. He did not, allowing sufficient time to make sure that no one had the gall to claim that Jesus' rotting cadaver had somehow recovered and left the tomb. Whoever did steal that corpse could not have found it a pleasant task."

"Why have you come here?" Lazarus asked. "Do I have the reputation of a body snatcher?"

"Fuck, no," Longinus growled. "The houses of all of Jesus' most prominent followers are being checked to satisfy Pilatus' curiosity."

"Pilatus?" Lazarus questioned, "or his doppelganger in the Temple, High Priest Caiaphas? I suspect the prefect doubts that any man could survive a Roman crucifixion. But Caiaphas constantly displays his fears about anything or anyone that could disrupt his efforts to maintain the status quo."

"I don't care about Caiaphas," Longinus said dismissively. "All Pilatus told me was that some Jews had come to him saying that Jesus' body had been stolen. Next, he said, he'd have other Jews claiming that it wasn't stolen at all, but that Jesus had come back to life."

"Then why not just wait and see if that is true?" Lazarus poked fun. "Save yourself a lot of running around in the middle of the night."

Longinus laughed.

"Duty is duty, Lazarus, or I'd stop right now and come in for a cup of wine."

"Why not do that anyway?" Lazarus offered. "Let your men rest for a few minutes. Enter and have a drink with me."

Longinus couldn't see why not. After all, he had inside knowledge of what had really happened to Jesus' body, and he knew that Lazarus had nothing to do with it.

"I accept," he told Lazarus. He ordered his men to stand down and pulled off his steel helmet, taking care not to rip its dyed-red horsetail plume. He held it by one of its steel cheek protectors and followed Lazarus into the formal dining room, a lavishly decorated space with mosaic floors, colorful hand-knotted carpets, black silk drapes, and an array of mahogany chairs, tables, and couches from Asia Minor. Lazarus offered Longinus a chair at a table.

"May I bring you anything besides wine?" he asked.

The officer shook his head.

"A Spanish red, unmixed with water?" Lazarus suggested.

"Perfect," Longinus said, admiring his host's manners. Lazarus left to fetch the wine. This elegant Jew was so unlike the vast majority of inhabitants in this piss-poor hinterland. Violent hinterland, truth be told. He had never served anywhere else where the occupied people carried such grudges against Roman rule. Even children barely able to walk were taught to spit on soldiers' boots. And they got away with it.

Emperor Tiberius Caesar favored the Jews, but only because he had met the cultivated Lazarus-types in Rome or Alexandria, never having set foot in this land where the rest of the Jews lived and complained endlessly about everything Roman. And what did the fucking Jews have to be so proud about? A wedding cake temple and a long list of civilizations who'd kicked their Hebrew asses throughout history over this scrubby bit of desert.

He should have known that allowing Jesus' body to be ransomed was going to plant seeds of mischief all over Judea. Half of the maniac population—merchants, traders, bankers, leaders of commerce—would now be protesting to Pontius Pilatus that he couldn't keep a second-rate politician in the grave where he belonged.

The religious morons—the unhinged other half of the natives—would declare that

Osiris-like Jesus had been resurrected from the dead by Jehovah to mount a rebellion against the Romans. Oh, sure. If Jesus hadn't been able to protect himself from the big bad Latin bullies before they crucified him, what chance would his reanimated cadaver have confronting the best soldiers in the world this time around?

Longinus shook his head, disgusted. He shouldn't even be thinking about such shite. And, as a matter of fact, what he *should* be thinking about was where in Spain he would be buying his retirement estate thanks to the fortune in gold he'd accepted for the dead man's removal. Thank you, Jesus!

Lazarus returned with a tray bearing two large silver goblets of red wine and a tall silver flagon filled with more wine. He handed a goblet to Longinus who nodded his thanks. Lazarus sat down with the other.

Longinus raised his goblet to Lazarus. He studied his host's face. Clean-shaven, handsome even features, well-styled curly dark hair, and young. Was he even thirty years old? Longinus had been serving Rome as long as Lazarus had been alive. But his twenty years of service to the empire was finishing up. He was fifty years old, almost twice the age of Lazarus. Would he live ten more years? Probably not. But it didn't matter. Whatever time he had left promised to be the best years of his life.

Lazarus' eyes were drawn past Longinus to the entrance of the dining room. Jesus' disciple Simon the Zealot had entered and was running toward Longinus with a sword raised high.

Lazarus cried, "Longinus, behind you!"

In an instant, the centurion pulled his sword and swung around to face Simon. The short, swarthy fisherman chopped his sword down at Longinus who stepped aside then thrust his sword deep into the assassin's chest. Simon collapsed, dead before he hit the floor.

"Are there more?" Longinus cried.

"I do not know," Lazarus shouted.

Longinus pulled on his helmet and ran for the front door. He pulled it open and rushed outside. The half-dozen soldiers he had left outside were all lying on the ground, heads hacked from their bodies. Two Jewish men stood on the road facing the house. One was holding a sword and watching Longinus. The centurion went straight for him with his sword extended, but crashed to the ground when someone leapt from the roof and landed on him.

Longinus struggled to rise, but the man who had taken him down thrust a twisted Sicarii blade under his jaw all the way up into his brain. Longinus' breath rushed out, as did his life, face down in the dirt of the land he hated so much. The man who killed him stood up and wiped his blade on the dead man's leather skirt. It was the disciple Judas.

"What have you done?" Lazarus cried, staring at the pool of blood spreading beneath the dead centurion.

"This is one Roman who will never threaten our Lord again," Judas declared defiantly. The two disciples on the road came closer. One was Simon and the other was James. Behind them stood John, crying and afraid.

Lazarus looked at the men accusingly.

"Do you realize what you've done? The governor and Jerusalem's entire garrison of legionnaires will hunt you down and hang you on your own crosses."

"Not necessarily," Judas said. "We have a wagon and a driver, and we can remove the bodies to a place where they will never be found."

Lazarus shook his head, furious at the massacre.

"If we don't, Lazarus," Judas continued, "your life is forfeit along with your sisters and your servants."

Lazarus looked at Simon and James, and then at Judas again.

"Have it your way," he said, "but this dishonor blights the return of the Lord and will surely come round to dishonor us all."

"Yak, yak, yak," Judas mocked. "Keep your superstitions to yourself and let us get this cleaned up. Where is the Zealot?"

"He is lying dead in the kitchen," Lazarus responded. "He tried to murder Longinus from behind. For his effort, he got a sword through the heart. And speaking of his cowardly tactic, did you murder these Roman soldiers when their backs were turned?" No one answered. "I thought as much," Lazarus spat out.

Judas and Simon brought the wagon up to the house. The Roman soldiers were dumped inside, bodies, heads, swords, and helmets. The body of Simon the Zealot was brought out of the house and laid on top of them. Lazarus had his servants fetch blankets to cover the bodies and clean up the blood stains soaked into the dirt in front of the house. By torchlight they scraped up the wet soil and poured buckets of fresh earth over the whole area.

Judas stood in front of Lazarus.

"When you see the master, tell him that we will wait for him in Galilee."

Lazarus grimaced.

"Too bad the stories about your hanging weren't true," he slammed the killer.

Judas smiled.

"Who says they weren't, Lazarus, son of Cyrus? There are darker devils in this world than the Roman ones."

Lazarus stood stunned. Judas turned away and bid the waggoneer be off. James walked on one side of the wagon and his brother John on the other. The young boy suddenly turned back and ran to Lazarus.

"I swear to you, Lazarus," John said, his voice anxious and faint, "that dead Roman centurion was the very man who took our money at the tomb in exchange for Jesus' body. His coming here was a betrayal. A flat-out betrayal. I thought you should know."

"As dishonest as his deed was, John, it was not an action deserving of death. Someday I hope you realize that there is no occasion, not one, not ever, when Jesus would approve taking a man's life. Not one."

John left without answering, running to catch the wagon heading east towards the Jordan River and the mountains of Edom. Who knew where the dead Roman soldiers would be secretly hidden forever?

Lazarus went into his house, picked up his goblet, and drank the wine down. It was odd to feel sorry for a Roman, yet the thought that centurion had been murdered in cold blood only months before he would have retired to Spain made Lazarus feel truly sad. The Lord giveth and the Lord taketh away. True even for the conquerors of the world.

Lazarus filled the goblet again and shook his head in despair. In a span of three days he had been plunged into deep mourning over Jesus' torture and death, then was shocked into hysterical joy when he beheld him alive again. Now he was on the verge of panic over the murders of the soldiers and the fact that the authorities were hunting for Jesus. Worried and upset, Lazarus forced himself to focus on how to get Jesus out of Judea and to prepare himself for how he would answer when Roman officials came searching for Longinus and his soldiers.

Lazarus finished the wine and filled the goblet a third time. He went to his bedroom where he changed into a warm wool robe for night travel and tucked a fortune in Roman gold sesterces into a good-sized leather sack and hid it in a pocket inside his robe. Then he went out the front door and turned south towards Jerusalem, ransacking his brain for the best way to get Jesus out of the boiling pot of human madness called Israel.

Long before dawn, Lazarus was welcomed into the Jerusalem home of Mary's cousin, Elizabeth, who had not only been sharing her home with Mary, but was now sheltering Jesus and Mary Magdalene as well. Elizabeth was a thin and intense elderly woman with a lined face and milky blind eyes. She knew Lazarus' name when he gave it and opened the door wide to her one-room house. Her small home was simply furnished with a wooden table and a half-dozen plain wooden chairs and stools. Jesus was seated at the table with Mary Magdalene. His mother was sitting in a chair next to him. Jesus rose to greet Lazarus and gave him a kiss on the cheek.

"I am so glad you're all right," he said.

"Thank you, Lord," Lazarus replied. "Things have spun out of control since you left my house. Simon and Judas killed a half-dozen Roman soldiers while I was inside talking to the commanding officer. Simon the Zealot tried to murder him in my house, and Judas killed him when he stepped outside. He was a centurion named Longinus. Do you remember him?"

"Of course, I remember him. He was in charge of the Roman detail that crucified me."

Lazarus nodded.

"By now he's buried in some nameless pit between Bethany and the Jordan River."

"He got what was coming to him," Jesus' mother responded, her voice full of spite.

"He was only doing his job, Mother," Jesus chided her.

"I can't argue with that," Lazarus said. "However, John told me that it was Longinus who also commanded the guard at your tomb. He took the money that he was offered to let your disciples enter the tomb and carry your body away, then betrayed everyone by seeking it at my house."

"Where I was," Jesus added.

"Only not quite in the state he expected."

"He's in hell now," Mary said.

"He's dead, Mother," Jesus told her. "A little kindness is in order."

"From me?" she mocked. "Kindness for the man who hung my son on a cross and watched him die? Not likely. My only hope is that *he's* suffering now."

Jesus and Lazarus exchanged glances. Hell was an unknown concept in the Hebrew Scriptures. It had sneaked into Jewish religious discourse and then into Judaic tradition during the Hebrew captivity in Babylon where generations of Jews were exposed to the fire god Ahura Mazda. Self-righteous and violent, he sent the souls of evil doers straight to eternal hell. It made sense that the Jews thought him very like Jehovah.

Jesus taught that there was a heaven, but he had never accepted the reality of hell despite using metaphors akin to such a place where the rich and the selfish were doomed to spend an unhappy afterlife. Lazarus once asked Jesus if he was going to hell because he was rich. Absolutely, Jesus told him, and winked. Since Longinus had not been a Babylonian, but rather a traditional Roman with a soldier's religion,

Jesus guessed he was more likely drinking wine and gambling in the Elysian fields, Imperium Romanum's heaven.

Elohim had never said that he was the only god, but demanded that the Jews put him above all others. Using that as a foundation for his own thinking about non-Hebrew religions, Jesus tended to give credence to their beliefs and assented to the possibility that there were other gods with their own revelations and rules, rewards, and punishments, capped by how they judged their adherents, good or evil, when their lives ended.

If his followers disagreed with such liberal tenets, they never expressed it. When the Temple authorities, on the other hand, encountered such opinions, it was simply more tinder for the fire being fanned to consume Jesus' life. So much for free-flowing religious discourse.

"The Roman soldiers were carted away and secretly buried in the wilderness," Lazarus continued. "Even if Prefect Pilatus cannot discover who murdered them, he will very likely blame your disciples anyway. He is very likely fearing for his own life right now."

"From your lips to God's ears," Mary said. All eyes went to her. "What?" she asked. "Am I supposed to believe that I'm the only Jew in this house who would like to see that pitiful excuse for a governor dead?"

"More blood?" Jesus asked astounded. "Men have died tonight, Mother, murdered in cold blood by Simon and Judas."

"I think they are brave men," Mary countered, "and Judas is my hero."

"He's a betrayer *and* a killer," Jesus said.

"He put the aspirations of his country first," Mary replied undaunted. "We all thought that the confrontation he set in motion between you and the Romans would force you to call Israel to arms and overthrow the oppressors."

"It didn't quite work out that way, did it?" Jesus asked. "I have said since the very beginning of my ministry that my kingdom is not of this world."

"Pray tell then, which world are you waiting for?" Mary snapped. "You are the risen Lord, the son of the Living God. Yet you still can't figure out that your duty is to set Jehovah's people free?"

Jesus refused to answer. His vision of the world of men was far larger than the narrow confines of Judea, and his crucifixion was more than a pin-on badge allowing him to lead frustrated Jews in a suicidal war against the world's greatest military power. His goal was and remained to bring empathy, kindness, and love to the world, not swords and spears.

Lazarus broke the silence.

"Jesus, you must leave as soon as possible. I have a merchant ship in Jaffa that will carry you to Gaul."

Jesus stood and walked over to Mary Magdalene. He offered her his hand.

"Will you come?" he asked. "Will you accept my offer of marriage here in the presence of my family and friends?"

Mary took Jesus' hand, kissed it, and then rose and looked into his eyes.

"I will come and I will marry you, staying by your side wherever you may go, serving you with love and honor until my breath leaves my body."

"Hear, hear!" Elizabeth cried, her worn face smiling, tears of happiness welling up in her blind eyes.

"Hear, hear!" Lazarus echoed.

John ran up and hugged Jesus.

"May I go, too?" he begged.

"You are still your father's son," Jesus replied gently. "I will come back for you, I promise."

John clung to Jesus and buried his face in his robe.

Lazarus walked to the front door.

"We must leave while it is still dark," he urged. "I have asked Miguel to travel with you. He is smart and resourceful and will carry money necessary to not only fund your travel, but to see to your settlement in the new land as well."

Jesus gazed at his mother, Elizabeth, John, and Lazarus.

"Bless us, son," Mary said.

Jesus raised both of his wounded hands and spoke emotionally.

"The Lord bless thee and keep thee. The Lord make his face shine upon thee, and be gracious unto thee. The Lord lift up his countenance upon thee, and give thee peace."

"Amen," sounded around the small room.

Hugs and kisses were fervently exchanged, and as Lazarus and Mary Magdalene waited at the open door, Jesus held his mother and told her goodbye.

She put her head against his chest and wept.

"You die, you live, you disappear," she told him. "A normal son you aren't."

"I will be back, Mother."

Mary dried her eyes with her sleeve and looked up at Jesus.

"Don't bother unless you bring me grandchildren," she said.

"Shall I regard that as a blessing on my betrothal?" Jesus asked.

"Well, you can take it as a certain kind of encouragement anyway," Mary answered.

Jesus gave her a last hug and kiss and then left the house shutting the door behind him. He wondered how long it would be before he opened that door again. He could not have guessed that when that day finally came he would be twice as old and that everyone in the house would be dead or exiled.

He would not be able to bring his wife, Mary Magdalene, for she would lie buried in Gaul. The Jews of Israel would have revolted against Rome whose armies would slaughter millions of Hebrews including his first-born son, and perhaps the most telling of all the changes, the great Temple of Jehovah would be burned and razed to the ground.

Would Jesus still have left Jerusalem had he known that all of these things would happen? Of course he would have. As a mystic follower of his would write a millennia and a half later, "Man proposes, God disposes." No life was destined to be any more invested with pain and suffering, love and honor, than Jesus of Nazareth. In shutting the door to that house in Jerusalem and turning his face to the Roman west, he did so knowing that whatever triumphs and sorrows, blessings and losses, lay ahead in his life, one thing would always be true—The Lord giveth, and the Lord taketh away. Blessed be the name of the Lord.

Jesus pulled the door to Elizabeth's house shut. Taking Mary Magdalene's hand, he walked into the next three decades of a new life in Gaul, a world away from Jerusalem and the Promised Land.

The End of Part I

CHAPTER SIX

Jesus and Mary rode in the back of one of Lazarus' covered mercantile wagons filled with bags of salt from the great Salt Sea en route to Joppa on the Mediterranean. Pound-for-pound as valuable as gold, the salt would be shipped to Gaul and traded for tin, which would then be brought back to Judea and sold at a premium to metal smithies for coating the edges of iron tools for Jewish farmers and steel weapons for Roman soldiers.

Miquel had ridden in front next to the wagon driver, Alejandro, a muscular young Spanish Jew who had stowed away on one of Lazarus' inbound ships from Spain and had been promptly recruited by Lazarus to work for him. He managed the transport of cargo to and from Joppa for Lazarus' import and export company in Jerusalem, a responsibility that gave him honor and dignity and made him fiercely loyal to Lazarus.

The wagon ride took three days with stops for food and drink and bodily needs. They had not stayed at any of the inns along the way for obvious reasons. Miguel and Alejandro fetched food when the wagon was pulled over and reported that everyone was talking about the fact that not only had Jesus' tomb been opened and found empty, but he had been seen alive by numerous people who swore on Jehovah's name that it was Jesus himself back from the dead.

Such rumors made it that much more important that Jesus not be spotted on the way to Joppa—not by gossips, not by believers, and especially not by any authorities. This was actually welcomed by Jesus and Mary who reveled in their confinement, spending their time together in the wagon sharing stories with each other shyly, but happily setting the foundation for their future life together.

"Did you ever notice me all the years I followed you and the Twelve?" Mary asked. She was wearing a beautiful red wool robe made in Tyre and imported by an expensive shop in Jerusalem. Her lustrous hair—so black it looked shadowy blue—was knotted and wrapped on top of her head, but she had foregone wearing a headscarf inside the wagon. Was she flirting, she wondered to herself? But was that even possible with the man she had agreed to marry?

"Is that a serious question?" Jesus answered in a teasing tone. "I *always* noticed you. You were attentive, but not intrusive. Always ready to help with meals, yet never one to ask someone else to wash dishes. Judas also told me that you frequently contributed large sums of money towards our expenses."

Mary frowned.

"He wasn't supposed to do that."

Jesus shrugged.

"Judas has his own set of rules."

"I never liked him. He was greedy and violent."

"Not on my watch, he wasn't," Jesus objected.

Mary arched an eyebrow.

"So, you're not including the fact that Judas betrayed you to the cross and your death?"

"But he didn't," Jesus answered. "He pushed things into motion hoping to ignite a revolutionary fervor in Judea that would lead me to declare that I was the messiah ready to overthrow the Romans."

"He wasn't the only one who wished for that," Mary commented. She herself had believed for a long time as one of the last remaining Jews of the lost tribe of Benjamin that Israel would be ruled by Jesus, God's Son himself. Later that dream was replaced by a true understanding of his teachings and his mission. His fellowship was of the conscience, of the spirit. His kingdom had nothing to do with governments or formal religion. As he had said repeatedly, it was not of this world.

"When did you first notice me?" Mary asked.

Jesus shook his head gently.

"Un-uh," he said. "It's my turn to ask a question. When did you first notice *me?*"

Mary gazed at him and smiled.

"You will never remember. It was years ago, and I was still a young girl. I was at my cousin's wedding in Cana. You were there." Jesus frowned, remembering all too well. Mary laughed, delighted that he recalled the episode. "You might try and deny it now, but you made so much wine that my uncle and his friends were stunned."

"Didn't mean to," Jesus muttered.

"Well, of course, you did," Mary corrected him. "I was seated near to you and I overheard your mother telling you that the wedding wine had run out. You got right up and told the steward of the feast to have the purification vases filled with water. Each one of those—and there were six because I counted—held thirty gallons of water, and after they were filled you told the steward to drink from one. He did and was shocked to find that the water had been changed to wine, good wine, *one hundred eighty gallons of good wine.*"

Jesus stayed silent. The fact that he had changed water into wine as his first public miracle still bothered him. He could have made a lame man walk or cured an outcast leper, but instead he had made so much wine that the wedding guests drank themselves blind.

Mary watched Jesus' face.

"You have nothing to say?"

"Nothing but an apology."

"Oh, quit. You saved the wedding."

"I gave a lot of folks hangovers."

Mary laughed loud and hard. It was not a very lady-like laugh, but it was joyous and fun.

"You may have, but I don't think God disapproved. The Lord gives, and in this case, he gave wine. In fact, I remember your mother trying to tell you what a blessing it was, but you were pretty angry at her."

"I was," Jesus admitted. "I felt like a fool."

"That wasn't her fault. It was yours."

Jesus stared at his betrothed without answering. He loved women for their kindness, their social graces, and their willingness to sacrifice for the well-being of their families. He wasn't sure, however, that he was a big fan of some women's fondness for pointing out one's foibles. His mother had performed that role for him for thirty-three years and now it appeared that in some mysterious right of transmission that responsibility had passed to Mary Magdalene.

On the other hand, if Mary's observations could help him see what he had done right or wrong, would that not be a true blessing from his helpmate? He'd have to become more patient though to receive her corrections, there was no doubt about that. He had once boldly declared that the truth would set you free. Good chance it would set you on edge, too.

"True enough," Jesus responded at last. "I don't think I ever apologized to her."

"Well, you still can if you're not a stubborn—"

"Jew?" Jesus interrupted.

"Man," Mary corrected him. "Stubborn man."

Jesus grinned. "I promise I will apologize to her face-to-face with you present when we see her again."

"Not before there are grandchildren, you won't," Mary reminded him.

"I will diligently work to make sure that happens first," Jesus said, realizing a moment later the unintended suggestiveness of his remark. He blushed, and Mary laughed her loud and raucous laugh again.

"What I meant—" he started to explain.

"I know what you meant," Mary cut him off, "and I'm going to damn well hold you to it."

Jesus blushed again.

Mary laughed again.

"Now it's my turn," Mary said. "When did you first notice me? And when did it become *important* for you to notice me?"

Jesus nodded amused by her choice of words.

"The first time I remember seeing you, which is really not the same thing as *noticing* you, was the day I was baptized in the River Jordan by John the Baptist."

Mary instantly remembered the occasion.

"After I had walked into the river," Jesus continued, "I knelt and dipped my head below the surface. When I stood up the Baptist hugged me and urged the crowd to be baptized and repent of their sins. Many did. You did, walking into the river all by yourself. You didn't look like you were even twelve. I did not know then that you were an orphan living with your father's brother and his family in Magdala. All I knew was that you were the only child who came forward that day to be baptized."

Mary nodded, but didn't speak.

Jesus continued.

"I was well aware of your presence over the next years and noted that my mother made it a point to invite you to join her and the other women who accompanied me and the Twelve. Still, I never spoke to you until the time I was visiting Lazarus and you came into his private garden, knelt by me, and poured perfumed oil on my feet. You shocked everyone when you undid your tresses and dried my feet with your hair.

"When you rose to leave, I bid you stay, and you did. Even though you were not much older than a young girl you opened my eyes to your maturity as you spoke about the Scriptures, confidently offering your own interpretations and questions. From that day on, I eagerly looked forward to our discussions, and always asked Lazarus to invite you to join us when I stayed at his home."

Jesus smiled tenderly, took one of Mary's hands, and went on.

"At some point during those occasions, I thought that of all the women I had met in my life you were the only one who provoked thoughts of marriage and children. From then on you were never far from my mind. I did not speak of such things to you, or to anyone, because it was becoming undeniably clear that I was going to crash headlong into the Temple authorities and the Roman ruler.

"The Sunday I rode the donkey into Jerusalem marked the end of my mission. My preaching was done, my lessons were taught, and my ministry was finished. Then came my arrest and trial, conviction, and the cross. I saw you there with my mother. My disciples were not there. Lazarus was not there. But you were there. I knew then that I loved you, Mary, with a longing and passion that I had never allowed myself to feel before. And when at the end I surrendered myself to God, I looked at you and gave up the last thing that could have kept me on Earth."

Jesus paused, then finished his story.

"That is not to say that I surrendered hope. Even in the moment I died, I struggled to believe that God would bring me back to continue my life as Jesus of Nazareth. I have to admit, though, that I did not imagine this part about sitting in a wagon filled with bags of salt."

"With your wife," Mary offered gently.

"Yes, technically," Jesus agreed. "Your consent to become my wife is legally tantamount to being married, but when *I* call you my wife it will be on the day you rise early in the morning to make breakfast for me."

Mary flushed deep red.

Jesus burst out laughing.

"Somewhat adventurous talk for a man who has never even kissed me," Mary said. Then she lifted her face toward Jesus and closed her eyes. He leaned down and gently put his lips on hers. Mary licked them with her tongue and kissed him hard. She kissed him again and again, urgent and unceasing. At last Jesus sat back and looked at Mary.

"It is clear to me that you won't be getting up early to fix breakfast for me. Which is fine, actually. I'll be too tired to wake up and eat it."

Mary laughed loudly, stood up, and wrapped her arms as far as she could around Jesus' chest.

"My, what a big chest you have," she whispered in his ear.

Jesus grinned, but did not answer.

"Anything you want to say to me?" Mary whispered in Jesus' ear.

"Maybe you could hug me a little less hard. I'm still pretty sore."

Mary pulled back, her face stricken with remorse.

"I'm so sorry."

"No, it's all right."

"I didn't mean to hurt you. Was I too forward?"

"No more than Ruth."

"Yeah, but only if you believe she slept at Ruben's *feet* to get his attention."

"Ho!" Jesus responded. "Alas, I am not as robust as my ancestor. At least not right now. I may be back from the dead, but I probably could use a hospice."

"*I'll* take care of you," Mary declared, instantly.

"I accept. Cancel the hospice."

"We're talking like a couple teenagers being coy with each other," Mary said, smiling happily.

"One of us *is* a teenager," Jesus answered, "and we *are* being coy."

"Not for long. Plan on lots of kids."

"That would be nice."

"I am already working on names," Mary announced. "My father's name was Saul and I would like to name our first son after him."

"I love the story of Saul. He was a great hero and a great king."

"The very first king! And he was from the tribe of Benjamin, my tribe. I also like the name David, after the greatest king, from your ancestry and your tribe."

"My mother says I have his red hair and freckles."

"Had his red hair," Mary said touching Jesus' white locks.

"Strange isn't it?" Jesus replied.

"Doesn't matter," Mary said gently. "You still have his blue eyes and handsome face."

"My father Joseph used to tease me that David killed the giant Goliath for messing with his harem."

"That would explain how tall you are," Mary teased.

"I'm not *that* tall. Besides, Goliath never had any children."

"Because he was killed?"

"No. Because he was gay."

Mary sat and thought about that.

"Moving on," she said, "I think we should have lots of sons and daughters."

Jesus smiled.

"What?" Mary demanded. "If you can make all those gallons of wine with a single command, you can certainly manage to give me all the kids I want. Just maybe not six hundred and eighty."

Jesus laughed.

"Our first-born daughter shall be called Mary," he said, "after you and my mother. Our next girl shall be called Ruth so she is encouraged to be bold and daring like you."

Mary poked Jesus gently.

"Be serious."

"I am! If I wasn't serious I would have said Sarah, or Hagar, or Michel, or Jezebel. All women with attitudes."

"So, why didn't you throw in some really famous women like Calpurnia, or Livia, or even Cleopatra?"

"Because they're Gentiles. Who cares about them?"

Mary stared at Jesus, then burst out laughing.

"I think this is going to be a very interesting marriage," she said, her eyes twinkling.

"Between our discussions and working on the grandchildren," Jesus replied, "I can't see how it wouldn't be."

"Amen, husband," Mary intoned.

"Amen—" Jesus said, then paused. He held out his hand to Mary. She took it with both of hers and snuggled up close. "—dearest wife," he finished.

— ⚜ —

The morning of the fourth day on the road the travelers reached Joppa. It was a sprawling seaport city with endless rows of wooden piers stretching into the sea. Ships from all the great trading nations of the world were packed in slips on both sides of each dock. Miguel and Alejandro went in search of the captain of the ship that would take Jesus and Mary to Gaul.

The young lovers were left to enjoy the sun and the sand, sitting on the beach eating fresh dates from Jericho and drinking a sweet white wine from the Greek island of Crete. They watched the bustle of bare-chested stevedores loading and unloading gold and ivory from Punt's mysterious jungles, cowhides from far away Londonium, large clay amphoras of red wine from Italy, ingots of tin from Gaul, and the most luxurious of all materials, dyed and printed bolts of silk, the wonder of China.

"Do you know that some people in the world own more than one set of clothes?" Mary asked Jesus.

"Yes," he replied, "but I've never understood the point of that. It's like having extra feet or two more hands. What do you do with them?"

"The ability to own multiple sets of clothes demonstrates the wealth and status of the owner."

"Blessed are the owners of multiple outfits," Jesus teased. "They shall inherit the envy of their neighbors and lots of laundry bills."

"Stop it. I'd like to go shopping for some silk for my wedding dress."

"Well, why didn't you just say that? It's a lot different than filling up chests with clothes that you'll hardly ever wear."

"I want to shop now."

Jesus arched an eyebrow.

"That surprises you?" Mary teased.

"No," he replied. "But you might ask Miguel or Alejandro to accompany you. They know the captains and the quality of their goods, and they also probably speak just about every language bantered about on the piers."

Mary nodded and reached inside the fold of her wool gown and pulled out a very substantial painted leather purse. "From India," she said holding it up. She loosened the bag's leather strings and pulled out a handful of large golden coins with the head of Tiberius on them. She held them out to Jesus. He opened his palm, and she placed the coins on it.

"Money for wedding rings, husband. You might ask Miguel or Alejandro to accompany you. They know the captains and the quality of their goods, and they also probably speak just about every language bantered about on the piers."

Jesus gave Mary a droll look.

"Ha!" she laughed, and clapped her hands together. "But I'm serious. I want everyone who sets their eyes on you to know that you're taken."

"I would never even notice someone who sets their eyes me."

"I will."

"Rings are so, so—"

"Gay?"

"No!"

"Materialistic?"

"No."
"Ostentatious?"
"No."
"Roman?"
"Close."
"Pagan?"
"Yes! That's it. And Jews don't wear wedding rings."

"But Jews *do* wear rings. The more well-off they are, the more rings they wear."

Jesus frowned and shook his head.

"Does that sound even remotely like something I would do?"

"How bad can one ring be?"

Jesus studied Mary's face for a long moment.

"Just one? Well, maybe," he said, kindly, "as long as it's a wedding ring."

"You are so wonderful!" Mary cried happily, and leaned forward to hug Jesus. She put her arms around him and gave him a peck on the cheek. Then she lifted up her left hand for Jesus to see.

"I would like a plain gold ring, size five. You will need to be sized and I want you to pick out something that is huge and forbidding. I want every woman who thinks about flirting with you to fear the wife behind the ring."

Jesus' eyes went wide. He bit his tongue to keep from responding. It was the first of many lessons he would experience learning to be a good husband. He and Mary finished off the dates and the wine, and minutes later she was off with Miguel to buy Cathay silk while Alejandro took Jesus into the port city itself in search of wedding rings.

— ✤ —

Finding a perfect gold ring for Mary was easy. Jesus and Alejandro were inside a small, dark shop with its owner Chukwu, a short, fat black man with a shaved head. There was a small table in the center of his shop where Jesus and Alejandro sat sorting through a mound of gold rings that Chukwu had brought all the way from Punt, his homeland in eastern Africa. Many were plain gold bands of various colors, wrought by combining the gold with alloys of copper, nickel, or silver. Jesus had set a rich, dark gold band aside for Mary. Pure, with only a bit of copper to stiffen the gold, it was somewhat soft and could be bent with effort. Strong but pliable, it was the perfect symbol of the give-and-take of a good marriage, he thought.

Jesus pulled a ring out of the pile. It was huge, a thick band of gold with a beautiful blue stone set in the center. He tried it on his left hand. It fit precisely on his fourth finger, the digit before his smallest finger which rich men like Lazarus tended to use for signet rings. The ring fit snugly without being too tight.

"What kind of stone is this?" Jesus asked Chukwu.

With a serious expression the shop owner answered, "Lapis from Egypt."

"I like it," Jesus said, "and it fits me."

Chukwu nodded. The customer was always right, even if the gold ring had a cheap alloy and the jewel was fake. Neither would prevent him from charging a premium price.

Alejandro frowned and shook his head.

"For all its size it's a bit underwhelming," he spoke up.

"I like underwhelming," Jesus told him.

"Underwhelming as in piece of crap."

"What?"

"The band is at least half nickel and the supposed jewel is nothing but glass."

Chukwu didn't react.

Alejandro poked through the rings piled up on the table top. Jesus glanced at the face of the stoic shop owner.

"Does your name have a meaning?" he asked.

"It is the name of god."

"The name of *your* god?"

"Who else? Actually his name is Chuk. I added the Wu which means son. So I am the son of god."

Jesus looked at the proud expression on Chukwu's face.

"Well, good for you, Chukwu," he told him. "That name might get you in trouble in certain circles though."

"Not with the women," Chukwu answered, shaking his head. "Oh, no, not with the women."

Alejandro grinned. Jesus blushed and stared at the rings. Alejandro pointed at a thick gold band with an intricately wrought gold star on the top.

"That's the one!" Alejandro exclaimed. He reached for the ring. "Made for a big man, too." Alejandro slipped it on Jesus' ring finger. It slid off. Jesus put it on his middle finger. He saw that the star was made from two pieces of gold, one mounted over the other to create a star with six points.

"The star is a hexagram created from two equilateral triangles," Chukwu explained.

"I bought it from a Jewish widow in Alexandria. She called it the Star of David and told me that Jews all over the empire were adopting the symbol allowing them to secretly identify each other." Chukwu shrugged. "Who knows if what she said was true."

"Star of David," Jesus repeated, reverently. He turned to Alejandro. "Did I tell you that King David was my ancestor?"

"Whichever giant owned this ring was your ancestor, too."

Jesus looked at Chukwu.

"I'll take the Star of David and this plain gold band," he said. He handed the rings to the shop keeper. Then he looked at Alejandro. "Please pick out one for yourself."

The Spaniard was surprised.

"For what reason?" he asked.

"For your help."

"We are not finished with this adventure, my Lord, not by a long shot," Alejandro protested. "Gaul is very far away."

"Pick something anyway," Jesus told him.

Alejandro nodded respectfully, then carefully investigated the hoard of rings again. He pulled out a thin silver band mounted with a black pearl.

"It is made of white gold," Chukwu told him, "and the pearl is from ocean islands in the middle of a sea un-sailed by men other than the dark seafaring tribes who live there."

"I've never heard of such a place," Alejandro said.

"And you've never seen a black pearl either."

"True."

Alejandro tried the ring on the forefinger of his right hand. It fit a bit snugly, but he was able to get it on and off over his knuckle.

"Was this ring made for a woman?"

"It was made for you," Chukwu replied smoothly. "If it was owned by a woman before you, she would have been a princess, brown and naked except for that ring."

"How much is it?" Alejandro asked.

"Let *me* discuss that with Chukwu," Jesus interrupted. "With three rings I am sure we will save Mary some money, who, in fact—" Jesus paused and reached inside the pocket of his robe for her coins, "—sent money expressly for our purchases."

Chukwu rose and brought a clay pot filled with a hot liquid mixed with honey. He served Jesus, Alejandro, and himself, filling small enameled glass tumblers with the beverage. Everyone drank. It was a strong yet pleasant drink, and the honey left a sweet aftertaste.

"It's called tea," the merchant said. "I first tried it in the land of the Turkmen across the Unfriendly Sea."

"You mean the Black Sea?" Alejandro asked. He'd sent ships there on Lazarus' behalf.

"Trust me, it's unfriendly."

"Isn't tea actually from Indus, the land beyond the Ganges River?" Alejandro asked.

"It is, indeed. Have you had it before?"

"Without honey, and honestly, it was not that memorable. This version however, is worthy of the gods."

"Yes," Chukwu said, "it is." He glanced at Jesus. "See? Sometimes being the son of god can work out nicely."

Jesus, Alejandro, and Chukwu sat together for a long time drinking the sweetened tea and talking about the world, small and large. Chukwu said the seaport was filled with endless speculation as to what happened to the body of Jesus of Nazareth. Many, many people believed that sometime in the morning on the third day after his interment his followers had stolen his body.

Pontius Pilatus ordered his tomb opened. It was said that the funeral wrappings wound around the body had been undone and dumped on the floor. The burial chamber was empty. Jesus' body was gone. The guards who had been posted at the tomb had been dismissed before the discovery, and the centurion in charge of the detail had gone missing. It was widely assumed that he had been murdered by Jesus' followers.

And where was Jesus' body now? Most likely buried in a hidden location known only to his closest friends. But that didn't mean things were over. Servants to Pilatus let loose the word that the governor was fearful that Jesus' rumored resurrection would ignite a popular revolt, fueling the very rebellion that Pilatus thought he had prevented by executing the would-be messiah. He had called the half legion of soldiers stationed in the Roman capital of Caesarea to Jerusalem and had sent special messengers to Rome warning the emperor that he might need more than those five thousand legionnaires if indeed a Jewish revolt was brewing.

Chukwu said that he was dubious that Pilatus' message would find its way into Caesar's hands. The septuagenarian ruler of the Roman Empire was holed up in the grotto of Capri surrounded by scholars and young men. Books and boys were all that the declining Tiberius seemed to be interested in.

Rome itself was being run by the Senate and the empire's wealthiest families, and they all sacrificed daily to every Roman god and goddess praying for the lecherous ruler's longevity. And why not? The emperor's chosen successor was Gaius Julian Caesar Augustus Germanicus, still known by his childhood nickname Caligula, Little Boots, whose main interests in life were his sexual preferences, currently his three sisters and his favorite horse.

After discussing other local and world news, Chukwu looked at Jesus and told him that a very good price for the three rings he had chosen would be six hundred gold sesterces. Alejandro reacted like he was having heart failure. He grabbed his chest and struggled for breath. Chukwu watched him with a poker face. Alejandro never opened his mouth once.

"A generous price," Jesus responded, "but for a dozen rings not three. Three rings should be something more like seventy-five sesterces." He took a sip of tea. "I love the bit of mint you added in this last serving," he said.

Chukwu smiled slowly.

"You are a funny man. I like that. But who taught you to bargain? If I were not a gentleman and an easygoing fellow, I should likely be insulted. Five hundred gold sesterces."

"I would never intend such a thing," Jesus apologized. "My father taught me to bargain in answer to your question. He traded with itinerant merchants who journeyed to Sephora where he worked most of his life on Roman construction projects. One hundred and fifty."

Chukwu squinted, pondering Jesus' information.

"Your father was a laborer?"

"My father was an artisan with many men in his employ. He loved to have Phoenician pirates work for him because they appreciated the steady work and the guaranteed income. They were also the ones who trained my father to barter. He copied their tattoos on his body and wore a golden circle in his left ear."

"That meant he was a homosexual," Alejandro piped up.

"No, it meant that he was *not*," Chukwu corrected him.

"I think he might have even bought that gold earring from traders bringing gold from Punt," Jesus added. "Maybe people you might know."

"Chuk be praised," Chukwu said piously. "In such a case, how can I not offer you the rings for four hundred sesterces in honor of your father?"

"Four hundred?" Alejandro spoke up at last, clearly offended. "Jesus, if you accept such a price, then remove my ring. I will not be party to such robbery."

Chukwu's eyes narrowed.

"Not necessary, good Alejandro," Jesus assured him. "And I would appreciate it if you'd work at recovering your good manners. The price for the rings is not just a matter of what they should cost. It is also important that the final agreed-upon price be a blessing to both parties."

"Yes? Well, at four hundred sesterces, only Chukwu is being blessed."

"Ho!" Jesus replied. "Amusing, but not helpful."

He turned to the fuming merchant.

"How would you feel if I offered you two hundred and fifty for the three rings?"

"Almost blessed."

Jesus looked him in the eye.

"And if I offered three hundred sesterces?"

"From the son of a man who learned to barter from pirates? Damn lucky!"

At that all three men laughed. Jesus extended his hand and Chukwu shook it.

There was another round of tea and more tales. Chukwu talked about the wild animals in the jungles of Punt. Alejandro spoke of the ancient Egyptian monuments he'd seen sailing up the Egyptian Nile. And Jesus told stories about his father Joseph arm wrestling his employees to see who would be buying the first round of wine when a job was done.

Chukwu stood up and went to the back of his store. He looked through some bags he had stashed there, then returned and sat down. He laid out a few gold earrings on the table and looked at Jesus.

"Are any of these similar to the one your father wore?"

Jesus pointed at a simple gold circle with a diamond set at the inside bottom.

"Whoa," Chukwu exclaimed. "Pirate plunder indeed. That one was offered to me right off the ear of a Wagonhaginian sea rover who needed money."

Jesus picked it up.

"It's identical," he declared, studying it carefully.

"Then it's yours," Chukwu said. "In remembrance of your father."

Jesus looked at the shop owner.

"But only," Chukwu went on, "if we pierce your ear right now and you wear it on your way."

Jesus gazed at Chukwu and thought of the lifetime of love Joseph had showed him even though Mary maintained that it wasn't Joseph, but Jehovah, who was his true father. He reached out and shook Chukwu's hand again.

His earlobe hurt afterwards, and he was a bit worried about what Mary was going to say. On the other hand, his father would be proud that he had successfully negotiated for and purchased three beautiful rings for his wife, his friend, and himself. Jewelry, jewelry, jewelry. Wow. It felt really good. No wonder pagans smiled a lot.

— ⚜ —

Mary was waiting at the wagon with Miguel. She ran to greet Jesus and told him that she had found a dress for herself, something for him, and that she was starving. Could they all go into town and eat? Miguel took them to a small Dacian inn where they shared flatbread and lentil soup, roast lamb served with a sour herb dipping sauce, and a skin of red wine from Galicia, the verdant countryside at the very northwestern tip of Spain. It was a place of aboriginal Iberian tribesmen where the land jutted into the vast and lonely Sea of Atlantis. No one knew when those blue-tattooed folk began making wine, but its fame now extended through the Roman Empire to its farthest reaches.

There was talk and laughter, but both Mary and Jesus were ready to have time alone. Leaving the inn, Alejandro and Miguel went off to visit friends in port. It was almost dark when Mary pulled out her purchases inside the wagon. They were wrapped in thin papyrus paper and bound with twine made from rushes. She held up a vermillion silk dress and then one that was deep blue. Both had embroidery on the sleeves and around the necks depicting dragons and calligraphy of far-off China. They were the most beautiful gowns Jesus had ever seen. Mary was thrilled with his reaction and then pulled out a paper package for him. He opened it slowly and lifted up something he did not recognize.

"They are called pants," Mary told him, "made in the Persian style."

"I'm not wearing them."

"I think they'll go perfectly with your new earring."

Jesus flushed. It was Mary's first acknowledgement that he had had his ear pierced. Mary handed him another package. He opened it and found a long-sleeved silk shirt the same scarlet color as the pants.

"You wear them together, day or night."

"They're pajamas?"

"They're called a suit. Your friend Lazarus owns several pairs. Miguel told me."

Jesus put the clothes down and took Mary's hand.

"Thank you, sweet. Are you ready to see the rings?"

"Not yet," Mary said. "Let's take a walk on the beach and snuggle up in some secluded spot, and then you can show me."

"Done," Jesus replied.

As the sun set over the sea, Mary and Jesus walked far beyond the commercial piers looking for a spot on the sandy beach where no one had trod. They sat and Jesus handed the pouch with the wedding rings to Mary. She pulled the strings open and felt inside searching for the bigger band. She pulled out the heavy gold ring with the fused stars and stared at it.

"I have heard of this symbol," she said. "It's a Jewish star like the one that hovered in the heavens signaling your birth."

"You've been talking to my mother."

"Doesn't make the stories any less marvelous."

Mary put it on the ring finger of Jesus' left hand. Then she removed it and put in on his middle finger. Without a word she pulled out the petite gold wedding band that was for her.

"It's perfect," she said, happily. "Thank you." She took Jesus' face in her hands and kissed his mouth. "I affirm before God and man that you are my husband, Jesus, son of Joseph."

She gave her ring to Jesus who gently placed it on the ring finger of her left hand.

"I affirm before God and man that you are my wife, Mary, daughter of Saul."

They kissed long and passionately.

"It's almost dark, dear husband," Mary said softly.

"Do you think we should go back?"

"No, no, no," Mary said, taking Jesus' hands. "We should do what new husbands and wives do."

"Here?"

"Here and now."

Jesus hesitated.

"What would Jehovah say?" he asked.

"Amen!" she cried.

It was a persuasive argument to which Jesus had no response other than to gently lay his wife down on the sand. Amen, indeed, he thought afterwards, holding Mary in his arms. He doubted that he'd ever be able to utter that word again without thinking of loving his wife on this beach. Could the reserved, even pious part of his soul ever accept that? All he could think of was, Amen!

CHAPTER SEVEN

Mary suffered from seasickness the entire three weeks she was aboard the old Phoenician bark on which Alejandro had arranged passage for her and Jesus to Marseilles. The ship spent its own sweet time bobbing up and down along the northern shore of the Mediterranean with but a single mast and sail. It was almost impossible for Mary to do anything except sit up in bed with Jesus' help and take barley crackers, bean soup, and tea.

After landing at last in Marseilles, the largest Mediterranean seaport in Gaul, Alejandro and Miguel spent two days buying foodstuffs, basic household supplies, and arranging transport to a vast parcel of rural land in southern Gaul owned by Lazarus. Jesus' friend and benefactor had deeded a large valley out of those holdings to him and had renamed it La Valdieu, the Valley of God, in his honor.

The land had been cultivated in an age long before this one, and a large stone house still remained. Its stones needed stabilizing and all the glass was broken. Over the next months, the stonemasons, carpenters, and glaziers that Alejandro hired in Marseilles restored and expanded the building into an elegant manor house, redoing the windows with clear modern glass and building a stone road from the main highway to the house.

The interior was cleaned and scrubbed and filled with elegant furniture created by a team of master carpenters. Innumerable wonderful things purchased by Miguel and Mary on shopping trips to Marseilles filled the interior: German porcelain vessels and mugs, Frankish crystal glasses and pitchers, heavy Italian damask drapes, several large Persian carpets, Maghreb lampstands of brass, Hindustan candle holders studded with pieces of colored glass, and a host of kitchen tools and devices all the way from the city of Rome itself for preparing meals worthy of the king that both Alejandro and Mary perceived Jesus to be.

Everything had been paid for with funds given to Alejandro by Lazarus, and he had recently sent word that he was promoting Alejandro to estate manager and Miguel to house supervisor if they chose to remain and serve Jesus and Mary. They did. Alejandro laid out ambitious plans to develop the whole property. He wanted to make the land profitable by cultivating grapevines and citrus orchards, and dedicating hundreds, even thousands of acres for grazing sheep and cattle. He also asked permission in the fullness of time to marry and have children. Jesus gave his blessing to everything.

Lazarus had confided to Alejandro that he originally purchased the abandoned estate in Gaul as a precaution should he be forced to flee a Jewish rebellion against the Romans. He had chosen a place far away from Judea where produce and husbandry could be peacefully tendered, allowing him to live well and prosper, welcomed and respected by his neighbors.

Lazarus had given a full half of his holdings to Jesus, retaining ownership of the other half should he need to join Jesus in exile. The tens of thousands of acres that Jesus now owned would provide a permanent source of income that would allow him, his wife, and their children to live without need or want.

Without allowing himself to feel prideful about being able to create a wealthy landowner's position in Gaul for Jesus, Lazarus did at times ponder if his act of generosity was why God in his wisdom had given him a second opportunity at life. Hallelujah, if such were the case. But who knew? He was a hard one to figure out, this Jehovah.

Jesus had spent three years proclaiming that the God of Abraham, Isaac, and Jacob was a God of love, but Lazarus wasn't so sure. Jehovah seemed hard to him, vengeful and unforgiving of even the smallest apostate behaviors. He was touchy, unreliable, and absent more than present, declining to save the Jews as war after war swept through tiny Israel undoing Jerusalem and destroying the first Temple built by Solomon.

Lazarus paused for a moment waiting to see if God would strike him dead. Nope. Okay, he thought, and shook his head. Jehovah might not be a God of love, but a case could be argued that he was a God of patience.

Snow lay upon the ground and a sharp wind blew through the bare trees on the spring day that Saul, the first-born son of Jesus and Mary, was born. Alejandro had fetched a local midwife with gray hair and a confident manner to assist with Mary's birthing. While Miguel and the crew of artisans, house servants, and farm hands went about their tasks, Jesus waited in the master bedroom where Mary lay, a room she had lovingly decorated with Oriental carpets, silk hangings, and tall lampstands holding multi-spouted bronze lamps that lit the room with a subdued light.

A large stone fireplace warmed the room, and Jesus tended the blaze while the midwife comforted Mary and reassured her that the wrenching cramps she was experiencing were normal and not to be feared. They were propelling her baby into the outside world. Mary didn't cry out, but during the moments the labor pains seized her she called to Jesus who came to her side and held her hand, amazed at the strength of her powerful grasp.

Her fierce grip also enlivened the ancient pains of his martyred hands, each one still bearing a hole greater in width than his thumb, created by the nails that had fastened him to the cross. Jesus shook his head. He tried never to think about his death on that instrument of torture. The agony, the crown of thorns, the blood and sweat, urine and feces, flushing down his naked body. And what purpose? To demonstrate that if one was faithful to God it required a loyalty even unto death?

If that had been his Father's intent, then Jesus had certainly given his last measure to fulfill its necessity. Once. He didn't believe that Jehovah would ever ask such a terrible sacrifice of him again, but a dark fear dwelled deep in his soul that if God's call to faithfulness unto death should ever issue again from the Divinity's lips, he didn't know if he could cry out as the prophet Isaiah had, "Here am I, send me, send me."

"The baby is crowning," the midwife said, and beckoned Jesus to join her at the foot of Mary's prostrate form. His wife lay on her back in their bed, arm over her eyes, legs spread and propped high on satin pillows. Jesus looked at Mary's female parts, the fount of all life beginning with Eve herself. He could see the small round top of the baby's head. Its hair was vermillion and luxuriantly full.

"Push now, Mary," the midwife commanded. "Push hard!"

Mary cried out with the force of her effort. Suddenly the baby's whole head emerged from her body.

"One more time, dear girl!" the midwife urged. Mary cried loudly again and pushed the baby all the way out into the waiting hands of the midwife. Jesus felt tears rush down his cheeks.

"What is it?" Mary cried.

Jesus moved to her side and took her hand.

"Saul has arrived, sweet love. Red hair, ten fingers, and ten toes!"

Mary burst into tears and cried on Jesus' hand, holding it tightly against her cheek.

The midwife, humming with happiness, cut Saul's umbilical cord and bound the remainder tightly with a heavy thread which would allow it to dry up and drop off in time. She washed his ruddy little body and wrapped him in swaddling cloths. Then she tenderly laid him on Mary's chest. She moved between Mary's legs again to prepare for the afterbirth.

"Oh!" she cried out and anxiously waved Jesus over. Jesus put Mary's hand down and hurried to the midwife's side. A great wash of blood was flowing out of Mary's body, soaking the blankets and pillows supporting her.

Jesus stared, then looked at his wife. Mary's face was pale and her eyes were closed. He shook his head furiously.

"No!" he cried. "This shall not be!" He placed both of his hands on Mary's belly. The bleeding stopped at once. Then the afterbirth came, washed out of Mary's body by clear pure fluid.

Perhaps Baby Saul had heard his father's refusal to give up his wife, or perhaps had simply smelled the milk in his mother's swollen breasts, but either way he opened his eyes and searched for his mother's face. He found her and opened his mouth. Undoing her robe Mary put the newborn at her nipple and fed him.

God be praised, Jesus thought. Saul was safe and so was Mary. He was somewhat astonished that God had allowed his healing powers to remain intact. Astonished *and* thankful. Suddenly his quest to understand what he would be doing while he and Mary raised their family became clear. He would do what he had always done, use his gift of healing to restore the minds, the bodies, and the souls of the needy. Thank you, Father, he mouthed silently. You give and you take away. Blessed be your name. Especially on this day when you gave and did not take.

Jesus squatted behind a bush watching a deer forage only feet away. The wind carried the deer's smell to him. If it had blown the other way, the animal would have bounded off and escaped Jesus' intentions of taking it down and carrying its flesh back to his family. Sitting on his thigh was Saul. At five he was a small boy, shorter than his peers and weighing no more than thirty pounds. But Jesus, having squatted long minutes before the deer appeared, grit his teeth against the weight of Saul on his strained thigh. His legs were sore and his patience was thin. He wanted to kill this deer and go home.

He and Saul had done this before, though Alejandro, Jesus' estate manager, was usually the one who took Saul hunting. He had been absent three months now, traveling through Gaul and Spain to buy himself a wife. Not that Jesus would say it that way to his face. The fact was though that Alejandro had ridden off with a bag filled with Roman gold searching for of an olive-skinned virgin beauty with dark hair and flashing eyes. Would there be love in that kind of transaction, Jesus wondered? That was not for him to judge. Not every man could be as fortunate as he was, having Mary Magdalene to have and to hold. He wished his friend luck in finding the kind of mate *his* heart desired.

Jesus watched the deer grazing. Was his willingness to kill it any less arbitrary than Alejandro's need for a woman to satisfy his manhood? No. And there was something to be said for buying a mate versus having to take her down with a sling.

He looked down at the sling in his hand. It had a smooth oak handle several inches long with both ends of a rawhide sling embedded in the top by an iron spike. The middle of the sling had a rawhide pocket that held a stone weighing up to four ounces. The trick was to choose a stone light enough not to affect the trajectory, but sufficiently heavy to provide a fatal strike.

Slings were as old as the Canaanites who had come down from the hills and intermarried with the Israelites who had arrived from across the sea. The sling was their gift to the Hebrews. The sling slew bear and lion. The sling slew Goliath. The sling slew soldier, horseman, and charioteer, and had for centuries.

When a brigade of scouting Egyptians had once encountered Jews hunting in Gaza they laughed at the men without swords or shields, banding together with only slings in their hands. They laughed until they were cut down like wheat, felled by stones smashing their faces, crushing their temples, ramming their throats, and breaking their necks.

Then the sling-bearers rushed forward and cut the throats of the pagan spies sending them off to their appointments with black-faced Anubis. None of the Hebrews took weapons from the dead Egyptian soldiers. What use would those be?

Jesus gently eased Saul off his thigh. He nodded at the sling that his son held in his own hand. Joseph had trained Jesus to use the sling at a young age, but it had never been more than a boy's toy for him, a bother for birds and rabbits and nothing more. For Saul however, it was a deadly weapon. He had already used it to kill vultures and hawks and had tried to bring down foxes and coyotes as well.

Jesus looked at Saul's pale skin, red hair, freckled face, and eyes as blue and deep as the sea. They concealed a bloodlust and violence such as he'd never seen in a child. Fifty generations of his ancestors had gone to sleep with their fathers since King David had died, yet the famous king's ferocious spirit had risen unquenched in Saul who desired nothing more than to wash himself in the blood of beasts, and surely in time, the blood of men slain by his own hand. It was what it was, however, and Jesus was sure that he could not save his son from it.

Saul put a smooth stone in his sling, rested it over his shoulder, then hurled the stone at the unsuspecting deer. The rock crushed in the side of its face, smashing the deer's eye and driving fragments of bone deep into its brain. It fell dead, very likely having never felt a thing. Saul ran towards the animal.

Jesus' mother Mary had taught him that sin and violence had entered the world when Eve ate the forbidden fruit. He had somehow known even as a child that her fable was a rabbi's erroneous tale. He had believed in his young heart that sin had entered Creation when the first animal seized another animal in its teeth and ate its flesh. *That* was the act that had changed the world, not an idle whim to take a bite of fruit.

Saul knelt down beside the deer. He pulled his hunter's knife out of the leather sheath tied to his calf, bent the deer's head backward, and slit its throat. Blood burst out of the wound covering Saul's face and hands. He looked at the blood, then rubbed his hands together, bathing them in the animal's blood.

Jesus spoke to his son.

"Back to the house, young man," he told him. "We need to get your clothes changed before your mother sees you."

Saul looked up at his father.

"It's only blood."

Jesus gazed at his son. It's only blood. Had he no comprehension of the meaning of dying?

"What do you mean, it's only blood?" Jesus asked him.

"I mean I wasn't hurt," Saul answered. "The blood splashed on me. That's all."

"Would you feel different if it was your own blood?"

Saul thought for a moment.

"If it was shed stupidly, yes. And I would curse my carelessness. If it was a fight required to protect family, or friends, or our country, I would shed it willingly."

Jesus put his hand on Saul's shoulder.

"That you are King David's heir, there can be no doubt."

Saul stood erect and smiled proudly.

"King Saul, too?"

"Present in your flesh as well. You surely have the blood of both of those valiant kings flowing in your veins. Spend it wisely."

"I swear by Almighty God that I will, Father."

"Your word is good enough for me, son."

"I just wanted you to know how serious I am."

"I accept that. Now let's hike home. I'll send some of the kitchen staff to fetch your kill."

Saul took Jesus' hand and they began the walk back to the house. It was early spring and soon the woods would be green and full, so different from Jesus' childhood in the brown hills that nestled Nazareth.

"Do you know who killed the first deer?" Saul asked as they walked.

"No, but I know who killed the first man."

"Was he a hero?"

"No. He was a coward. His name was Cain and he murdered his own brother, Abel."

"Why?"

"He believed that Jehovah blessed Abel's sacrifice and not his. He killed his brother out of envy and spite."

"That wasn't fair!"

No, Jesus thought, it wasn't.

"Did God kill him for his crime?"

"He did not. Jehovah forgave him."

"That wasn't fair either."

"I don't think Jehovah was trying to be fair. More like trying to make the best of a bad situation."

Saul pondered that.

"What are you thinking, son?" Jesus finally asked him.

"I think that Jehovah should have killed Cain."

"And not forgiven him?"

"Not for murder."

"Then this is the first time that you and God do not see eye to eye."

Saul nodded solemnly.

"And what should I do when I think God is wrong?"

"You can get angry. You can bear a grudge. Or you can just decide to accept his will."

"What about forgiving? Could I forgive God?"

"No. For although you may think that God is wrong, the fact is he is never wrong."

"How do you know that? Maybe he does whatever he wants, right or wrong."

Jesus didn't answer. He had shared Saul's suspicion on more than one occasion.

"In that case I think it is important that you forgive God."

Saul nodded and had no more to say on the topic. Jesus, however, kept thinking about the subject. God's puzzling actions among men had gotten little attention from him during his ministry. Why did the good die? Why did Roman's rule? Why did corrupt men control the Temple? And, of course, why did he have to be sacrificed on the cross?

Since his resurrection, his flight from Israel, and his new life with Mary, Saul, and their friends, God's seemingly capricious actions had not entered his mind so often. When they did, he chose to believe that all things, good and bad, were the result of conscious actions by his Father to help the Jews, and yes, to help him as well. Without that belief, the bloody events in his life and the lives of others were just accidental circumstances, in which case he'd have to think long and hard about whether *he* was willing to forgive God.

Jesus and Saul were met at the house by Julius, a new servant born and raised in Gaul and named by his parents after the great Latin general who had conquered this land. He was of medium build, blonde and handsome, with a hooked nose that would have made Caesar proud. Miguel had hired him and made him the master of the outside servants. He was their spokesperson when dealing with Jesus or Mary, or with Miguel and the indoor servants of the manor.

"Any luck?" he called out to the returning hunters.

"Greetings, Julius," Jesus called back. "Saul has the answer to your question."

"We took down a big buck," his son announced proudly. "I bled it out so the meat wouldn't taint. Its body lies about five hundred paces before the place where water seeps from the cliffs." Saul was referring to an outcropping of volcanic obsidian that loomed hundreds of feet above the land at the property's western boundary. "The beast took my missile right in the eye. It was a shot that would have put Goliath down," Saul bragged.

"Good news, then!" Julius cried and nodded respectfully as Jesus and Saul approached. He smiled at Saul. "For your stomach's sake, I am glad that you decided on the deer and not that uncircumcised Philistine. Not sure at all how he would have tasted!"

Saul laughed, though he wasn't completely sure what a Philistine was.

"Alejandro has returned," Julius went on, "with a wife and six pairs of Arabian stallions and mares. It appears that he fancied a Moor's daughter in Seville and paid what he was asked to make her his wife. The Arab horses are a dowry from her father who recommends that they be raced against the local Spanish breed descended from the wild horses of La Mancha's high plateau.

"He also sent six knights along with their wives and families to raise and train the new herd. So Alejandro is pleased with both his new wife *and* his little cavalry. He says the new troops will also make our growing numbers safer, day and night."

Jesus nodded, somewhat surprised that Alejandro had left to find a wife and had come back with a village.

"Take one or two men and dress the deer," he told Julius. "We'll roast it tonight in honor of the bride and groom."

"Yes, Lord," Julius said, and turned to go back to the manor house.

"Is she pretty?" Saul blurted out.

Julius spun back around and looked Saul in the eye.

"So pretty she could steal your heart. My advice is to watch out." Julius winked at Jesus and went on his way.

— ⚜ —

Jesus stopped at the well and lowered a wooden bucket on a rope to draw water. Before he could haul it back up however, Mary appeared with fresh towels. She kissed Saul on the cheek and Jesus on the mouth. Twice. Then she pulled up the bucket herself, dipped a towel in the cool water, and began washing her son's face and hands. Jesus watched, charmed by Mary's mothering instincts and, as always, enamored with her beauty.

He had heard that some men in other cultures stopped whatever activity they were engaged in to pray to their gods six or seven times a day. Honorable. Even admirable. Yet, all in all, he had to admit that he was more inclined to interrupt an activity to harvest kisses from his wife six or seven times or day. He felt a bit sheepish about that but rationalized his choice by figuring that he could make up for lost prayer time when he was old and bent. What else would he be doing?

Mary spoke to her son while she scrubbed him.

"I presume seeing blood on your hands and robe that some animal has been hunted down and killed?" Mary used a fingernail to scrape out the blood under her son's nails.

"I took down a big deer," Saul answered, "and I bled it out making the first cut while it still lived. The knife opened a vessel and the blood gushed out on me."

Mary blanched. Saul noticed and felt proud that the animal's blood and gore had not bothered him. Blood was life and seeing it squirt out of the dying animal affirmed the animal's demise and his triumph. He would never be afraid of blood, animal or human. Some instinct told him that this was not the moment to reveal that to his mother. Keeping it secret, however, didn't make it any less true.

Jesus spoke to Mary.

"Julius told us that Alejandro has returned with a bride."

"A princess would more like it," Mary responded. "She is a beautiful girl, fourteen or fifteen, elegant and refined, the daughter of a Moorish Spanish king and his royal Frankish wife."

Jesus studied Mary's face. She was not happy.

"And?"

"And I haven't been introduced yet. She told Alejandro that she wants to be presented to you first as the Lord of La Valdieu."

"It's just protocol, Mary. Silly rules that prop up royal wannabes."

"She *is* royal, Jesus, and lives by your so-called protocols. She brought six male knights to tend to a herd of horses she brought, plus their families and six personal ladies-in-waiting, virgins all, just as willing as their mistress to get married, *and* six dozen trunks and hundreds of crates and bags filled with everyone's personal possessions.

"I put the bride in a guest room in the manor house, the ladies-in-waiting are in guest rooms next to the bride, and the six knights and their families in tents outside for now." Mary shrugged helplessly. "The ladies are girls really. They are young and friendly and get along fine. They entertain the princess during the day, and every night they seem to think it's a slumber party. It's making me feel old and left out."

Jesus put an arm around his wife and kissed the top of her head.

"It will all work out, my love. Our role is to ensure that Alejandro's bride knows that she is a welcome part of our family. Alejandro himself will be responsible for their living accommodations, the lodging of his wife's courtiers and ladies, and will manage their duties here on the estate. He will also have to erect homesteads for the knights and their families. Did you meet any of them?"

Mary snorted.

"They're typical men-at-arms, bored to tears unless they're slashing and bashing each other, striving to disembowel whoever is closest at hand."

No sooner had Mary finished her litany of complaints than Alejandro appeared at the well. He was stern-faced and all business, but before anything else he knelt and showed homage to Jesus.

"Welcome back from the hunt, Master. Julius and his men have gone to fetch Saul's trophy." Alejandro's stern expression gave way to an anxious one. "I beseech you, Lord, to change into clothing suitable for the introduction of my bride."

Jesus raised an eyebrow at Alejandro's remark.

"I am a simple man and simply dressed," he replied. He was sitting in his warm outdoor leather robe wearing heavy leather sandals. "What are your expectations?"

"My bride, RoxAnna, is a daughter born both of a Moorish king and her mother's Frankish royal blood. She wants her presentation to you to be formal and requests that everyone dress in court attire. Please, Lord, just for this one special occasion, please ask all the members of the household to turn out in elegant costumes to honor her introduction to you, the ruler of La Valdieu." Alejandro gazed at Jesus' robe and sandals. Manor casual. "Perhaps you could wear the red silk Persian suit Mary gave you?"

"The one with the pants?" Jesus asked and frowned.

"The very one. Tailors in Babylon call it the Alexander Suit because it was modeled on one that he wore hunting after he had conquered the city."

"Hunting? I thought you could wear them as pajamas."

Jesus looked at Mary. She avoided his glare, inspecting Saul's face and hands for spots of blood.

"I will do it this once, Alejandro," Jesus replied.

Alejandro was ecstatic.

"Once would be magnificent. Thank you, Lord! May we meet in the great room? At midday?"

Alejandro had coined the term great room for the largest and most utilized room in Jesus' home. It had a huge stone fireplace and an oak dining table that seated twenty in carved wooden chairs. There were big overstuffed couches, large Oriental carpets, divans, silk pillows, and ottomans tossed all around the room like flotsam and jetsam. There were hanging bronze candelabras for candles and bronze oil lamps set on side tables.

Tucked away in one corner of the great room was a desk made of cedar and ivory that Jesus used. He had devoted many hours there writing his memoirs and recording commentaries on the stories of the Hebrews recorded throughout their long history. For all of the room's size and elegance, however, Jesus, Mary, and Saul loved using just one cozy corner near the fire place for family conversations and meals.

"Midday would be fine," Jesus told Alejandro. "One more thing, my friend. What are your plans for the six retainers, their families, and the six handmaidens RoxAnna brought with her?"

"I shall have a proper fortress erected for my bride atop the rocky outcrop that overlooks your land. It was Lazarus' property, but he has deeded it to me and given me funds to build a suitable keep for her and all the new folk. In exchange, I have vowed to continue to watch over your estate as well as ours."

Jesus was surprised at Alejandro's words.

"What do you mean watch over? You manage every estate operation already. Quite brilliantly, I am happy to say."

"Actually, I meant that I will also take on the obligation of protecting your home and property. Gaul is Roman and peaceful, but that does not mean we need not be vigilant. Random gangs of former soldiers and opportunistic highwaymen cross these lands snatching up food and women whenever an opportunity comes their way. The more our structures look refined and wealthy, the more they will attract the notice of such ne'er-do-wells."

Jesus nodded. Alejandro's proposed castle on the rocky heights overlooking the valley would certainly attract attention. Such an edifice would be noticed by everyone entering La Valdieu. Yet for all of its visibility, the castle would also function as all-seeing eye, gazing upon those who beheld its strength and beauty and warning them by its power and might that its lord had the wherewithal to defend his land and its inhabitants.

Bravo, Alejandro, Jesus thought, and thank you, Lazarus. Not for the first time, he wondered what he would have done after fleeing Israel if his generous friend had not acted on his behalf.

Alejandro left to see to RoxAnna and gather her party. Jesus went to the kitchen to order wine for RoxAnna's presentation. Mary scurried everywhere directing servants to clean and tidy the great room. Jesus stared in amazement at his wife's effort. Saul appeared bathed and wearing a fresh white robe.

"Some part of me would like to sneak out and go look for another deer," Jesus whispered to him.

"Not me, Father," Saul said. "You probably met many famous people in your day, but I haven't met any."

Yes, Jesus reflected, that I have. King Herod Antipas, High Priest Caiaphas, Prefect Pontius Pilatus. Woo hoo. And of course there were the two harpies, Herodias, wife of King Antipas, and her daughter Salome, who danced her way into Herod's heart at a drunken party, then asked for and received the head of John the Baptist who had insulted her mother.

"Fame is not always a creature of beneficence," Jesus told his son.

Saul stared at his father, not understanding.

"Fame is rarely the progenitor of goodness."

Saul stood still, eyes blank.

"Fame can cause a lot of trouble."

Now Saul understood. Yep.

"Were you famous?"

"I'd prefer to say that I was well-known."

"And that caused you a lot of trouble?"

"Someday I will tell you just how much."

"Anything to do with the holes in your hands and feet?"

"Everything to do with them."

Saul didn't speak for a moment.

"Will RoxAnna have holes in her hands and feet?" he asked finally.

"No, but her beauty has already left a hole in Alejandro's heart. Make sure it doesn't happen to you."

"With another man's wife?"

"It wouldn't be the first time."

Saul shook his head and steeled himself for meeting Alejandro's wife.

"What about you?" he asked his dad.

"I will be fine. My heart is filled with your mother. There is no room for any other woman. Even one famous. And beautiful."

Saul nodded. Maybe being old like his father had its benefits after all. He looked at his father's thick white hair done in cornrows and hanging down his back. Cool. But still old.

Thirty minutes later, Mary was still frantically staging the great room. She had placed one of the wooden dining chairs in the center of the room for Jesus, and others on either side of it for Saul and herself. She had the servants lay a red carpet runner from the entrance to the room all the way to Jesus' chair, and had tall Chinese silk banners hung on gilded wood poles behind each of the three chairs to give the look of a royal dais decorated with heraldic banners.

Granted, the gorgeous flowers and wild birds embroidered on the banners weren't exactly totems of conquest like lions, dragons, and weaponry, but they would have to do until some proper ones could be made.

Jesus had seated himself in the center chair at Mary's request, but was obviously uncomfortable wearing his Persian shirt and pants. Really red Persian shirt and pants. Mary sat down in the chair to his left. She was wearing a blue cotton robe with a white sash across her chest and a small circlet of gold on her head. That made Jesus look twice. Where did his wife get a crown? Modest as it was, it might well affront RoxAnna. Yes, Mary was in the line of King Saul, but Israel's first monarch had lived a thousand years ago. Was there some time limit to claiming blue blood?

Alejandro appeared at the entrance. He was wearing a black robe with a silver belt. He scanned the faux throne room, then turned and beckoned. Two men in full battle dress entered the room, followed by two more and two more after them. Each of the men was impressively tall, at least six foot in height, giants by the standards of men in Spain and Gaul who measured five foot two or three.

All of the men wore thick leather pants, leather belts which were hand-tooled and painted, and plain heavy leather sandals. They were bare-chested with large blue scarves around their necks that spread across their shoulders. They had long scabbards on their belts, seven foot spears in one hand, and a painted leather rectangular shield in the other. Each wore a brilliantly shined conical copper helmet with worked silver and copper flaps to protect the temples and ears, and a two-foot-long iron trident covered with colorful feathers, scarves, veils, and sleeves given as good luck tokens by admiring females.

When the knights reached Jesus' chair, all six bowed, then split to form an honor guard lining either side of the carpet leading up to Jesus' throne. All six ladies-in-waiting entered the great room. They were dressed in the colors of spring flowers, wearing gowns that fell from shoulders to toes in pink, blue, and violet.

Each woman wore a thin circlet of silver on her head embedded with turquoise, lapis lazuli, and carnelian carved with their noble family's coat of arms. One at a time, the young women approached Jesus and bowed low. He acknowledged their obeisance and pedigree by extending his hand and bidding them rise. Each girl then turned left or right and placed themselves inside the two rows of knights standing at attention.

Then RoxAnna walked into the room holding Alejandro's arm. Jesus and Mary both gasped, as did Saul, as did every house servant watching from the dark corners of the great room. RoxAnna was short and petite. To overcome this, she wore platform shoes with decorative leather tops cut like lace. She wore a long crimson wool dress which dropped from her neck down to her feet.

She had on a half-dozen gold necklaces, each an inch wide and studded with three dimensional icons of bulls, eagles, lions, and men. She wore a snug leather cap from which gold-braided ropes hung from the sides and back dropping to her shoulders and terminating in bell-shaped chunks of gold. On her head sat a triple-layered crown of gold, with large golden balls molded in between each tier. And that wasn't all. Sewn to each side of her cap was a pair of golden spoked wheels bound together, each one spanning a stunning twelve inches in diameter.

The effect of RoxAnna's royal costume was stupefying. The little princess exuded a hubris unmatched by the richest royalty of Egypt, Greece, or Persia. No queen, no *goddess*, had ever appeared in such a way. Her father and mother belonged to some of the largest land-holding families in Gaul and Spain yet had only been elevated to Roman titled nobility. This new prominence probably explained the gaudy beauty of RoxAnna's outfit. Nouveau riche, their French offspring would declare self-righteously centuries later.

No one had asked RoxAnna how she felt about her costume. If they had, a quite self-possessed princess would have told them that her appearance was only a faint and humble reflection of heaven's royalty, of which the very Son of God himself reigned here on Earth. Her union with Alejandro would bring forth children and grandchildren that would one day marry directly into the messiah's line and produce divine kings and queens that the world would envy. Goodness. Arrogant, overdressed, calculating little tart.

Yet within seven hundred years, the world would see that RoxAnna's prophetic calculations were correct, the climax of her manipulative aspirations occurring when her great-grandson many times over would be crowned Charlemagne, the first Holy Roman Emperor of Christian Europe. Goodness. Confident, perfectly arrayed, trusting little soul.

Everyone in the room was speechless as RoxAnna, the youngest daughter of King Charles of a Moorish kingdom in Spain and Princess Isabella of a Frankish kingdom in Gaul proceeded down the red carpet toward Jesus. She stopped before him, bowed her head once, then looked directly into the eyes.

"I beg permission to become part of your household, my Lord. I will acknowledge Alejandro as my lawful husband, but my fealty I will give to you alone, Jesus of Nazareth, Son of the Living God, King of the Universe."

Jesus rose and extended his hand to RoxAnna. He smiled gently, and spoke.

"Greetings, RoxAnna, daughter of Charles and Isabella. Your praise is best reserved for Jehovah, but for my own part I am honored to respond by saying welcome to your new home."

RoxAnna took Jesus' hand and kissed it, touching her lips on the scarred flesh of the wound left from his crucifixion. She looked at Jesus' face again, and said softly, "Thank you. I will prove worthy of your love, and my offspring will prove worthy of your name."

Mary rose and approached RoxAnna. She kissed her on the cheek and embraced her. The knights and the maidens shouted out their hurrahs and amens. When the prolonged cries of adulation and approval died down, RoxAnna spoke quietly to Jesus again.

"Would you be terribly offended if I took some of this stuff off?"

Jesus laughed and nodded.

RoxAnna beckoned to her ladies-in-waiting who proceeded to take off the large golden wheels, the crown, the cap hung with garlands of gold, and every other decorative object she wore. In the end, RoxAnna stood barefoot wearing only the simple cotton shift she'd had on under her heavy crimson dress and golden bling.

"Now that's more like it," she said. RoxAnna stood up on her tip toes and spread her arms wide, embracing her freedom from the weight of her costume and all that it represented. She shook her long blonde hair and laughed. Alejandro stepped forward and picked her up with his hands. He twirled her around again and again until she squealed with delight.

Mary reached for Jesus' hand.

"Do me!" she teased.

"I would," he vowed, "if I didn't know how much more you'd rather have a glass of wine."

Mary smiled.

"Well, of course," she said, amused. "But how could you know?"

"Five years of a happy marriage, my love," he replied, coyly.

Mary used her index finger to beckon him closer. Then she reached her hands up to his face and kissed him on the lips. Everyone in the great room cheered anew. Whatever lay ahead for Alejandro and RoxAnna, and for Jesus and Mary, it would all spring from the happiness of this day, remembered forever in their hearts and cherished forever in their offspring's hearts, whose rise and triumph would change the flow of human history forever.

CHAPTER EIGHT

THE FIRST SNOW OF THE winter covered the meadows and woods of La Valdieu valley, but left only traces on the craggy heights above, blown off the unfinished walls and towers of Alejandro's castle by a swift bitter wind. The fortress had been ten years in the making and was perhaps half done. The inner keep with double stone walls and Spartan living quarters was finished. When the residential apartments and the mighty outer walls were completed, this heart of the castle would be the inhabitant's last stand should the main walls ever be breached.

A portion of the outer walls was finished, two parallel stone walls twenty feet high and twenty feet apart with hundreds of tons of rock and dirt dumped between them, leveled, and paved in stone to support hundreds of archers and countless defenders. Roman siege engines could pierce Alejandro's fierce walls, but no one else in the world could. He had built it to last and at the same time he had begun a family to carry on his line. He now had two sons and two daughters and his lovely little waif RoxAnna was pregnant again.

His oldest son, Arduous, was handsome and strong-willed, displaying the royal traits of both his Spanish and Frankish ancestors.

He had an olive complexion and dark hair which he wore down past his shoulders. He had fine manly features and fiery blue eyes. He was outspoken and spent his time bossing his siblings around, hunting in the estate forests, or challenging the sons of the knights of his father's court to mock combat.

Alejandro's younger son, Vercengetorix, was named for the great Celtic chieftain who had opposed Julius Caesar's conquest of Gaul. He was blonde and thickly built, preferring to go shirtless with a braid of hair falling down his back. Almost fully grown at sixteen, he was hot-tempered and quick to take offense. Like his brother Arduous, Vercengetorix often fought serious armed bouts against a duo or even a trio of the castle knights' young adult sons.

No one was willing to battle him one-on-one any longer. He was too violent, driven mad with the passion of winning at any cost. He was barely civil to his father and mother. Alejandro and RoxAnna had thought seriously of raising an army of irregular soldiers with Vercengetorix at its head and contracting them as mercenaries to Rome. What stopped them was a very real fear that their violent son would go rogue roaming their own lands with soldiers turned thieves and murderers.

There were now over two hundred and twenty knights in La Valdieu, most of them recruited from the local gentry, and all married and raising families. The newer knights lived on farms spread out behind Alejandro's castle. It was a rich agricultural community with fealty to Alejandro and a universal and undying loyalty to Jesus, lord of the manor and ruler of the long established knights occupying farms in the valley below the castle. Whatever Alejandro's knights tilled and harvested, ten percent was given to Alejandro. Jesus' knights tithed to him, but all the knights, whoever their lord, were allowed to keep the lion's share of the wealth they generated from the rich soil of Gaul.

Jesus and Mary had welcomed two more children into the world as well. A second boy was born when Saul was seven. They named him David after Jesus' famous ancestor. Their first and only daughter, Mary, was born when Saul was fourteen and David was seven. Mary had given birth in the spring six months earlier, so baby Mary was just now sitting up and quietly observing her new world through yuletide eyes.

Saul, the first born, had become a formidable warrior. He had mastered sword and dagger, spear and sling, and had spent countless hours fighting against Arduous, first-born son of Alejandro and RoxAnna. Though he was five years younger than Saul, and much shorter, Arduous was already as strong as Saul and even more determined to be the best warrior in the land.

Saul was almost six foot tall, which gave him a huge advantage over Arduous. He was a half foot taller than *any* other male in La Valdieu with the exception of his father Jesus, who at six foot six was considered a giant. Arduous was only five foot six, identical in height and size as his father, Alejandro. His stature only mattered when he fought Saul, but just holding his own against his towering friend helped Arduous defeat anyone else he faced.

Over the years, Mary and RoxAnna had become intimate friends. Their lives in the castle and the manor house were very similar: raising children; gossiping with the servants; monitoring the state of stores and larders; and insisting that all the children be polite and educated, learning Greek and Latin taught by a scholar sent to Gaul by Lazarus.

There was a distinctly different feel, however, to both of the women's households.

Mary and Jesus lived without conflict, enjoying their children. Jesus welcomed a steady stream of neighbors and folks from nearby towns who suffered from various ailments. Many of these hopeful pilgrims were healed, from small nuisances like sprained ankles and broken fingers to serious debilitations like blindness and skin disease.

Not everyone got healed, which was odd to observe and impossible to explain, departing from La Valdieu with tears and shattered hopes. Mary would hold Jesus' hand sometimes at night and ask him why some people hadn't been healed that day. I don't know, he would say. Once Mary asked why a certain rich man whom she personally found grasping and greedy had been healed. Jesus told her, I don't know.

Mary thought about that a long time, finally falling back on what she'd learned about her husband through the years. He did what he did for the love of God. But Jehovah, for his part, remained inscrutable and abstruse about who he healed or why. *Deus Absonditus* is how the children's teacher described God. Not of this world, living and dwelling behind a façade of silence and aloneness. Mary thought it was the perfect description of Jehovah.

What a burden it had to be for Jesus to carry on day after day, trying to live up to the expectations of a divine Father who to her knowledge had never reached out to his son. But carry on Jesus did, brave and true to the beliefs he had about a loving and forgiving Deity.

Living quite a different life, RoxAnna put up with the constant racket of stonemasons hauling, sawing, lifting, and fitting great granite stones into the rising castle walls and residential compounds built around the castle keep. The completed fortress would have some forty rooms for common use, a dining hall, kitchens, armory, offices, and bathrooms, another forty rooms for servants' quarters, and for family residents and their guests still another forty rooms.

Alejandro pledged to make each room as luxurious as any villa in Rome. He returned from visiting Lazarus every time with ships loaded with lampstands, stained glass, ivory-inlaid furniture, Asian carpets, dining ware and glasses, all in such quantities that he was easily able to make good on his extravagant promise.

Lazarus himself had never yet journeyed to visit La Valdieu, the land he had so generously bestowed on Jesus, having further relinquished his ownership of the holdings behind Alejandro's castle to him, and doubling the size of Jesus' kingdom of La Valdieu. After a hundred years of Roman occupation, there was still unrest in Judea.

But at fifty, Lazarus now accounted himself too old to flee even if a revolt occurred.

Roman officials, soldiers, and citizens were assassinated frequently, and Rome's violent countermeasures filled Calvary with crucified rebels, dead patriots all. Some overnight sensations claiming to be the messiah popped up then and again, but their claims expired on crosses as surely as the hopes of the patriotic Zealots crucified next to them.

No authority, Roman or Jewish, had ever figured out how Jesus of Nazareth had survived his crucifixion. Some believed he had not died, but swooned, and had been revived afterwards. But those who saw the centurion thrust his sword into the midst of Jesus' chest and cleave his heart in twain had no doubts whatsoever that the Nazarene had died, thereby leaving only two possible explanations. His body had been stolen and secretly reburied, or he had been brought back to life by Jehovah. But if that last scenario was the case, then where was he and where had he gone?

Only a few people knew those answers, and no one was speaking up. The number of eyewitnesses who believed they had seen Jesus risen from the grave was steadily declining. Lazarus was old and both of his sisters, Mary and Martha, had died during a bout with a plague that had swept up from Egypt.

James, Jesus' older brother, had been killed by King Herod Agrippa, as had John's brother James, son of Zebedee, both for proselytizing Jews. Jesus' mother Mary had been taken to Ephesus to live with friends, safely out of the reach of Herod and the ever fearsome religious parties rounding up and murdering Jesus' followers, the Pharisees and the Sadducees. The ever shrinking group of disciples and friends who had known Jesus still endured, praying, breaking bread together, and believing with all of their hearts that someday the teacher would return to rule over the just.

Alejandro had just returned from a trip to Judea and had brought back unspeakably long and thick cedar beams from Lebanon for the ceiling of the castle's great room, which he was showing off to Jesus.

Still under construction, it was a giant version of the great room in Jesus' manor house. The beams would be raised and bolted into place on an iron framework already erected above the great room.

Alejandro had flirted with the idea of building a castle made from white marble, but had decided on building with local white granite instead and cladding the interior walls with marble. He had already ordered and paid for the marble, procuring it from the finest Roman quarry in Carrara, Italy.

"You said that Lazarus looked old," Jesus said to Alejandro, pulling his winter cloak close.

"That he did," Alejandro answered. "But his step remains unhindered and his grip firm. He works hard and plays hard too as he likes to say, and to be candid I've never seen another man who could consume as much wine as Lazarus and still remain sober."

Jesus shook his head remembering the nights he had been Lazarus' guest. The food, the wine, and the conversation never stopped.

"He remains very active in the mercantile business," Alejandro went on, "but has little interest in anything else except news about you. He has abandoned all contact with the Temple and the powers that be, but he does make sure to bribe whichever Roman official has been assigned to govern Judea, currently Procurator Tiberius Julius Alexander. The man is actually quite sympathetic to the Jews by the way, having been selected by Emperor Claudius for just that reason. Claudius shares his old mentor Tiberias' interest in the Jews and rumors are everywhere that when old King Agrippa dies, Claudius will appoint his son Herod Agrippa II as king, the seventh and last of the Herodian rulers."

"Agrippa II has no heir?"

"Has no *interest* in an heir. He's as gay as a spring romp through the flowers with his favorite boys."

"I won't shed any tears. Herod the Great's loins produced two generations of poisoned minds and vicious hearts every bit as evil as his. Good riddance to that line."

"You have offset his brood of snakes with your pious and righteous sons."

"So have you, dear Alejandro. I have no doubt that great dynasties will be established by the sons and daughters brought into the world by you and RoxAnna. Long after the Roman Empire has fallen into the dust, your heirs will rule."

Alejandro reached into a leather pouch hung on a strap across his work shirt. He was wearing leather pants, a leather shirt, and a long jacket all made from the same deer hide. He handed Jesus a piece of fruit. It was large, round, and hard, with a reddish hue streaked with bolts of gold. Jesus looked at it and then at Alejandro.

"It's from Asia Minor," Alejandro explained. "It is called an apple by the Greeks." He held it out toward Jesus. "Have one."

Jesus was surprised at the loud crunching sound it made when he took a bite. He smiled as he tasted it.

"It's splendid."

"Indeed, and literally worth its weight in gold. I have dozens of bags of those crisp, hard apples being sold in Marseilles."

"Castle taking a toll on your finances?" Jesus teased and took another bite of the apple.

"No, though the cedar roof timbers and the marble cladding for the great room were pricey. As you know, there still remains several years of work on the residential rooms, the great plaza, and the exterior walls. But all that will be funded by proceeds from my new venture: I brought back seeds to plant apple orchards." Alejandro paused and looked at Jesus. "You actually have the best land for apples. I will personally manage the planting, growth, and harvest of the apples, splitting all the profits with you if you grant me permission to plant the orchards in La Valdieu."

"Done," Jesus said. "Pick your location and proceed."

"Thank you, Lord." Alejandro bowed his head respectfully.

"What other news of Lazarus?" Jesus asked, steering the conversation back to his old friend and benefactor.

"He lives alone now. He takes flowers to the tomb where his sisters are buried and where someday he expects to be buried as well. It feels a bit odd to convey to you this next piece of information. Lazarus wants you to know that he purchased Nicodemus' tomb and has deeded it to you and your descendants. Just in case, he told me somewhat wistfully, that you someday desire to have your remains brought back to your homeland."

Jesus looked away from Alejandro and gazed at the valley below. Surely this was his homeland now. He had been buried in that Jerusalem tomb twenty years ago and could not imagine any circumstance that could tempt him to want to be buried in it again.

"I don't want it," he told Alejandro.

"I figured as much. However, Lazarus has had it recorded in your name and stipulated that you must be present in person if you wish to sell it or register it in another's name."

"Why? I'm never going back to Judea."

"Lazarus is not so sure about that."

"Meaning?" Jesus said, a bit churlishly, and finished his apple.

"He believes that you are the messiah and that your fate is to return to Judea."

"And God told him that personally? Jehovah hasn't mentioned it to me."

Alejandro laughed out loud.

"Who knows? I'm just the messenger." Alejandro offered Jesus another apple. Jesus shook his head, no. "Oh, one more thing," Alejandro added. "Lazarus said that he was able to purchase an article from a retired Roman soldier that he had taken from your crucifixion. Lazarus asked me to tell you that he is saving it for your return."

"What is it?"

"The sign Pontius Pilatus had the soldiers affix to the top of your cross.

'Jesus of Nazareth—'" Alejandro began.

"'—King of the Jews,'" Jesus finished. "Pathetic old bastard. Everyone who saw it was offended, and they should have been."

"From the mouths of fools God speaks his truths," Alejandro replied. "Lazarus is not the only believer waiting for you to return and ascend the throne of your ancestor David. Your own mother believes it, having saved the crown of thorns she removed from your head when your body was washed and anointed in the tomb. Lazarus has that now, too."

Jesus shook his head. Lazarus could toss both of those useless relics into the tomb he had purchased for Jesus and roll the stone in front of it once and for all. When the time came for his days to be finished on Earth, he would not sleep with his fathers in Judea. He would be buried here with his Mary in Gaul, forever remaining in the land that had provided the only happiness he had ever known. And not now, or ever, would he abide any future circumstance that would try to force him to give it up for anything or anyone else.

Two evenings after Alejandro's return, Jesus and Mary welcomed him and RoxAnna to the manor for dinner. They were seated around the large oak table that Alejandro's craftsmen had made almost two decades ago. The wood had split here and there, shooting jagged cracks like lightning bolts toward the heart of the table. Mary and RoxAnna were dressed in simple white wool shifts against the winter cold. Alejandro had on a red wool robe over a gray wool shirt. Jesus was wearing the red silk pants suit his wife had given him long ago. Yes, he supposed he looked Persian wearing it, but it kept his legs warm. Sooner or later, everyone was going to wear pants. He was sure of it. In the meanwhile, if he encountered an amused look now and again from family members or servants, his legs knew better.

RoxAnna was in the last weeks of another pregnancy. Her belly was large, but she didn't try to disguise it. Her body had given

Alejandro pleasure and God had blessed their union. Not quite so joyous were her swollen feet, and she was bathed in sweat even though it was winter. The small copper braziers on the floor warmed the room against the worst of the cold, but RoxAnna was perspiring as though she'd gone blackberry picking in August. Her hair was damp, its raven tresses tangled with sweat. Mary's beautiful face was pristine and noble, but poor RoxAnna's was beaded in sweat with puffy bags under her eyes and new lines in her forehead. She was suffering for her baby and its father.

Jesus gazed at her admiringly. What man would be able to fill her role and do her duty? Not him. Not Alejandro. No man he knew had the courage and fortitude to carry, bear, and raise a child like a woman could. No wonder Jehovah had chosen Eve and not Adam to bring new life into the world. In moments of unspoken meditation, he had almost persuaded himself that jealous chroniclers had decided to blame Eve for the fall into sin, forging a dishonest aura of guilt and blame around Eve to disguise their overwhelming fear of women's reproductive power. Women were the equal of God in that regard, able to create life and bring it forth to walk upon the earth.

The house servants served dinner—venison, mushroom gravy, autumn squash, carrots, and potatoes—along with fresh baked bread from RoxAnna's kitchen and new white wine from Alejandro's wine cellar. He had stored the wine in beautiful blue bottles from Gaul, and stoppered them with cork plugs from Roman Lisbon on the River Tagus.

When Mary complimented him on the gorgeous bottles Alejandro told her that he'd been searching the shops of Marseilles for colored glass for the castle windows and had been swept off his feet when he had beheld the blue bottles. Most wine in the empire was stored and transported in clay vessels, but when Alejandro began exporting wine in his signature bottles all that changed overnight.

"My friend," Jesus commented, "you are a genius at making money. The apples, these bottles."

"I have a lot of mouths to feed, my Lord," was Alejandro's coy reply.

"*And* he does love to make money," RoxAnna added.

Everyone laughed, but with sincere appreciation, for who amongst them had not benefitted from Alejandro's generosity? Jesus studied his friend's handsome face. He had just turned forty, but he seemed as youthful and vital as ever. Granted, he had some early lines in his forehead and the sides of his black hair sparkled with silver in the right light, but Alejandro was still youthful and in the prime of his manhood, witness his pregnant wife.

But apparently the same was no longer true for their mutual friend, Lazarus. Did he have wrinkles now? Had his strength begun to retreat? And there was nothing to be done about it. Everyone walked the same path through youth, middle-age, and finally, old age. Well, maybe not everyone. No one spoke of it, and even though Jesus' hair had turned white as snow since his resurrection, his face was unetched, and his muscled chest and stomach still had the appearance of an athlete bound for the Olympian games.

In almost two decades, Jesus had not aged a day. It didn't matter for now, but in two more decades he would be a freak, all of his friends old or dead, and his grown children appearing as if they were his brothers and sisters. And his dear wife Mary? He stopped his mind from going there. The future held fates and truths that he was not ready to confront. For now things were good. For now things were perfect.

The two couples conversed freely over dinner. Mary talked about Saul being all grown up and how he and Arduous competed constantly. RoxAnna laughed and nodded. Thank God they were friends she and Mary agreed, never coming to angry blows when facing off against each other. Arduous rarely defeated Saul, but in one contest he reigned supreme. With overdeveloped biceps and large hands, he could beat his friend at arm wrestling even given Saul's longer reach.

Saul wisely agreed to arm wrestle Arduous whenever his friend's lack of victories against him needed a clear win to restore his spirits. Both of the young men excelled at spear throwing, sword fighting, and wielding the sling, though each thought to himself that it was an antique weapon from Jesus' yesteryear. Real men killed their foes with spears and swords. At best, the sling was an archaic weapon best suited for killing dumb animals.

Jesus and Mary's younger son, David, a vigorous and strapping eight-year-old, was enamored with the Sicarii dagger that Alejandro had brought him from a used goods market in Jerusalem. He was delighted with Alejandro's tales of its dark history as an assassin's blade and smuggled it around inside of his robe daydreaming of sneaking up on the first Roman soldier he spied.

Jesus was not happy with Alejandro's gift. The Spanish Jew was a great admirer of the brave and patriotic Sicarii of Judea. Jesus was not, but declined to tell Alejandro the tale of Judas' betrayal. Popular rumors said he killed himself. But Jesus knew that he had not. Delusional chap probably still thought that Jesus was the messiah. Maybe he could have Alejandro sell Judas the King of the Jews plaque from the cross and the crown of thorns for a bit of money.

Jesus smiled at the thought, then remembered to finish chewing the bite of squash in his mouth, laden with fresh butter and wonderfully seasoned with the rarest of cooking spices, salt. He was sure the almost priceless commodity was in the mansion kitchen because of Alejandro's generosity. Thank you, Alejandro. Oops. Wait a moment. Jesus remembered that he himself had given money to Alejandro to bring back five pounds of salt from the Great Salt Sea. Thank you, Jesus.

"A new Jesus sect has arisen in Judea," Alejandro told everyone. His tone was nonchalant, but Jesus could tell that this was an important bit of news that his friend had deliberately held back until now.

"That's unexpected," Jesus responded. "Most people decided a long time ago that I died and my body disappeared. What's the point of some new group venerating an absentee rabbi?"

"Your take is a little bit understated," Alejandro answered. "The various appearances you made to your disciples after you were risen, *literally back from the dead*, have provided evidence to a new evangelist who has seized on it. He maintains that your death on the cross was instrument of God's salvation and he vindicated your sacrifice by raising you from the dead."

Jesus frowned.

"My death on the cross was personal, not universal."

"I hear what you're saying, Lord, but Lazarus says that a brilliant and forceful Pharisee is preaching those exact things and lobbying ceaselessly to obtain recognition from Simon and the remaining disciples."

Jesus' face showed his surprise.

"A Pharisee? That would be a first."

"And not only a Pharisee, but a very persuasive Pharisee, schooled by Rabbi Hillel himself."

"Pardon the ignorance of a local girl," RoxAnna spoke up, "but what are you two talking about?"

"You're not ignorant, dear wife," Alejandro responded, "though it is true that you worship dried sticks instead of the one true God."

Jesus and Mary both smiled. They knew that RoxAnna was a devout Celt worshipping her god Dagda, the Good God, and practicing a good and virtuous life.

"Sticks?" RoxAnna said indignantly. "You know full well, husband, that I believe in the great Universal Source and dutifully practice the very same things you've always admired about Jesus—honor, loyalty, hospitality, honesty, justice, and courage. The dried *sticks* you disdainfully refer to are only handled by the holiest priests who divine them for information about the future."

"Gibberish, if you ask me," was Alejandro's unkind retort.

"Granted, their messages may appear obscure," RoxAnna answered, reigning in her temper, "but they are not indecipherable. The enigmatic nature of the wisdom gleaned from the sticks safeguards those unprepared to see the future. And I ask you, which individual really wants to know their future?"

"Not me," Jesus said.

"Nor me," Mary chimed in. "I'm not that brave."

Jesus looked at Mary, searching her eyes even as RoxAnna went on.

"Mr. Big Pants here," she nudged Alejandro with her elbow, "thought that he wanted to know *his* future and had the ancient sticks thrown and read by a renowned Celtic priest. *An unexpected star shall rise in the firmament, and from its fires new stars will issue forth with the divine right to rule the world.*"

No one spoke. What was there to say? It *sounded* like the best of all prophecies, yet not one single detail was discernable, and the tone of the message suggested that its prophetic fulfillment lay so far in the future that no one at this table would live to see it.

"So," RoxAnna said and looked at Jesus. "Now that we have the dried sticks out of the way, may I ask what you know about the teachings of the new sect that Alejandro is referring to?"

"Of course," Jesus told her. "The man leading it belongs to a religious group in Judea called the Pharisees, politically influential lay conservatives who often objected to my teachings. It seems particularly odd that one of them would be promoting ideas of mine." Jesus looked at Alejandro. "Did Lazarus give you any details?"

"He did. First of all, he claims he was tracking down Jesus' followers when God caught up with him on a trip to Damascus, where, he claims, you blazed in the sky above him, blinding him and causing his horse to throw him. He begged for mercy and says that you ordered him to visit one of your followers in Damascus where he received both vision and forgiveness. He has been repeating this story all over Judea telling people they need to repent and believe that your sacrifice washes them clean of sin."

"Jewish-sounding," Jesus commented, irritably, "but *not* Jewish. Which prophets or rabbis ever taught that the messiah would supersede the Temple and become the ultimate blood sacrifice?"

"None," Alejandro answered, "yet he is teaching exactly that. The blood of Jesus Christ cleanses us from all sins, he says. There is no Temple in his theology, no sacrifice, no laws or rules. Just the redeeming death of Jesus for the sins of the world."

Alejandro watched Jesus for a long moment. His master was clearly upset with Paul's transformational definitions of his life and death.

"What is this man's name?" Jesus asked.

"Saul of Tarsus, though as a Roman citizen he uses the Latin version of his name, Paul. He travels through Asia Minor sharing his vision and people apparently can't get enough of it. Assemblies, called churches, are being formed to worship you and practice this new religion. The speed at which these things are happening defies precedent."

Alejandro shook his head. He looked at Jesus who responded in a surprising way.

"Would it be possible for me to meet this Paul? He would have to come here, but I would make time to hear him out."

"Interesting that you should propose this. Lazarus says the traveling preacher has expressed his desire to preach to the Jews in Spain and Lazarus offered to pay his way with the proviso that he come and see you first."

"He did?"

"He did. Lazarus is convinced that the day will come when the appeal of Christianity—that's what Paul's followers call the movement—will not only overshadow Judaism, but will eventually displace it."

"That's a pretty big stretch. Lazarus really fears that?"

"He does. It's why he wants Paul to visit you. Lazarus calls it religion on easy street, salvation without discipleship, without hardship, and without sacrifice. Lazarus calls it *Jesus Light*."

"Ha!" Jesus laughed. "I like that."

RoxAnna excused herself for a moment, left the table, and returned moments later with a tray full of white ceramic mugs. She passed them out and raised her own mug in a toast.

"To Jesus, may he be as sweet as an apple forever."

Everyone toasted to Jesus without a clue of what RoxAnna was up to until they took a drink. Frowns appeared on every face.

"What is this?" asked Alejandro.

Jesus sipped at his a second time, then declared, "It's apple juice, but fermented and turned to alcohol." He looked at RoxAnna for confirmation.

"It is," RoxAnna said, and smiled. "If you sip slowly, you will taste apple. If you drink quickly, you will taste vinegar. But if you drink *lovingly*, as though enjoying a rare and special wine, you will taste a dry and exquisite apple-flavored alcohol, aged, fermented, and spiced with cinnamon and sugar that lights up your taste with fire and flavor. Enjoy."

RoxAnna smiled and took a drink from her mug.

"Marvelous, my love," Alejandro said, tasting his cider again, "and just in time for a cold winter's night."

"Or a cold winter's afternoon," Mary amended.

RoxAnna refilled everyone's cup, and the four friends toasted to God's bounty, to RoxAnna's brewing, and last, but not least, to Jesus' opportunity to straighten out Paul of Tarsus. His quest of drenching the world with Jesus' blood was a misunderstanding of Jesus' entire mission. His teachings were about being alive and whole. In fact, it was *only* about being alive and whole. Our Father who art in heaven, hallowed be thy name. Thy kingdom come, thy will be done, on earth as it is in heaven. Give us this day our daily bread, and forgive us our trespasses as we forgive those who trespass against us. Pretty elemental. Nothing to do with blood.

Who was this Paul of Tarsus?

CHAPTER NINE

"FATHER, FATHER!" SAUL'S URGENT CRY broke into Jesus' sleep even as it woke Mary lying next to him. Their bedroom was just beginning to reveal its shapes and colors as the sun rose in the east. Their son Saul stood next to Jesus' side of the bed bleeding from his shoulder and his chest where two arrow shafts protruded from his body. Without a word, Mary rose and put her face against Saul's cheek, then hurried off to get towels and water and an iron plier that Saul himself had often used to recover iron arrow tips from his fallen prey.

Jesus took his son's hand, as large as his now. Saul was twenty years old and had grown to the same height as him, six foot six. Jesus had him sit down on the bed.

"How hurt are you, son?"

Saul began to weep.

"My wounds are not fatal, Father, but I cannot say the same for the rest of the hunting party that left with me last night to stalk elk."

Jesus frowned, knowing that the worst news possible would come from Saul's mouth.

He sat down next to his son.

"Tell me what happened."

"David, Alejandro, and Arduous were with me. None of us saw who attacked. A swarm of arrows descended on the stand where we huddled waiting for elk to come and feed before first light. David took multiple arrows and Alejandro and Arduous were struck by countless arrows as well. David died in my arms, then I crawled away in the dark bearing the shafts of the arrows that you see embedded in me."

"The others are dead?" Jesus choked on his words.

Tears filled Saul's eyes. He wiped them away and tried to remain strong.

"No one remains alive."

"But why the attack at all?" Jesus cried. "Murdering innocent men attempting to provide for their kin?"

"I know not, Father, but the trail of the assassins will be in the snow. We were deep in the woods, perhaps a half a mile directly behind the castle."

Mary came back into the bedroom accompanied by maid servants bearing lamps, towels, and water. Mary carried the pliers. She looked at Jesus. He rose and took her in his arms.

"Unknown assailants have ambushed our sons and our friends. Saul was hunting with David, Alejandro, and Arduous. He is the only one who survived." Jesus' voice cracked with grief. Mary cried out and burst into tears. Jesus held her as the other women began to tend to Saul. He raised Mary's face and looked at her. "Tend to Saul while I gather men-at-arms." He let Mary go and kissed his son on the forehead. He hugged Mary again and whispered in her ear. "Saul held David. He died in his arms."

"But you can save him!" Mary cried, suddenly hopeful. "Oh, please tell me that you can save him!"

"I will try, angel." Jesus held her tight and looked into her panicked eyes. "Bear in mind that I am the one who prays, but it is God who answers."

Mary stared at Jesus.

"Then I will be praying to *your* Father for *our* son," she said. She turned to Saul and held his face in her hands.

Jesus spoke to his son.

"Saul, take care of your mother. We will bring back the bodies of our loved ones." Jesus paused a moment to push his sorrow down. "And then we will bring back the bodies of those who killed them." Saul's eyes grew large. Was he really hearing his father speak this way?

Jesus dressed in winter clothes for the trek into the woods where the body of his sweet boy lay dead. Where the bodies of his precious friend Alejandro and *his* son lay dead, slain without seeing the faces of their killers. I shall seek out their faces, Jesus swore, consumed by both grief and fury, as he walked out of the house toward the castle in a deer hide suit, leather boots, and a bear coat that dropped to his thighs. I shall punish them for this sin. Mark my words, God in Heaven, the blood of my son and of my friends calls out to me and not in vain, not in vain.

Jesus was met by a guard at the castle entry, not the great gates whose wood and iron double doors were swung wide to welcome family and friends, but a small metal door equipped with a spy window. The guard recognized Jesus. He opened the door and stepped out. He was a tall man, the son of a local Gaul who had been recruited by Alejandro to join his castle guard. His name was Pepin, a distant cousin of RoxAnna's family.

"Good morning, M'Lord," he said. "I worry that some tragedy has brought you to our door at this hour."

"It is true, Pepin. I need at least two dozen men-at-arms to hunt down a party of monsters who ambushed and slaughtered your liege Alejandro, his son Arduous, and my own son David. The hunters became the prey and lie dead in the forest beyond the castle. We must also rouse another dozen knights to guard this gate, and dispatch a further dozen to the manor house in case said foes approach either abode while we are gone."

Pepin bowed and ushered Jesus into the castle courtyard leading him straight to RoxAnna's chambers. Only a few knights and their families resided in the castle to protect the royal family. All the others had homes and farms on land behind the castle. Servants approached Pepin, and he ordered them to fetch the knights who lived closest to the castle. RoxAnna herself, garbed in a heavy wool robe and a fox cloak, came down into the courtyard. Jesus took her hands.

"Dearest friend, were you aware that Alejandro and Arduous went out this night to hunt?"

"I noted the absence of my liege from my bed, but I did not know that he had left the grounds."

"He and your son joined Saul and David on an elk hunt. They were set upon by unknown assailants. Saul alone, injured and bleeding, made it back to the house to get help."

RoxAnna stared at Jesus as though she could not accept what he had just said.

Finally she murmured, "My Alejandro?"

Jesus nodded slowly.

"I must go to him," she said.

"I asked Pepin to send servants out to ask knights of your retinue to come here. Some to accompany us to the site where our kin were attacked. And some to guard the inhabitants of the castle and the manor house in case either place be the rogues' destination."

RoxAnna nodded. She drew her hands away from Jesus. Her face was a mask of stoic acceptance, but she would not let herself face the truth of Alejandro's murder until she beheld his body with her own eyes.

"I am going to change," she said, and hastened back to her chambers.

Within an hour, four dozen knights stood with Pepin and Jesus in the castle courtyard. It was clear and cold and the sun was just beginning to lift into the heavens. The knights wore leather kilts, heavy woolen shirts, leather vests or coats, leather boots, and caps.

Some copper helmets were in evidence, but every man had a spear, a bow and a quiver of arrows, as well as one or more weapons for close combat—axes, knives, clubs, maces, ball and chain.

Jesus knew every man. From the newest and youngest Gauls and Spaniards, to the older Celts and Jews that had first joined Alejandro. They were all sturdy, hard men, many with sons of their own, their faces struck by shock and awe at what had happened to their beloved master and the boys who had accompanied him.

Jesus addressed them all.

"Loyal friends of Alejandro," he began, "for that is what you have always been to your lord. He has been most foully ambushed in the woods beyond the castle, he and his son, he and my son. Saul, my eldest boy brought me the news, having escaped with his life and his terrible tale. A party of archers reigned arrows down upon our folk while they waited in a hunting stand. We do not have a motive, and we do not know how many men carried out this crime.

"Those of you who are the most experienced will guard the castle gate with half of your number deployed to the manor house below. Those who are best with sword and spear will walk with me in leading the party to the scene of the ambush. Those who know the bow to be their best weapon will form a rear guard. If we are attacked, I expect the archers to destroy those who are trying to take us down with their own arrows."

"Our champion archer is your own son, Saul," one of the knights spoke up.

"And he is here," a voice said from behind Jesus. He turned to see Saul approaching with Pepin. He was dressed in clean leather pants, a wool shirt, leather boots, and a wolf-skin coat. He did not walk as if his wounds had debilitated him, and Jesus refrained from asking his son why he had come. He knew why he had come. Saul walked up to his father and handed him his sling.

Jesus had used it to bring down deer, bear, even a wild boar, but he had never used it to hunt a man. He reached out and took it, accepting as well a bag of river stones that he had gathered. He had never dreamed that a day would come when he would desire with all of his heart to corner a man and crush his skull with one of these stones. Imagined or not, that day had come.

The knights began to divide and regroup, with a dozen moving to the castle gate and another dozen leaving for the manor house. The remaining knights arranged themselves as frontline combatants or rear guard archers.

RoxAnna reappeared dressed in winter leathers, boots, and an ermine fur coat. She had brought six serving women with her carrying medical tools and supplies, bags of bread, dried venison, apples, and goatskin bags filled with water. Jesus looked at RoxAnna. Her head was held high, her heart steeled for the search for her husband and son. She knew that departing the castle would surely lead to the destruction of her world and the ruin of her heart. She was prepared anyway. It was no one else's task but her own.

The party left the castle led by Augustine, one of the original men-at-arms that had accompanied RoxAnna to her life here with Alejandro. He had almost pure white hair braided down his back, but his face was youthful and the strength of his body had not diminished. He asked everyone to be on guard against a new attack and spread the knights and servants wide, putting space between them and behind them. Every warrior carried one or more shields to protect himself and the women if another rain of arrows was unleashed.

The new snow was just deep enough to slow everyone down, forcing the search party to take careful steps while keeping a vigilant eye on the tree line of the forest ahead. Jesus and Saul walked together behind Augustine. Saul carried his bow and had a leather quiver of arrows slung over his shoulder. Jesus held his sling in his right hand and carried several good-sized stones in his left. The holes in his hands made clenching the handle of the sling painful and holding the stones difficult. So be it.

He wondered if he would actually use his weapon if the occasion arose. He had never harmed another human being in any way, but on this day that might very well change when the attackers were found and confronted. At that moment he was determined to do whatever his heart dictated. He had allowed himself such freedom only once before in his life, when he had asked Mary Magdalene to be his wife. When she had accepted it was the greatest and happiest moment in his life. Today his anger and his desire to avenge his son now once again opened him to do whatever he wanted to do. This time for blood, not love. Terrible, but no less critical to the calling of his heart.

No one attacked the knights as they approached the tree line. Augustine asked Jesus and Saul to accompany him into the forest to the scene of the massacre. He asked everyone else to wait, remaining alert to a surprise attack. The three men entered the woods following the tracks made hours ago by the hunting party. After a few minutes they found their bodies. Arduous lay on his side with arrows protruding from his shoulders, neck, and chest. Right next to him lay Alejandro, shot with at least a dozen arrows. He had died with his arm around his son as though somehow trying to shelter him. Augustine knelt next to them.

Jesus and Saul found David lying on his back. His shoulders and chest were pierced by a flood of arrows, his leather coat stained crimson with his blood. One eye was open staring at the sky. The other had a bolt shot through it which had pierced his brain and ended his life. Saul sat and held his brother's head on his lap. Jesus sat because he could not stand and wept for his dead son.

He wept and prayed, beseeching Jehovah, always so silent and far away, to take pity on his agony and restore life to his son. He reached out and took one of David's hands. His son had been dead long enough that his arm was stiff and his hand cold and hard. Jesus choked on his sorrow and put his son's hand down. David would never again rise to be embraced by those who loved him.

Jesus watched numb with grief as Saul pulled out the arrow that had pierced David's eye and threw it away. He dug through the snow and filled the bloody socket with soil to hide the maimed remains of his brother's eye. Then Saul began to pull the rest of the arrows out of his brother's corpse. Jesus watched, unable to help, unable to stop his tears. He could not think. He could only feel, overwhelmed by a sorrow so intense that it exposed his every emotion and flayed each one raw. He gazed at his son's corpse. Even seeing David dead and disfigured, he couldn't accept that he was gone.

Jesus glanced over at Augustine. The faithful retainer was removing the arrows from Alejandro's body. Jesus crawled on his knees over to Arduous and began pulling out the arrows that had killed him. Jesus warmed Arduous' cold eyelids with his fingertips and closed them. The young man's face revealed the agony of his dying. Jesus was unable to smooth away the terror etched on his frozen features. Arduous' future had been stolen. The man who was a prince and should have been a king was now only a corpse.

It was one thing to think about burying a man like Lazarus who would carry a lifetime of happiness and accomplishments to his grave, but how terrible it was to contemplate that young Arduous would bear only the years of his childhood into the hole that would eat his flesh. Again Jesus reached out to Jehovah. Would it be so hard for you to bring this young man back to life, back to his mother and his father? But even as Jesus lifted up his heart's desire he knew that his prayer was in vain. It was not that the task was hard. It was God's heart that was.

Jesus stood up. He could see that Saul was clearly suffering from his own wounds. Jesus went to him and supported him with an arm around his waist.

Augustine stood up and pointed toward the deepening woods.

"The killers came here and searched the bodies. You can see their tracks." Augustine swept his arm around the stand. "They took nothing, for truly there was nothing worn or carried by Alejandro's party to take. Four men stood here. They may have been part of a larger party. How they saw our people, I do not know, nor can I understand why they murdered them. There was no sex. There was no lucre. They killed everyone just the same, from a distance, without dialogue or challenge." Augustine shook his head.

The three men covered the bodies of Alejandro, Arduous, and David with their own winter coats. Augustine asked to be allowed to follow the tracks the killers had left in the snow. Saul stayed to guard his fallen brother and his friends. Jesus turned back to bring the men-at-arms and the women who would tend to the dead. Augustine left without a word, garbed in his leather armor, copper helmet, shield, spear, and sword.

The sun rose full in the sky as Jesus led the women and knights to the site of the massacre. He was glad that his wife Mary was not there. His son David's wounds were washed and cleaned by one of the women. She washed the soil and matter out of his eye socket and filled it with a small roll of clean cloth and then patched it over with a larger one.

Keir, son of Thrain, one of the newer knights to pledge allegiance to Alejandro brought one of the enemy's arrows over to Jesus. Keir was a young and mighty Celtic warrior who had done mercenary service for lords all across the Roman Empire, particularly in Asia Minor where citizens were continually threatened by Armenian kings and Turkic cavalry in the east. He held the shaft of the arrow in front of Jesus and slowly turned it until the shaft revealed a small branded image.

"It is the portrait of the goddess Kali from the land of Indus," he told Jesus.

Jesus knew of that land, east of Judea, east of Persia.

"Kali is the goddess of blood and death." Keir looked at Jesus. "This arrow was made by nomadic Hindus called Gypsies by the Romans and Gitan by the Iberians. They roam western Asia and Europe as well, stealing, pillaging, and looting. As despised as they are, I have never heard tales of murder laid at their door.

"I suspect these four killers left their camp without permission and waylaid our lords on the off chance they had objects of value. If we can identify them, the Gitan will not allow such a crime to subject their whole encampment to punishment or revenge. Perhaps even more importantly, they will not allow it to jeopardize their freedom to roam freely through the land."

Jesus studied the symbol on the arrow Keir had handed him. Kali's face was stern, her hair wild and uncontrolled. If there was a face of death, hers would do. And if Keir was correct about the identity of the killers, then Augustine should find that the tracks in the snow would lead him to a nearby Gypsy camp. They would all know soon enough.

Jesus watched the last of the preparations to take the bodies back to the castle. Several knights had fastened ropes to their cloaks to pull the dead home atop them. Jesus looked at RoxAnna. Her world had been ripped open. Her man and her eldest son taken without a farewell. She knelt by Alejandro holding and kissing his hand, a look of utter despair in her eyes.

Some part of Jesus believed that Alejandro and Arduous were safe in Jehovah's paradise along with his dear boy, David, all of them now far removed from the sorrow and grief in this place. Yet another part of Jesus feared that his David had died alone and abandoned, his soul cast into the black maws of death even as his mouth shrieked, "My God, my God, why have you forsaken me?" Jesus shut his eyes and whispered. "The Lord giveth, and the Lord taketh away." Jesus stopped. He could not say the rest.

Keir returned. "My Lord, RoxAnna has ordered that a dozen knights take the bodies back to the castle and escort the women. She has ordered me to lead the remaining knights and join Augustine. She fears that what he discovers may require all of our presence and she would much prefer not to lose her most faithful knight today of all days."

"I understand," Jesus said. "Saul and I will accompany you as well."

"We are honored, but are you sure Saul shouldn't return to the castle for care and rest?"

Saul overheard Keir and responded, his eyes flashing with fury.

"I am going, Keir. This day I avenge my brother. When we find the one who murdered him, I will rip his heart out with my bare hands."

"What are you saying?" Jesus asked horrified.

"I am going to eat his heart while he is still alive."

Jesus stared at his oldest son. Bloodlust consumed him. Neither Jesus nor anyone else in the search party would be able to prevent Saul from singlehandedly killing everyone in the Gypsy encampment. Jesus kept silent, struggling with his own desire to kill the one who had taken the life of his son David.

The knights were ready to bear the dead men to the castle. Keir and another dozen men-at-arms were ready to follow after Augustine. Saul stood beside Keir at the front. Jesus went to say goodbye to RoxAnna. She looked at his face and hugged him fiercely. Jesus put his hand against her head and held it to his chest. After a few moments she stepped back. Her face looked preternaturally calm, her eyes emotionless, her face regal and other-worldly.

"No one dies who did not fire an arrow at our kin," she said. "Swear that."

"I swear," Jesus replied. "I will do my best to see that only the guilty are punished and the innocent left unharmed. Comfort Mary. We will return to honor Alejandro, Arduous, and David."

RoxAnna bowed and turned away. Jesus went to join Keir and Saul. The day was bright and the air crisp and cold. The knights had dressed for an outdoor trek and were armed for combat. Keir pointed out where the raiders' footprints retreated through the forest after they had ambushed Alejandro and the boys. Keir followed their prints through the woods for more than two miles, the tracks gradually shifting toward the east and intersecting a branch of the Oltis River, which would in turn flow into the Rhodamus, a mighty river boasting schools of enormous fish and great clouds of waterfowl.

Saul had been there before to hunt and fish though it was a good ten miles from the manor. He'd gone alone bringing home salmon and trout and braces of wild geese. He told Keir that he had never seen Gypsies encamped along the river, but if they were there now, it would be an ideal place for shelter, food, and water.

Keir pressed on for another two hours, eventually leading the men to the grassy banks of the Rhodamus. It was here that Augustine was waiting for them. He pointed to the far side of the river, a quarter of a mile wide, where a half-dozen large wagons with wooden roofs were encamped. Wagon chimneys were smoking, and horses were grazing. Only light snow lay on the ground. Augustine told them that no more than three hundred paces ahead a small but sturdy rope bridge had been strung which crossed over to the Gitan camp.

Keir nodded and spoke.

"We will cross and gather on the other side of the river. I will attempt to call out the leader of the Gitan for parlay, telling him our purpose and explaining our intent to see justice meted out to those who slew our lord and our kin. Hear me well, however, for we will be vulnerable even with helmets and shields to protect us if our answer is the same hail of arrows our hunters received."

"I don't believe it wise," Augustine spoke up. "Why waste a single life offering generosity to murderers? I propose that we set fiery arrows into the roofs of their conveyances and cut down everyone who flees the burning vehicles."

"And what about children?" Jesus asked.

"If we spare them, they will die unattended," Augustine answered.

"So you'll kill them, too?"

"There will be no one left to care for them," he answered, a hard tone in his voice, but bearing no disrespect.

Jesus looked at Saul. His son's face was blank. He did not speak against the proposed massacre. No one did. Whoever was in the

Gypsy camp, men, women, children, young and old, every knight here, including his own son, was ready to kill them all. He turned to Keir.

"May I see again the arrow that you found?"

Keir pulled the alien shaft from his quiver and handed it to Jesus.

"I am going to approach the Gitan with this arrow in my hand. I will ask to speak with their prince. I will come back afterwards, if I can."

"And if you don't?" Keir asked.

"Then I will have failed to prevent your men from doing what they intend to do."

Jesus gave his son Saul a strong hug, and Saul embraced him back. Then Jesus hiked to the rope bridge with Keir and Saul and the rest of the knights following him. He crossed even as a pair of Gypsy men stepped out of a wagon and approached him. They had swords in their hands and bows and quivers slung over their shoulders. They wore thick wool caps, heavy wool coats, and knee-high leather boots. Both men raised their swords.

"What seek ye here?" one man asked in a Frankish tongue. He was short with a young face and intelligent eyes.

"I seek an audience with your leader," Jesus replied in the same language. "I believe men from this encampment ambushed and killed vassals of mine last night, a dozen miles from here. One of the men used this arrow. Note the totem burned onto the shaft."

Jesus handed the arrow to the Gypsy. He looked at the small figure of Kali charred into the wood. He recognized the symbol and knew who its owner was. Jesus was sure of it. The man handed it to the other Gitan, a hawk-faced, middle-aged man with long black hair streaked with silver. That man looked at it, also recognized the maker's mark, then looked at Jesus.

"The owner of this arrow will not come out to face you. He does not expose himself to adversaries. While it is entirely likely that he and his accomplices did indeed ambush your kin hoping for precious things to steal, my advice would be to return to where you have come from rather than raise the specter of your own death."

"You would tolerate the presence of a murderer in your clan?" Jesus said offended.

The Gypsy smiled a thin, amused smile.

"Shall we say that actually it is he who tolerates us? The man you seek is the leader of this gathering, Adheesh Sarvin, King of the Archers. He serves Kali, the goddess of retribution and death."

"There is no Kali," Jesus spoke angrily. "The greed and lust in Sarvin's heart is what leads him to do evil."

"So say you," the Gitan snapped.

"Indeed, so say I."

The sharp-faced, sharp-tongued man swiftly pulled the bow from his shoulder and notched an arrow to its hide string, but got no further. An iron-tipped arrow drilled into his forehead killing him instantly. Jesus looked down at the fallen man, then looked at the young Gypsy trembling before him. He met Jesus' gaze and threw his sword on the ground.

"Someone has slain Adheesh Sarvin," the man whispered, terrified. "It is he who lies dead at your feet."

Saul crossed the rope bridge behind Jesus holding an arrow in his bowstring aimed at the man facing his father. The young man raised his hands in the air.

"Where are the men who killed our kin?" Saul asked.

"They are barricaded inside their wagons."

Saul turned around and beckoned to the other men who had come with him. Keir and his knights crossed the bridge.

"You followed me across the bridge?" Jesus asked his son.

"It seemed prudent. You had your opportunity to speak to the Gitan. We made sure that it didn't cost you your life."

"The man you shot was your brother's killer. You have avenged his death."

"Not quite."

Saul dropped to one knee and pulled his hunting knife out of his belt. He cut open the coat Sarvin was wearing and ripped apart his shirt exposing his naked chest. Keir and the rest of the knights watched him silently, granting Saul the violence of his blood feud. He cut into Sarvin's chest just below the rib cage, reached his hand into the wound, and pulled out the Gypsy lord's heart.

He held it high and cried out, "Blessed are you, Jehovah. Great is your strength and great is your vengeance. This pagan's heart shall be eaten and his body disgraced." With that Saul chewed off a piece of Sarvin's heart with his teeth and ground the rest of it into the mud with his boot. He then picked up the gypsy's dead body and threw it in the river. Laden with heavy winter clothes the corpse sank immediately into the fast-moving water. Saul watched his brother's murderer disappear into the river while Keir called out to those hiding in the roofed wagons.

"Hear me, ye peoples of this camp. Your leader Sarvin lies dead, killed by the man whose brother he murdered in the land of Alejandro, Lord of the Heights, and Jesus the Christ, Lord of La Valdieu, the valley below it. Two more of our kin were slaughtered last night by Sarvin and three others. If the guilty men are brought out to us, all others may trust to our mercy."

The door to a wagon opened slowly and an old man came down the steps. He was dressed in stitched wolves' hides and had leather boots tied up to the top of his thighs. His face was lined and pitted by a lifetime in the sun.

"I am Vyas," he said, "one of the elders of this group. You have already struck down the evildoer who usurped the rule of this troupe. Hiding in that covered wagon," he pointed to a wagon next to the bridge Jesus and the knights had used, "is Sarvin's wife and his two teenage sons. They are the ones who accompanied him, wielding bows and arrows on his murderous ambush. Call the woman and her sons out to stand before you. Settle your score with them according to the ways of your rule and your religion. We have no feud with you, and we will not stand in your way."

Keir signaled to Saul and spoke to him softly. They walked up to the wagon where Sarvin's wife and sons were hiding. Keir climbed the few steps to its door. He smashed it open with his foot and crouched as Saul covered the interior with an arrow pulled taut in his bow. No one spoke. No one moved. Keir stood up, pulled his sword, and entered the wagon. Saul followed him.

Inside was a scene of carnage. Two young men, boys really, were dead on the floor. Both lay on their backs, their chests stabbed, and their clothes covered with blood. Their mother sat in a chair, her head tilted sideways against her shoulder. She was dead as well, having slit her throat with the knife still in her hand. Her dress was soaked in blood, drinking her life as it gushed out over her chest.

Keir and Saul looked at the murder-suicide. The woman had watched her husband cut down by Saul's arrow and had chosen to spare her sons and herself the punishment that had befallen him. Keir and Saul walked out of the wagon.

"Sarvin's woman killed her sons and herself," Keir reported to Jesus. Vyas, the Gitan elder stood nearby listening. Other men and women emerged from their wagons and listened as well. "The circle of violence is now complete. Those responsible for its birth and blood are no more."

Jesus nodded. Seven people dead. For what? For nothing. Not for gold or silver. Not for honor or truth. Just for greed and revenge. The Gypsy family had been annihilated for their crime, but he and Mary—and RoxAnna and her family—would bear the scars of this evil for the rest of their lives. Patterns of love had been broken and would not be mended.

David would never come for a goodnight kiss and hug. Alejandro would never linger over dinner flirting with the wife he cherished. Arduous would never puff out his chest and challenge his hero and friend Saul to race, or wrestle, or hunt. The wounds of these losses would be cauterized by time, but the scars would not fade and the sad longing for the vanished lover or son would never end.

Jesus and Keir exchanged looks, then Jesus walked towards the rope bridge and started home. Saul caught up with him. The fury of the manhunt was over, and the shed blood of his brother and his friends had been expiated by violence and death. It was time to perform the last services for his brother, David, for his dear friend Alejandro, and for Alejandro's son whom Saul had loved, Arduous.

It was time to kiss their cold brows goodbye. It was time to bury them and do what grieving families and friends had done since mankind's sins had first yielded up hatred, death, and revenge. It was time to mourn what was lost and then begin anew. The Lord giveth and the Lord taketh. Blessed be the name of the Lord.

The End of Part II

CHAPTER TEN

TEN YEARS PASSED. ROMANS CALLED it a decade. Jesus called it a mix of good and bad. He had been away from Judea for more than thirty years, having now spent half of his life in Gaul. When he was in a philosophical mood, he supposed that he had lived a normal human life. There had been disease and death, children welcomed and mourned, money spent and happiness sought, all the kinds of ups-and-downs he expected when he had sought and wedded Mary Magdalene.

But when he was feeling sorry for himself, he was sure that his life had been marred by trauma and sadness, suffering and loss. Maybe he was just too sensitive, or maybe he'd just had some plain bad luck. The Lord giveth, and the Lord taketh away. Blessed be the name of the Lord. What else was there to believe?

Paul of Tarsus had been to visit. He had been forceful and brilliant in his interpretation of Jesus' passion, death, and resurrection. He was wrong, but that did not stop him from traveling the world preaching that Jesus was the Lamb of God who'd shed his blood for the sins of the world. He founded Christian congregations in Asia Minor and Europe and sent his foundling churches short and powerful missives exhorting them to live up to his high standards of Christian behavior and chastising them when they fell short. He routinely sent copies of these letters to Jesus. What makes him think I care, Jesus wondered? Cheeky bastard. Jesus read the scrolls end to end.

RoxAnna mourned two years for her dead husband, Alejandro, at which point Jesus' son Saul requested permission to court her for his wife. He was twenty-two when he asked, and RoxAnna was forty-six. Jesus said yes, and they had married. She had born Saul a son they named David after Saul's brother, a male heir now three years old, who RoxAnna reckoned united her Spanish-Frankish royal heritage with Jesus' heavenly blood thereby creating a demi-god who she believed would sire a line of divine sovereigns. She had not forgotten the prophecies of the Celtic priest. *An unexpected star shall rise in the firmament, and from its fires new stars will issue forth with the divine right to rule the world.*

RoxAnna reminded Jesus of his own mother Mary who'd set him on his life's path as the putative messiah as soon as he could be coached, fervent in her belief that he was God's anointed one. She believed it right up to his crucifixion on Calvary. Then she waivered, confused. After Jesus rose from the dead, however, she felt vindicated and proud. She and RoxAnna were both kingdom builders pursuing their own promised lands.

So was Paul of Tarsus, come to think of it. Jesus shook his head. Why didn't anyone ever get it? The kingdom of God was not dependent on castles erected on rocky crags, golden crowns won and worn, or bloodlines planned and incarnated. It was built on kindness and forgiveness, and its only foundation was love.

Lazarus had finally come to visit, old and bent, but wry and very kind. He wept when he gave his condolences to RoxAnna over Alejandro's death, but had a joyous reunion with Miguel. Lazarus noted that at sixty-three years of age, Jesus hadn't aged a day. Lazarus pondered the meaning of that in his heart. He himself had once been saved from the grave, but death was inexorably drawing him back. Jesus, on the other hand, did not look as if he had aged a single moment since his resurrection. What if the greatest man who ever lived, lived forever?

When Lazarus arrived, Jesus had not received any notice of his intention to come to Gaul. He just appeared at the manor door, and he had not come alone. His arrival was announced to Jesus in the great room where he was reading a scroll discussing the philosophy of one Siddhartha Gautama. It had been sent to him by a scholar in India hoping that he could secure Jesus' comments on the so-called Buddha whose philosophy of good works seemed in many ways to precede Jesus' own teachings. He had just begun the book when Miguel interrupted, laughing and crying simultaneously.

"My Lord," he said bowing, "our most wonderful friend and benefactor has come all the way from Judea to visit."

"Lazarus?" Jesus asked, stunned, jumping up and walking rapidly towards the front door.

"Yes!" Miguel affirmed, trying to keep up with him. "And he has two traveling companions whom he introduced as Judas Iscariot and Paul of Tarsus.

"Paul of Tarsus? Have you heard of Christians, Miguel?"

"Yes. They seem to be sprouting up all over. I don't know much about what they believe, but they seem confident that they're going to convert everyone in the world."

Lazarus was waiting outside the open door. Jesus embraced him without uttering a word. Then he held his friend by the shoulders and studied his face. It had been a long time since he had beheld the man who rescued him from his enemies in Judea and given him his new life in Gaul. Lazarus was still a handsome man, but he was showing his age. The skin on his face was wrinkled and his hair was silver.

"Don't stare," Lazarus said, a bit tartly. "It's been thirty years, after all. Things change..." His voice trailed off, his eyes hardly believing Jesus' youthful, almost beautiful face. They were exactly the same age. No one would ever guess that. "The decades have obviously not had the same effect on you," he told Jesus, then dropped to his knees and bowed his head. So did both of the men standing behind him.

Jesus touched Lazarus' shoulder.

"Come, old friend," he spoke gently. "Stand, up, please."

Lazarus got up slowly, Jesus grasping his elbow. He looked into Jesus' eyes and spoke fervently.

"Blessed be the Lord God of Israel for he has visited us and accomplished redemption for his people."

Jesus gazed at his old friend for a moment, not entirely sure what Lazarus was saying. He glanced past Lazarus and greeted the men who had traveled with him. One he recognized and the other he knew from his earlier conversation with Miguel.

"Salutations, Judas, and greetings to you, Paul of Tarsus. Welcome to my home."

Judas rose and approached Jesus.

"Hello, Master!" he said and bowed low. He was wiry, bald, and hawk-faced. His visage was etched like steel and just as hard.

"You look as cruel as you surely have become," Jesus told him bluntly.

"If by that you mean patriotic, then thank you! I have come to your house seeking a recruit for the war against Rome."

"The same war that you and the Sicarii assassins have stoked forever?"

"No," Judas answered, "I am talking *real* war. Rome is weak and vulnerable, ruled by a lunatic. We will rise together and pull the paper lion down."

"Together?" Jesus asked. "You use that word boldly. Have Judea's bitter factions united?"

"No," Judas admitted. "There is still division and disagreement, but four Hebrew armies are being raised which will allow a confederation of the factions to defend every part of Judea."

"How many soldiers can be fielded?"

"More than forty thousand."

"Those are significant numbers, but they will be facing the hardest, best trained troops in the world."

"We know that. We have swords, spears, armor, and shields, and the weapon that will win us the war, the sling."

Jesus' eyes opened wide. The humble sling? Only then did he remember Paul standing next to Judas.

"I beg your pardon," Jesus said. "I am Jesus, son of Joseph, born and raised in Nazareth."

"I know who you are," the man responded, shaking Jesus' hand. "You are the Christ, the Son of the living God."

The man stood triumphant, posturing like a victorious gladiator. He was very short, no more than five foot tall, but he had a full head of dark, wavy hair, with a perfectly sculpted male face that looked Greek. He had piercing black eyes, black eyebrows, and a small black moustache. He also had a very athletic build, a large chest, and bulked-up arms and legs. Little guy worked out, Jesus thought, uncharitably. At six foot six, Jesus was more than a foot and a half taller than this self-appointed Christian missionary.

Jesus stared at him.

"Thank you, Lord!" Paul bowed his head.

"Thank you," Jesus replied a bit nonplussed. "Come in. Come into my house."

Jesus asked Miguel to provide rooms for the travelers and to have the manor kitchen prepare wine and food for when they returned. He asked Judas to tarry while Lazarus and Paul left with Miguel. He wanted to introduce him to his son Saul, the heir to Jesus' kingdom.

When Jesus had first come to this part of Gaul, the people had been largely Celtic. But over time the men and women who had migrated to La Valdieu were mostly Frankish nobility, younger sons and daughters of rich families from adjacent realms who hoped to find their fortunes in Jesus' domain, now perceived throughout Europe as the richest of all the Frankish kingdom.

Jesus sent for his son Saul and bid him sit on a divan with him when he arrived. Judas pulled over a dining table wooden chair and sat facing them. The atmosphere was tense. Jesus and Judas had not seen each other since Judas had betrayed his master to the authorities, and neither man had heard about the other's activities since the night Judas and his accomplices had murdered the Roman centurion Longinus and his soldiers at Lazarus' house.

The servant who had fetched Saul warned him who was waiting with his father. Saul had never met Judas, but had heard about him all of his life. As a young boy, his mother had filled his head with hatred for the man who had led the soldiers to arrest his father. Saul had carried a grudge against Judas forever, and now he was seated in the same room where the man whom he had despised for so long was watching him.

"Why did you betray my father?" Saul asked Judas straight out.

Judas did not react immediately. He had, of course, been asked this question over and over in the years since he had done the deed and had honed his answer long ago. This was a singular moment, however, because this time the question had been asked by the son of the man he had betrayed. For all of that, however, Judas' answer was still the same.

"First of all, Saul, betrayal is the word my detractors have used to stamp my action. The plain fact is, your father knew what I was going to do and even told the other disciples at the final meal we shared. By bringing Jesus and the Romans face to face, I thought it would ignite a conflagration of Jewish fury that would lead to an uprising against the oppressors. I was wrong. It did not, and my actions cost your father his life."

Saul looked at Jesus.

"You knew?"

"Yes."

"Then why did you allow it?"

"God allowed it."

Saul looked at Jesus trying to comprehend his father's answer. God needed him to die? And if so, then why resurrect him?

Judas read Saul's confusion.

"However you choose to understand your father's duty, I ask you to accept that he does not bear a grudge against me. It is apparent, however, that you do. Am I mistaken?"

"No," Saul answered. "I think your betrayal was self-serving and a lie. You walked with my father for three years. Didn't you ever listen to what he was saying or witness what he was doing? He would never have led a mob to overthrow the Romans. He believed in forgiveness and peace."

"You are right," Judas answered, "and I told you I was wrong. However, I have not abandoned the dream of throwing out the Romans. They steal our livelihoods, mock our traditions, and line the roads with the crosses of our young men."

"What is your role?" Saul asked.

"I command the united Sicarii and the families associated with our order. I am raising one of the four armies that will destroy the Romans once and for all."

"Once and for all?" Saul was stunned. "Are you aware of how many legions Rome has?"

"Twenty-eight."

"And you really think that Rome will leave Judea if you actually manage to defeat *one* of those legions?"

"Yes."

"Nonsense. The emperor will simply send as many legions as it takes to kill every Hebrew man, woman, and child in the Holy Land. All you will have done is turn Judea into a wasteland."

"Big talk for privileged child," Judas snapped.

"No, *accurate* talk from a man who would willingly give his life if he could truly help free Judea."

"Prove it and come with me. Come and join the forty thousand soldiers ready to fight for their homeland and their loved ones."

"You speak as if you think you are the messiah," Saul said.

"There is no messiah. The deluded Jews who wait for such a figure stand by and witness Roman idolatry, murder, and arrogance every day, doing nothing." Judas looked squarely at Saul. "Maybe like you."

In a flash, Saul leapt out of his chair and grabbed the front of Judas' robe. He pushed him to the floor and put his knife up against his throat. Judas didn't move. Then he smiled slowly and spoke.

"Forgive my unkind words. They were chosen to provoke you. Saul, son of Jesus, *you* have the courage and the strength to be worthy of the great Maccabees who once led us to victory."

Saul pulled his knife away, stood up, and offered his hand to Judas. Judas took it and stood facing Saul.

"I apologize again for my words. But I had to see if you were the one we have been seeking. Word of your warrior spirit is on every Zealot's tongue, and the day the revolt is set in motion we pray that you will be part of the movement. Gaul is not your home. Judea is your home, and it waits for you."

Saul did not speak, dazed by Judas' words. Jesus had watched the confrontation between Saul and Judas with apprehension. He knew his son's temperament and was not surprised that he had attacked Judas. Saul's wiser self had prevailed, however, and there had been no blood shed. He was unprepared though for Judas' clever seduction of Saul. And after his old nemesis departed from La Valdieu a few days later, Jesus woke every morning dreading that Saul would come to him and announce that he was leaving to fight for Judea's freedom.

And then one day Saul did. He left. He fought. He lost. Judea was utterly destroyed and its inhabitants massacred. And near the end, when the revolt was breathing its last breaths, Jesus returned to the Promised Land after a thirty year absence to be with his son one last time. But for now, that lay in the future.

Tonight the great room was filled with guests celebrating Lazarus' visit. Its huge oak table seated knights, ladies-in-waiting, and special guests like Julius and Miquel with their wives at their sides and their children here, there, and everywhere, occupying all the small occasional furniture like locusts.

The great room had become truly great over the years, featuring a cedar beam ceiling forty feet overhead with ancient timber brought from Lebanon, four stone fireplaces each ten feet tall and ten feet wide, the oak dining table that sat as many as twenty guests in wooden chairs carved with Celtic motifs, dragons, axes, and chains twisted into single, double, and triple circles.

There were overstuffed leather chairs as well, large Oriental carpets, and divans with satin pillows. There was a large gold and glass candelabra hanging over the dining table made in Roman Pannonia. It was filled with lit candles and surrounded by hanging lamps of colored glass from Roman Africa. On the table was a small trove of bronze lamps, bellies full of olive oil and wicks lit. For all of the great room's size and grandeur, however, the muted light and color that Alejandro had chosen for the room so long ago gave it a warm ambiance that made it seem intimate even when filled with guests like tonight.

Jesus sat at the head of the table with Mary on his right and Saul on his left. Lazarus sat to the right of Mary and RoxAnna sat to the left of Saul. Outfoxed by Miquel, the master planner of the occasion, Judas had been seated far away from both Jesus and his son Saul. While no one had informed Miguel of the dagger attack Saul had made on Judas, it wasn't hard for him to see that oil and water shouldn't be placed anywhere near each other. He put Judas right next to Paul of Tarsus. My. Now that would be a conversation worth overhearing.

"You're holding my wife's hand," Jesus told Lazarus.

"That I am," Lazarus said, smiling happily. "I asked first though, didn't I, dear?"

Mary laughed and nodded. "See?" Lazarus said. "All is well. Remember when Mary was just a little girl, full of fire and grace? You hooked the finest woman in all of Galilee, Jesus. But you know that, don't you?"

Jesus smiled. He'd considered himself the luckiest man alive ever since Mary Magdalene had agreed to marry him, and even after all these years he was most content when he was holding her in his arms at night.

Their son Saul had the true makings of a king, and their daughter Mary was modest and graceful. Jesus liked to observe her playing, or being tutored by her Greek and Latin teacher Nicholaos. He was a brilliant Jew who loved all things Greek, but who also had great regard for Arabic mathematics, Roman science, and Judaic history. Mary, educated and worldly, would make a great queen someday, hopefully married to a man who was literate enough to sign his own name. Which was something Jesus' disciples could not do.

That hadn't stopped them from coming up with accounts of their times with Jesus, however, written to meet an exploding demand by new Christians hungry for information about the Christian Savior. Matthew had hired a Greek scribe to record his memoirs. Mark, a lackey who followed Paul around, had written down the things his master had heard about Jesus' ministry.

There was yet another Gospel set down by a Gentile named Luke who Jesus did not know, but who claimed to have become friends with the last remaining disciples. He also claimed to have done the first portrait of Jesus, a mosaic based on descriptions provided by eyewitnesses who had known him.

Paul, of course, had forwarded copies of all these Gospels to Jesus who found the accounts to be mostly faithful, differing only in inconsequential detail. What he did find fascinating was that virtually all of the Gospel writers had him departing Earth and ascending to heaven after his resurrection.

No one had written a word about the fact that he was alive and still around, living prosperously and happily in Gaul. He suspected that the ascension to heaven was a literary device that placed him out-of-reach and inaccessible, as well as kept him from challenging Christians like Paul who had transformed him from a rabbi into a redeemer.

Speaking of Paul, as the dinner progressed, the very man stood up and addressed Jesus from the other end of the banquet table.

"My Lord Jesus Christ," he said. All the guests stopped talking and craned their necks to see who was addressing the ruler of La Valdieu. "In front of this august assembly of your family and your friends, may I ask which teaching of yours comes to mind on such an auspicious occasion?"

It seemed like an innocent question, but Paul was a trained Pharisee belonging to an order of lay scholars and teachers who possessed both a profound mastery of the Hebrew Scriptures *and* a despicable willingness to twist and turn reason itself to suit their interpretations of God's Word.

Jesus answered Paul.

"Love the Lord, your God, with all your heart, with all your mind, and with all your soul."

"Thank you, Lord," Paul responded. "But what does a person do if they are unable to fulfill that command? Where do they turn for grace and forgiveness?" Before Jesus could answer, Paul went into a full defense of his belief that Jesus was the Son of God, incarnated in human flesh, the messiah sent by Jehovah to save people from their sins. "Holy Scriptures teach that you are the one whose sacrifice and blood offering forgives our sins and reconciles us with God."

Jesus arched an eyebrow. Paul had chosen this occasion to present his beliefs surrounded by interested listeners who might already lean his way, a trick the Pharisees had often used on Jesus during his teaching ministry, stirring crowds to anger who were unprepared for his unorthodox views. Jesus didn't really mind Paul's insistence on this audience, however. These were people who knew Jesus and were perfectly able to judge the truth of Paul's claims and Jesus' responses.

"Sacrifice and blood offering? What are your proof texts, Paul of Tarsus?" Jesus challenged him formally, signally that the debate was on.

"There are many, Master," Paul answered. "Hear and judge for yourself."

Jesus nodded. Mary reached for his hand. Saul sat erect as though ready to protect his father.

"The Scriptures declare that the messiah shall be king," Paul began, "a member of the tribe of Judah, belonging to the family line of Jesse and the house of David. You are the fulfillment of all those prophecies."

"Verses from Genesis, Isaiah, and Jeremiah," Jesus acknowledged. "Your selection of prophecies could apply to hundreds of thousands of male Jews, Paul."

"Yes, but that is not the point. The point is that those significant heritage factors apply to you."

Jesus nodded. Point for Paul.

Paul quoted another Scripture verse.

"The Lord himself will give you a sign. Behold a virgin will be with child and bear a son, and she will call his name Immanuel."

"My mother did not conceive me as a virgin," Jesus disagreed.

"I would think that your mother Mary would be the final authority," Paul replied unflustered. "Did she not claim that the Archangel Gabriel himself told her that she would give birth to God's son without the seed of a man?"

"But was that a dream, or a vision, or true reality? I don't know what Mary really experienced, and I never heard about a virgin birth. Where did you hear such a thing?"

"That Mary was a virgin is common knowledge," Paul protested.

"Did she tell you, or did you draw your conclusion from *your* common knowledge?"

Paul did not answer the question.

"Common knowledge around here, Paul, is that Mary's brawny husband standing over six foot tall might have had more to do with my creation than Gabriel thought. Although, given my height I probably should rethink the possibility of Gabriel's participation in my conception."

The diners howled with laughter, surprised and amazed that Jesus could be so lighthearted in his teasing about the circumstances of his conception and his birth, something Paul and his fellow Christians were working very hard to turn into a miracle. *Our Lord Jesus, conceived by God and born of the Virgin Mary.* Jesus had just punched a couple of holes in that.

Paul sat red-faced, but still defiant.

Jesus seized the moment to take another shot.

"You also mentioned that Isaiah said the messiah would be named Immanuel. A pious and special name. It means 'God with Us.' Sad to say my mother picked *Yeshua* in Aramaic, Jesus in Latin—neither one Immanuel. What was she thinking?"

Again the crowd laughed, and Paul had no answer. That didn't deter him from offering another Scriptural proof.

"Isaiah also says that the messiah will be our judge, our lawgiver, and our king."

"Paul, how can I even begin to address that list of things that I am not?"

"Ah, but listen to your own words, recorded by your own disciple John that declare, 'I can of my own self do nothing, as I hear I judge and my judgment is just; because I seek not my own will, but the will of the Father which hath sent me.' Would you say that this prophecy of judging and rendering God's will signifies your unique role as God's son, the Anointed One?"

Jesus shook his head.

"You are forgetting context, Paul. I made those remarks to encourage believers to free themselves of slavery to laws made by men and attributed to God. I offered myself as an example of a believer who allowed the Father to guide his will, teaching me how to judge my circumstances so that I could live my life in purity and truth. That, Paul, applies to every living person.

"Witness the words God reveals by the Psalmist, 'You are gods, ye are all children of the Most High.' You are struggling to limit God's presence to me, whereas my task was to invite *every* person to be a child of God. Neither you nor any other person needs an intercessor to access God, or to become a son of God."

There was a hush in the great room, but Paul was just getting more fired up.

"Then your greatest objection to the Christian message that proclaims you the Lamb of God, sacrificed for mankind's sins, is that you believe every man and woman can approach God without your sacrifice? That there is no need for a Redeemer?"

Jesus nodded.

"And you are ignoring Isaiah who says of the messiah, 'He was wounded for our transgressions, he was bruised for our iniquities; the chastisement of our peace was upon him and with his stripes we are healed.'" Paul stared at Jesus. "What say ye?"

"I say that I am not that man. I gave my life in obedience to God as have many sons and daughters whose holy lives are recorded by the Scriptures. No man or woman embraces the love offered by God, except by their own hand, and by their own faith. To teach other than that abandons Jehovah's eternal covenant with the Jews and inserts a middle man, a bargain maker, an offering that is neither true, nor viable. The Jews are the Lord's people, received by him as an offering without blemish, by his will, and by his will alone."

No one breathed.

"Well, that's good news for the Jews," Paul said. "What about the Gentiles? How are most of the people in this room going to be saved?

"They are saved, *even in their ignorance,* by God's love."

"What?" Paul cried out. "If that's the case, then there must be a lot more Gentiles in heaven than Jews."

"I suspect that's true," Jesus replied.

The grand room erupted with laughter and cries of bravo.

"Say of me what you will, Paul of Tarsus," Jesus spoke, "but the truth is that God's grace is free and abundant, not reliant on me or on any mortal man. It is free for the asking, for Jew or Gentile, lest any man, including Jesus of Nazareth, should boast. May God bless your own quest for his love."

The room exploded with shouts of joy. Paul turned away and walked out. He had heard with his own ears Jesus' denial that his life, death, and resurrection could be construed as necessary for another person's forgiveness and salvation. He would think on Jesus' words as he continued his missionary journeys. But whatever his heart and soul believed, his mouth continued to proclaim that God gave his only begotten Son that whosoever believed in him would be saved. This night was not the only time that Jesus and Paul would meet. Five years in the future, Paul would send word to Jesus urgently asking him to come and visit him in prison in Rome where he was waiting to be tried before Emperor Nero on charges of instigating religious riots in Jerusalem.

In the here and now, Paul was gone and the rest of the guests prepared to depart as well, leaving for the castle or for their farms on the high plateau behind it, or returning to their farms in the great valley of La Valdieu. They raised wheat and oats, beans and barley, potatoes and rice, and managed thousands of acres of citrus groves, grapevines, and nuts. The land was rich, and more families every year petitioned Jesus to enter La Valdieu.

Saul and RoxAnna spent many hours planning the future of the kingdom. Their sons and daughters would be princes and princesses, and someday RoxAnna would rule as Queen over the united kingdom while Saul ruled as king.

Jesus always smiled when he remembered the day when Saul had approached him about marrying RoxAnna. He found Jesus reading in the great room sitting at his ivory-inlaid olive wood desk. He seemed to spend more and more hours there every day, reading scrolls and piling them in wicker baskets strewn all around his desk. Jesus told Saul to pull up a chair. Both men were dressed in loose cotton robes. It was Saturday, a customary day of rest for everyone.

"Father, I have come to ask you, or tell you, depending on how the topic should be addressed to your liking, that I would like to marry RoxAnna. It has been two years since Alejandro was killed, and I know I want her for my bride."

Jesus was not surprised. He had seen them together often. It seemed a good match for everyone concerned.

"Is RoxAnna of the same mind?"

Saul nodded.

"Would you like to divide RoxAnna's holdings from our united kingdom?"

"No. We would like to continue the union of your holdings and hers as one property under your lordship."

"What about RoxAnna's son, Vercingetorix?"

"He's only eighteen, but will be my heir until such time RoxAnna bears me a son. After that he will still be regarded as a prince of the kingdom. Or if he prefers, he may take his inheritance as a monetary payment and leave these lands to found his own house elsewhere."

"It sounds fair for everyone, my son. When would you and RoxAnna like to be married?"

"As soon as possible."

Jesus looked at Saul's face.

"Is there an heir on the way?" he said, teasing only a bit.

"Possibly," Saul answered.

Jesus lifted his eyebrows.

"Possibly?"

"It might be a girl."

Jesus smiled. Of all the girls he'd met who would make better rulers than any men he had ever met, they included his mother, Mary Magdalene, his wife, and RoxAnna.

"If it is a girl, she may well deserve to be your heir," he told Saul. "No one in these parts denies a woman the right to wear the crown as queen with or without a male consort at her side."

"I'm sure RoxAnna wouldn't object to such an arrangement," Saul answered amused.

"If your daughter has half RoxAnna's skills and temperament," Jesus answered him, "you may as well think about stepping aside the moment she is born."

Both men laughed because they knew that what Jesus said was true.

"Do I need to speak with RoxAnna?" Jesus asked.

"She's already wearing a wedding ring, if that answers your question."

Jesus shook his head and smiled.

"Set the date, and I'll have Julius work with you two on wedding plans."

"Actually, he can work with just RoxAnna."

"Of course. What was I thinking?"

CHAPTER ELEVEN

RoxAnna sat in her bedroom at the beauty table, teasingly nicknamed that by her late husband, Alejandro. He had always claimed that nothing in the world could make her more beautiful—not henna, not tattoos, not creams, not powders, not pencils, not brushes, not paint. Maybe back then, she thought, but Alejandro had been dead twelve years now, and she had been married to Saul for ten. The servant girl hovering over her carefully blackened the roots of her hair disguising the white hairs that were laying claim to her scalp.

She also wore heavy make-up in the style of the Egyptian pharaoh's wives in Egypt. When Cleopatra had commanded the empire's attention as the very public mistress to Julius Caesar and then trumped that with her polygamous marriage to Antony, her gorgeous make-up made her look like a goddess. That was a long time ago now, but many women throughout the Roman Empire had permanently adopted eyeliner, blush, and lipstick in imitation of Cleopatra, and men everywhere wished they could watch such faces sucking their manhood.

Vercingetorix, RoxAnna's only surviving son by Alejandro, burst into her bedroom. He was fierce and famously hotheaded.

"What are you doing?" RoxAnna shouted at him. "Have you no respect?"

Her blonde son, short and squat, but built of solid muscle and featuring a rogue temperament, stopped short. His mother was the only person in the world he was afraid of. RoxAnna stood up and dismissed her servant girl with a wave of her hand. She was wearing a silk pajama shirt with a low-cut top and shorts whose bottoms rose almost to the top of her thighs. She watched Vercingetorix eyeing her breasts.

"Look me in the face, or I'll have your eyes cut out."

Vercingetorix flushed and looked her in the eyes.

"How dare you burst into my bedroom," RoxAnna snapped.

"How dare you give my father's lands away to the lackey you fuck every night."

RoxAnna took three steps towards her son and slapped him hard.

Vercingetorix didn't move.

"You can slap me as many times as you want," he told her, "but it doesn't change the fact that you are bedding Saul and that you are planning to give my inheritance to him."

"First, you little shit," RoxAnna spit out, "it's not your land. It was your father's land and now it's *my* land. By Roman law it passed from my husband to me, and as you obviously have heard somewhere, that land and Jesus' land will belong to Saul as Jesus' sole heir. You have been Saul's legal heir and will remain so until such time our son David sits on the throne. If that rubs you the wrong way, and God knows it doesn't take much to do that, we will grant you a cash settlement of fifty thousand gold aureus should you prefer to settle elsewhere and create a fiefdom of your own."

"What does that mean?" her son asked, sullenly.

"That means that you will receive enough money to purchase your own lands wherever you choose."

"And what will that amount of money buy?"

"As much land as we have here, plus ample funds to construct a fortified castle as large as the one your father built."

Vercingetorix pondered his mother's words silently. It was a lot of money and he could even declare himself to be a king.

"When would this sum be paid?"

"Within a fortnight. Saul and I are celebrating our tenth wedding anniversary this weekend. After we have celebrated with our friends and allies, we will dispatch a courier and an armed escort to fetch the funds from our bank in Marseilles."

"Swear that what you have told me is true."

He extended his hand.

RoxAnna took it.

"I swear by Aine of Knockhaine," she said.

Vercingetorix yanked his hand away.

"Who is that?" he demanded.

"It is the Celtic goddess of love and childbearing." RoxAnna pulled her silk panties down below her belly. Her tummy was distended, a sure sign that after waiting many, many years she and Saul were expecting a child again.

"Whore," Vercingetorix hissed. "I will live to spit on your grave."

RoxAnna reached out her hands and shoved Vercingetorix in the chest.

"Do you think you will always be able to talk to me like that, you misshapen lump of dung? Before the day comes when you go too far, think on the fifty thousand aureus promised to you, and try to hide your ugly emotions and animal wits." RoxAnna stared at her grown-up son with repugnance. "I cannot believe you are the product of my womb. Some devil must have had me in my sleep, and you are the result. Which means that none of these lands will ever be yours. Take your bribe and go to hell. The land is probably cheap there."

Vercingetorix clenched his fists and took a step towards his mother.

RoxAnna did not move.

Her son did not strike.

"Oh, my," RoxAnna mocked. "Have the gold coins stayed your hand? In Marseilles we buy protection for our shipments. I suspect your promised gold has purchased protection for me and Saul."

Vercingetorix turned and walked away from his mother.

"Do you know what insurance is?" RoxAnna shouted after him. "It is the act, system, or business of insuring property, life, one's person, and so forth, against loss or harm arising from death, disablement, or the like, in consideration of a payment proportionate to the risk."

Vercingetorix kept walking.

"Insurance, dear son. We are paying fifty thousand pieces of gold to stay free of your violent hatred. Do you understand?"

Vercingetorix slowly turned and faced his mother. He raised his right hand and gave her the most popular Roman gesture of insult. It involved making a fist towards her with all his fingers closed, and then lifting the middle one. RoxAnna shook her head and turned away. Vercingetorix left thinking of what he would do to Saul and RoxAnna after he received his money. They didn't have insurance. More like a stay of execution. Vercingetorix did something then that he very rarely did. He smiled.

Weddings were great occasions in Jesus' realm. When knights or ladies-in-waiting married, Jesus officiated using a version of the Jewish marriage ceremony (using less prayers and Scripture, more focus on vows of respect and fidelity). Jesus also deeded land to the new couple to farm and offered more to lease so they could be productive in the kingdom as well as in the bedroom.

When new babies arrived they were blessed and boys were circumcised if the parents chose. It was not taken as a sign of being Jewish, but rather as a promise that the boy would be raised to know and serve Jehovah.

Landmark anniversaries like Saul and RoxAnna's tenth were also accorded great appreciation. Children had been born. Fortunes had been made. And the next turn of that wheel would see those children married and their parents aging, beginning to prepare for the time when they were gone and their grown children would faithfully serve the ruler of La Valdieu.

Everyone in Jesus' kingdom was allowed to honor and serve whatever god or goddess they chose. The only exceptions were gods or religious rituals that advocated violence, licentiousness, or dishonor to other gods. Moloch, the Phoenician god who demanded infant sacrifice, was banned. Aphrodite and Bacchus, big on free sex and abundant wine, were banned. Mithras' worship, whose advocates slaughtered a bull and bathed in its blood, were banned. Jehovah of the ancient Jewish Scriptures was spared being banned, but only because he had been recast in Jesus' teaching as the God of love. Christianity was also banned for the simple reason that Jesus considered it just plain wrong.

The June day of Saul and RoxAnna's wedding anniversary drew nigh. Everyone living in the manor and castle was invited, as well as all the families and servants working the land's farms and vineyards. Kings and queens of adjacent kingdoms were invited as well, but most sent gifts of jewelry forged from gold and precious stones as an acknowledgment of the special day.

All in all, hundreds of guests would be in attendance according to Julius. The anniversary festivities would have to be moved outdoors to accommodate everyone. Julius made one more whirlwind shopping trip to Marseilles for suitable decorations and returned with six wagons filled with several painted canvas tent tops from Arabia, each capable of shading a hundred standing guests or keeping them dry if it was the wrong kind of day, dozens of long silk banners from China, stiff fabric pots with hundreds of flowers to fill them, and Julius' favorite find, handmade paper plates and cups from Egypt. What in the world would those people think of next?

"Paper cups?" Jesus asked, gingerly touching the rough surface of a papyrus drinking cup that his wife had brought to his desk. It was filled with chilled wine mixed with water. He looked at the contents, and he examined the outside of the cup for seepage or leaks. "Is this really made out of paper?" he asked Mary.

"Yes," she answered, amused. "Paper. The people of the Nile use a process where reeds are mashed and smoothed over a mold, dried, and then waxed to make it waterproof. And get this. When you're done, you just throw it away."

Jesus frowned.

"I haven't thrown anything away in my whole life. This," he pointed at the cup, "seems disrespectful of the earth and represents a hazard to its future. What if the population of the whole world took to using these? Millions of them would be thrown away every day."

"Julius told me they dissolve when buried, faster than clay or metal."

"Well, all right," Jesus murmured. "Maybe they have their place."

"There is another bonus to the process," Mary told him.

"No dishes?"

"Well, that too, but Julius brought something special for you." Mary handed him
a pile of papyrus pages stacked and sewn together.

Jesus took it and stared at it.

"It's made from reeds, just like the paper cups and plates. It can be filled with beautiful script and miniature paintings.

"It is wonderful."

"The cost is a hundred times less than a sheepskin parchment."

"That's wonderful," Jesus exclaimed. "People everywhere will be able to buy them."

"You could have Miguel procure some blank ones so you could write down your memoirs."

"You are so kind, dear wife." Jesus pulled Mary close and hugged her. "You would probably be the only one who would read them."

"Then write them for me, husband. And get going," Mary said, pulling back and looking up at Jesus. "I'm not going to live forever, unlike someone else we both know."

Jesus looked surprised, and then sad.

"You mean me?"

Mary nodded, and took one of Jesus' hands.

"You don't age, my love. You still look like the dear, sweet boy that I married."

"He was thirty-three. I am almost sixty-three."

"And have you looked in any of my bronze mirrors lately? You look like you are *still* thirty-three."

"Mary, I can't talk about this. It only breaks my heart to think that I might not have you forever."

"You darling thing. But if that's the reality that you will someday face, let's plan for it together."

Jesus kissed Mary's forehead.

"Thank you, love. I promise you that we will face my strange fate together."

"I love you, husband." Mary's eyes were moist.

"You own my heart, dear wife, ever and only you." Jesus took Mary in his arms and kissed her long and sweetly. "Only you," Jesus whispered to Mary one more time.

— ⚜ —

The well-wishers come to celebrate with Saul and RoxAnna assembled beneath the tent tops, smiling, laughing, and visiting. Three royal lines had been united a decade ago when they had married, Gaul and Spain from the bride's side and Judea from the groom. A fourth line which would supersede these and every other noble line anywhere in the world was incarnate in Saul as well, namely the flesh and blood of his father Jesus, the son of man, and the Son of God. Jesus never spoke of that heritage, but everyone in La Valdieu knew that the man who rose from the dead and became immortal was the King of kings, and Lord of lords, the only being worthy to bless yet again the union of Saul and RoxAnna.

Knights and merchants, ladies-in-waiting, and mistresses of manor, castle, and farm had dressed to reflect the glory of the occasion. Virtually all the women wore long gowns of satin like those worn in Rome, falling to their feet, but baring shoulders and back. They had on dainty dyed leather sandals whose laces snaked up their calves. And virtually all of the women wore multiple golden necklaces and bangles designed in the Iberian style favored by RoxAnna, thick and heavy, and not for the weak of heart.

Many men wore quilted Celtic skirts, white cotton shirts, and belts from which hung colorfully braided magic circles to protect their homes and clans. Others wore Persian pant suits made of red and blue silks fastened with braided cloth cinctures. Still others wore knee-length Frankish wool robes with leather symbols and coats of arms embroidered on the chests.

The assembly of guests represented hundreds of fiefdoms in La Valdieu, now famous all over Europe for its abundant produce, skilled knights, and beautiful women, all of them united under the rule of their Lord Jesus. He stood in front of the assembly with Mary on his right and Saul on his left.

Jesus wore a gray cotton robe that buttoned up the front, and Mary wore a long light blue dress with a white sash and a dark blue head covering. A plain gold circlet sat atop her head, resting part way down her forehead. Saul was dressed in a kilt and steel breastplate hammered with an image of the Temple in Jerusalem. He looked every inch the future king of La Valdieu waiting for his queen to appear and stand at his side.

The crowd began to cheer and applaud as RoxAnna walked slowly down a long carpet through the midst of the guests towards her husband. Walking next to her was the heir to Jesus' throne, ten-year-old David. He had a handsome face, strawberry blonde hair cut short, and a bearing that said he knew that he was the crown prince. He wore a silver robe and a silver belt. No one in La Valdieu had ever looked more like a royal heir, but all eyes were on his mother RoxAnna.

Mary gasped and Jesus shook his head in admiration when they saw what RoxAnna had selected to wear. For only the second time in all the years they had known her, she had on the brilliant gold-bedecked costume that she had worn when she had met Jesus the first time. A crimson gown fell from her neck to her ankles and she wore a half-dozen gold necklaces around her neck each at least an inch wide, studded with figures of bulls, eagles, lions, and men. She wore a snug black leather cap from which golden ropes dangled gold bells which chimed when RoxAnna walked. On her head sat a triple-layered crown of pure gold with large golden balls molded in between each tier. Finally, mounted on each side of her head were golden spoked wheels, twelve inches in diameter and bound to RoxAnna's crown.

The effect was stupefying. RoxAnna walked through the crowd, people bowing as she passed, and took her place next to Saul. David stood next to her holding her hand.

Jesus smiled at RoxAnna and spoke loud enough for her to hear him over the cheering crowd.

"Bet you forgot how heavy that whole get-up was, didn't you?"

RoxAnna rolled her eyes.

"You can say that again. But I swear this is the last time I'm ever putting it on. Took four hours, can you believe it?" She turned to her husband. "Saul, will you have someone make a model of me wearing this for a sculpture? Then we can melt all this junk down and spend the gold on stuff we really want."

Jesus laughed. Mary shook her head. And Saul leaned down and gave RoxAnna a kiss on the lips. And so the ceremony marking a decade of royal marriage between Saul and RoxAnna began. Jesus prayed for the Father's blessing and gave a brief message on love and loyalty in marriage. He knew as he spoke that if the world ever forgot him, the royal line these two would sire would not pass away from the face of the earth.

He wondered if even for a moment Jehovah had ever thought of him in that way. Probably not. His ministry of teachings about love and obedience had not changed the world very much, and whatever small heritage of good he had accomplished was being usurped and obscured by Paul and the early Christians spreading across the Roman Empire. Believe and thou shalt be saved. Just confess Jesus, and your worries are over. What had Lazarus called that? Jesus *Light*.

He could already foresee a future where practicing his teachings about living an abundant life by God's grace would be boiled down to a ten-second formulaic confession. Dost thou believe in Jesus Christ? I do! Dost thou believe that his blood forgives your sins? I do. Well, then, Amen! Thou art okay, brother! Be on thy way.

Mary looked over at Jesus, watching him as he spoke about the traits of ideal husbands and wives. Jesus had been an ideal spouse. He was kind, forgiving, protective, patient, and gentle. She had tried to be those things as well and had given him children to love and nurture. Alas, she would grieve about her lost David forever, but Saul had loved her twice as much to make up for his death. She looked at her son's face. So handsome, so strong. Whatever the course of his life would be, she would always be proud of her eldest child, loving him almost as much as she loved his father, her tender and wonderful Jesus.

It was her last thought. There was an explosive crash against her forehead, a flash of pain and fear, then Mary fell, the shaft of an arrow embedded in her skull. There was no blood. But Mary's brain had been pierced to its core, and she was dead in the blink of an eye.

There was a great cry of disbelief from the wedding guests. They pressed forward wailing and weeping as Jesus knelt at Mary's side, Saul searching the distance for the archer who had killed her. In that same moment RoxAnna was struck in the neck by an arrow, its iron tip crashing through her throat and thrusting out the other side. Saul grabbed her as she collapsed. Blood gushed out of her neck, then stopped as her heart failed. Her eyes glazed over as death approached. Jesus watched, holding the hand of his murdered wife. Mary was gone, and he knew in his soul that no prayer of his would bring her back. But there was still hope for the dying RoxAnna.

He moved immediately to lay hands on her neck. Jesus prayed from his heart. Not my will, but thine, O Lord. But I beg you not to break my son's heart on this day of all days. His mother's spirit is gone beyond any retrieval. Please spare him his wife to comfort and love him. Jesus broke off the arrow in RoxAnna's neck and withdrew both pieces. Her flesh closed up and she opened her eyes. Saul held her head against his chest, even as he and Jesus and the wedding guests saw Vercingetorix ride his war horse up the front lawn of the manor. Wearing only a simple woolen robe and leather sandals, he held a bow in his hand with a quiver of arrows slung across his back.

Jesus rose and looked at him. Saul laid RoxAnna in the arms of one of her ladies-in-waiting and stood as well, facing the coward who had just murdered his mother Mary and had almost succeeded with matricide shooting his own mother RoxAnna. Vercingetorix waved his bow as his horse shied and reared up. He forced the horse's front hooves down and addressed Jesus.

"Did you think money could buy me off, Lord of La Valdieu? Did you really believe that a *bribe* could somehow compensate for having my mother abandon me and give my father's lands, *my* lands, to your son? I vowed that it would never happen. The castle and Alejandro's lands shall come to me this very day!"

Vercingetorix faced his charger towards the crowd.

"What say ye, men of Alejandro? Who will say that this day they turned their backs on his faithless widow RoxAnna and joined Vercingetorix to carry on his father's memory and inheritance?"

Alejandro's only living son received his answer from the only knight who had come to the wedding with a weapon. Keir, son of Thrain, drew his bow and shot an arrow deep into Vercingetorix's chest, then a second one that passed through his belly and lodged in his spine. He fell from his horse and sprawled in the dirt.

Saul ran forward and fell on Vercingetorix's neck. With his own bare hands he choked him, his thumbs jammed up against his throat so hard that Vercingetorix could not speak, could not breathe. His wounds bled out of his chest and into his bowels while Saul's grip suffocated him. The dying man tried to struggle, but death robbed his strength. He stared at Saul's furious face as his sight began to darken.

"Your mother lives," Saul cried out. "But my mother does not. Hear my oath in this moment of your death, you coward. I swear to Jehovah above and on my father's wounds that I will leave your flesh in the sun so that vultures and wild dogs can pick your bones clean. Then I will gather them up and carry them back to Magdala, the place of my mother's birth. There I will scatter your bones in the dump, leaving them to rot in the shit of the village, a feast for rats and cockroaches. Take that image with you as you depart to face Almighty God!"

Saul released Vercingetorix's throat and the murderer's last breath wheezed roughly from his lungs. His eyes were frozen, his body limp. Saul stared at him a long moment then stood up and addressed the crowd.

"No one shall move his body," he called out. "I have sworn to leave Vercingetorix's corpse exposed to the elements and the animals and then to scatter his bones in the waste of my mother's village in Judea, and that I will do."

Saul walked back to the scene of the attempted massacre. Only by his father's intervention had RoxAnna been saved, and who knew who else might have been slaughtered if not for Keir's bow? Saul knelt by his mother's body. Jesus was sitting next to her, holding Mary's hand. Saul put his arm around his father's waist. At his comforting touch, Jesus broke down and cried out in anguish, staring at his wife's lifeless form, her eyes closed, her dead face blank. The Lord gave and the Lord took. And it made Jesus want to die.

He looked at RoxAnna, bareheaded and dazed, surrounded by her maids. She saw Mary's silent body and began to moan and cry.

"Go to your woman," Jesus told Saul. Jesus gazed at Mary's face. What now did he have to live for? How would he fill his days and nights without her? What would he do until it was at last his turn to die?

He rose and stood over Saul, and RoxAnna who looked at him. He spoke, devoid of emotion, but he said the words he wanted to speak.

"With the power invested in me as lord of this estate, I abdicate my ownership of this land and the power to rule it, to both of you, King Saul and Queen RoxAnna."

No one spoke. The crowd was completely silent, emptied of every emotion by the events they had witnessed. Jesus sat again and held Mary's hand, burdened by the thought of the innumerable years that he would face without her.

It was a good thing that he did not know then what would yet be required of him. A lifetime of twenty centuries lay ahead, filled with countless burdens and endless conflicts. Though he would struggle to do good and remain forever loyal to his vision of a God of love, he was weary of its cost at the end.

Yet in an oddly satisfying way, with the very last act of his life, he accepted at last that Isaiah's prophecy had indeed been meant for him, that he truly was the suffering servant, the Son of God, the messiah, demonstrating throughout his whole life that there was always hope no matter life's unrelenting assaults on one's heart. He had survived, and others could survive, could dwell together in forgiveness and peace, and could, above all other things, suffer, suffer so that others could be whole, even unto death, so that others could live.

> *He was despised and rejected of men; a man of sorrows,*
> *and acquainted with grief: and we hid as it were our faces*
> *from him; he was despised, and we esteemed him not.*

*But he shall see the travail of his soul and be satisfied,
He shall see his seed, and the pleasure of the Lord
shall prosper in his hand.*

End of Part III

CHAPTER TWELVE

KEIR, SON OF THRAIN, THE executioner of Vercingetorix and one of King Saul's most trusted knights, entered the great room of Jesus' manor house escorted by Julius. Keir, tall and blonde, originally from distant Nordic lands, was dressed in a Celtic skirt and leather sandals and was bare chested. His face was handsome and his features pleasing to the eye. One of two knights guarding the manor entrance this particular morning, he wore a pointed, cone-shaped copper helmet and carried a spear. A sword, a knife, and a sling were stuck in his leather belt. Julius wore a scarlet cotton robe, comfortable and perfect for early summer. His long black hair was pulled back in a ponytail thrown down his back.

Keir silently knelt in front of Jesus who was seated at his desk. Jesus did not hear him and kept reading a scroll of Hebrew mystic philosophy sent to him by a man belonging to a Jewish contemplative order called the Essenes. He and his celibate fellows lived lives of prayer and meditation in the remote Judean wilderness. This community was unknown to most Jews, and for that matter, the occupying Romans. Left alone, they had no interest in the increasing conflict between Rome and Jerusalem and received little news of the tensions and bloodshed occurring between the occupiers and the occupied.

Jesus did follow that conflict from afar, disturbed by its sharp escalation in the two years since his beloved wife Mary had died. His heart continued to mourn her, even while his mind became more and more obsessed with the Jews and their reckless hope that they could overthrow the Romans. He finally noticed Keir kneeling silently. He stood up and bid the knight rise. Keir did.

"Welcome, Keir." Jesus saw that he was dressed in his full soldier's gear. "Have you come here from guarding the manor entrance?"

"I have, my liege."

"What news do you bear?"

"Pepin keeps guard, watching a Roman soldier who approached on horseback and requested permission to see you."

"Is the soldier known to you?"

"No, Lord. He is not one of the local Roman legionnaires. He claims that he has come all the way from Rome. He asked for Jesus of Nazareth."

Jesus frowned. Only Romans who knew him from Judea would use that salutation.

"Did he give his name?"

"Yes." Keir looked at his bare arm.

"What are you doing?"

"I scratched his name with my knife so I wouldn't forget it." Keir looked at Jesus and grinned sheepishly. "It's pretty long."

Jesus couldn't help but smile.

"He says his name is Titus Flavius Vespasianus. He claims he's a Roman general."

Jesus did not know that name, but why should he?

"Tell Pepin I will come out and greet him. Make haste for the castle, and tell Saul that a high-ranking Roman officer has arrived from the imperial capital."

Keir nodded, bowed, and left. Jesus straightened up his desk, pushed in his chair, and asked Julius to have the great room tidied up and food and wine prepared for a meal in the guest's honor. Then Jesus walked to the front door of the manor to meet the so-called general whose long name had required Keir to scratch up his whole forearm.

Rome's envoy sat on a large, white charger and watched Jesus approach. He was dressed in a steel breastplate depicting the head of Medusa gilt in gold, a leather skirt, and heavy military leather sandals that strapped up to his knees. A large scarlet cloak covered his back and much of the back of his large horse. His galea, a polished steel general's helmet with a red plume, was strapped to the side of his saddle.

The man himself was considerably less impressive than his armor. He was short, maybe five foot one, and stout, enough so as to make it a squeeze strapping on his breastplate. His face, however, was quite handsome, and oddly, rather closely resembled the official marble sculptures of Emperor Nero that were placed all over Marseilles. The soldier had blonde curly hair and a very heavy beard that he shaved to the skin. Before Jesus could speak, the general did, trying to hide his astonishment at witnessing the giant who had stepped outside to meet him.

"Jesus of Nazareth?" he asked, in a high-pitched, yet strong voice.

"Jesus, son of Joseph," he replied.

The officer dipped his head slightly.

"My name is Titus, son of Vespasian, a general and the top aide to our glorious emperor, Nero. I serve my father with the rank of general as well."

Jesus did not know the man nor recognize his father's name, though as the top aide to Nero he had to be one of the most important men in Rome. As long as he managed to stay alive. The whole empire had heard the whispers that Nero had murdered his mother, two wives, and countless noblemen in a quest to protect himself from enemies, real and imagined. Genuine enemies had tried to kill the moody and mentally unstable ruler, and imagined enemies like Christians were his constant target because of their refusal to acknowledge him as a self-declared god. Like cockroaches, they somehow managed to survive his vicious pogroms, and, in fact, continued to grow in numbers everywhere.

"Welcome, Titus, son of Vespasian," Jesus responded. "Will you enter my home and break bread with me?"

"Willingly," Titus replied, "if you are not anti-Roman in your mind or in your heart." The general watched for Jesus' reaction.

"I bear no animosity toward Rome or its rule," Jesus replied. "Many gods are worshipped in this kingdom, including many loyal vassals who show fealty to Roman gods. I, myself, worship the Hebrew God, Jehovah, and him only do I serve."

"I presumed such," Titus said, and grinned. "Name like Jesus, son of Joseph, makes you a Jew for sure."

"I hope that you are not anti-Jewish in your mind or in your heart," Jesus said, daring to imitate the general's own words.

"Ha!" Titus exclaimed. "None whatsoever. Judea is a handful to be sure, but it's not *my* handful."

"You are welcome to be my guest and sup under my roof."

Titus held his hand up as though bidding Jesus stop.

"You may wish to hear my business before consummating that offer."

"Fair enough."

"I have been sent by my father to invite you to travel to Rome. I will be your escort. He is asking this because Nero has had extensive conversations with a man named Paul, a Roman citizen from Tarsus, who was sent to the emperor to stand trial. He was brought up on charges issued by the governor of Judea, Antonius Felix, on behalf of Jewish officials who accused Paul of fomenting religious riots among the Jews.

"In those conversations, which my father Vespasian witnessed, Paul claimed that the foundations of a new religion called Christianity were based on your person, your teachings, and your deeds. He specifically professed that you were crucified, dead, and buried some thirty years ago, but miraculously came back to life by the power of the Hebrew god. Nero was surprised to hear that you were still alive and ordered that you be found and invited to come before his presence. I have to say, however, that I cannot believe you are the same Jesus that Paul talks about. Despite your whitened hair you scarcely look older than me, and I just celebrated my twenty-fifth birthday."

"I am the man Paul is talking about," Jesus answered slowly. "In fact, he and I met years ago in this very house to discuss his beliefs. His claims about my death and resurrection are accurate." Jesus paused and held up his scarred hands for Titus to see. The general looked at both of them. He was clearly amazed and impressed. Jesus went on. "I was crucified and I died, but on the third was indeed enlivened and restored to life by Jehovah. You may know that Paul also teaches that the blood I shed on the cross is somehow magical or sacerdotal. That is his belief alone. My blood does not save sinners, and I am not the savior of Christians as Paul teaches."

Titus listened to Jesus' theological response, but more practical questions occupied his mind.

"How did you survive the cross?"

"I didn't. I died and I was buried. I was laid in a tomb on Friday evening and remained there undisturbed all day and night on the Sabbath, Saturday. On Sunday I opened my eyes and breathed again as a living man."

Titus' eyes narrowed.

"That's not possible. You had to still be alive. No other explanation is possible."

"Only the one you will not accept."

Titus shook his head stubbornly.

"You are familiar with how centurions administer the death blow for the crucified who stubbornly refuse to die on schedule?" Jesus asked.

Titus nodded.

Jesus undid his silk cincture and opened his robe. With his index finger he pointed at the large scarred mass just below his sternum. It was there that the Centurion Longinus had pushed his sword into Jesus' chest, driving it up through his heart and killing him instantly. Titus bit his lip and stared at the wound that had murdered Jesus.

Then Jesus moved his index finger to the spot above the wound. The letter L had been carved there by Longinus, the Roman centurion who crucified him. Titus stared at it without speaking, mulling over the fact that this man had been crucified, executed, and marked as dead. He looked up at Jesus and spoke.

"I am forced to acknowledge by the evidence witnessed by my own eyes that the good god Jupiter spared you in his great mercy and inscrutable wisdom. No one lives who has had a centurion's short sword thrust up his innards except by the god's grace. Why is it that you did not stay in Jerusalem after you came back to life?"

"Roman soldiers were sent to scour the city looking for me, dead or alive. My ministry was done, and I confess that I had no great desire to mount another Roman cross."

"Ha!" Titus grunted. "I think Nero is going to be very surprised and entertained when he meets the *real* Jesus. It's likely that we'll get to Rome before the emperor returns from Greece. That would give you an opportunity to see Paul again if you so desired. His execution has been stayed until Nero is back."

"I've heard even in this distant part of the empire how the emperor loves everything Greek," Jesus commented.

"That he does. He is in Olympia competing in the Games. He's already won the victor's laurel for the chariot race. Apparently he was thrown out of his chariot, but the judges awarded him first place anyway."

"Really?" Jesus was surprised. "Does that come with a monetary prize as well?"

Titus grinned slyly.

"It did for the judges. Nero thanked them by giving them a million sesterces."

Jesus arched an eyebrow.

"Such generosity is admirable."

Titus winked, entertained by Jesus' take on Nero's bribe.

"He will be in Greece for several more weeks. The Olympics have introduced new competitions for singing, dancing, acting, and dramatic poetry. The emperor is heavily favored to win them all, some 1,800 events leading up to a host of championship rounds."

"And you said your father is with him?"

"Yes, commanding a company of a thousand of the emperor's Praetorian guards. The guards will protect Nero, and my father will likely be asked to carry home his prizes."

"It is important for each of us to know our role," Jesus said, straight-faced.

"Indeed." Titus smiled a thin, knowing smile. "Does your offer of a meal together still stand?"

"By all means."

Titus dismounted from his war horse and handed the reigns to Pepin who had stepped forward to take them. Jesus walked up to Titus who was almost a foot and a half shorter than him. Unfazed, the general shook his hand with a grip of steel. He turned Jesus' hand over and looked at his palm.

"Sorry," he said, examining the scarred hole in Jesus' hand. "Did I hurt you?"

"I felt the power of your grip. You have unbelievable strength in your hand."

"I do," Titus acknowledged. "When you're pretty and fat, you learn how to take care of yourself."

Titus' eyes twinkled. Jesus couldn't help but like the man. He had great presence. He was a bright and witty conversationalist. He was also, despite his charming self-deprecation, the high-powered son of his highly placed father. For all that, Jesus seriously doubted that Titus had much of a future being short, pretty, and overweight, most likely being judged a lackey for his father, who was a lackey for Nero, the most hated man on earth.

He, himself, had had an unpromising beginning as a small town rabbi who earned a reputation as a troublemaker, who was turned over to the authorities by his own friend, killed on the cross, and deemed the most forgettable corpse of Passover. Yet despite all of that, he was alive and being actively touted as the founder of a religion that was giving the entire Roman bureaucracy fits and starts because of its converts' unwillingness to serve its emperor's desires. And on top of all that, he had now been officially invited to journey to Rome to meet Nero himself, the man who ruled most of the known world. *Emperorus everythingus.* Who knew?

Jesus held out his arm towards the front door of the manor house. Before he could invite Titus inside a great cry arose from a rider on horseback descending the road from the castle to the manor.

"Wait!"

Jesus, Titus, and Pepin all looked to see Saul riding hard towards them. Behind him rode Keir, who had informed the king about the Roman officer who had arrived.

Saul slowed his steed and halted a few yards away from Jesus and Titus. He was wearing his war armor, breastplate and helmet, leather pants and sandals, with a sword in his belt and a spear in his hand.

"Who has come calling?" he demanded to know.

Before Titus could respond, Jesus answered.

"Son, this is General Titus, son of Vespasian, general and aide to the Emperor Nero."

"Says who?" Saul responded belligerently.

"Says me," Titus responded and walked closer to Saul. "And who might you be?"

"Saul, son of Jesus, king of the lands you are standing on, Roman."

Titus turned to Jesus.

"Your son lacks manners."

Jesus shrugged.

"He worries that I don't protect myself," he told Titus.

"Commendable," Titus replied. "Still, manners wouldn't hurt." He looked at Jesus' son again.

"You're rude, King Saul. I'd be happy to instill some manners, if you are willing to be tutored. Say with spear and sword?"

Saul was furious. He pointed his spear towards Titus.

"To the death!"

"No, no, no," Titus chided Saul. "We're talking about manners. What good will they do you if you're dead? How about instead we each ante up 50,000 sesterces to be awarded to the winner?"

"You are so—" Saul was so furious he couldn't conjure up the word he wanted. Titus helped out.

"Inexpensive?"

Everyone grinned, except Saul. He fumed, waiting as Titus undid the spear bound to his horse's saddle.

"Have at it!" Saul cried and lifted his spear. Even as Saul pulled his arm back to throw, Titus threw his first. It hit Saul's breastplate with such force that it knocked him off the back of his horse. He smashed onto the ground, his head snapping back and hitting with such force that he was knocked unconscious even with his helmet on. When Saul opened his eyes, Titus was looking down at him, his sword tip resting on his throat.

"Okay," the general said. "Time for your first lesson, methinks." He looked into Saul's eyes. His adversary was conscious, and though fully aware of his desperate situation, unafraid. "How about, 'General Titus, welcome to my father's house.' Can you say that, do you think?"

"I'd rather die," Saul said through clenched teeth.

"Ah, ah, ah," Titus corrected him. "Fifty thousand sesterces, not death. We talked about this. You are a king, Saul, son of Jesus. Act like one."

"Then allow me to stand up, *General*."

"Nicely asked," Titus responded. He pulled his sword away and offered his hand to Saul. Saul gazed at the Roman warily, but he had never met a man who could unseat him from his horse with a single cast of his spear. He took Titus' outstretched hand.

"Thank you," he said, standing up. He stood no more than three feet from Titus.

"General, welcome to my father's house. I apologize for my poor manners."

"Accepted. Though you still owe me 50,000 sesterces." Titus winked.

Saul looked at Titus. While he himself was six foot six, his father's height, and stronger than any man he had ever met, this short, fat, Roman was stronger than him by far.

"I have never felt a harder blow than the one you dealt me," he told Titus, "and that includes a hefty river stone hurled into this same breastplate," Saul pointed at a large dent on one side of the steel plate, "launched by my father's sling. Also trying to teach me manners."

"Ha!" Titus laughed. "It's clear that you've had this problem for some time."

Saul smiled, relaxing now, and to tell the truth, a bit seduced by Titus' easy-going manner.

"Yes, but the lesson today may have been the one that worked."

Titus peered at the embossed art on Saul's breastplate. It now had another large dent where his spear had struck it.

"What is represented on your breastplate?"

"The great Temple in Jerusalem. Built of white granite and decorated in gold, it is held sacred by every Jew in the world."

Titus nodded.

"I've heard that it is quite magnificent. I've also heard that it is the rallying point for the Zealots seeking to overthrow Roman rule."

Saul did not comment. Neither did Jesus, who was listening to their conversation a few feet away.

"Do you think there will be a rebellion?" Titus asked Saul.

"Very likely from what I hear, but I suspect the Judeans will call it a war of independence. Resentment over a hundred years of Roman domination has come to a boil with Emperor Nero's demand that his image be honored and worshipped in every part of the empire."

Titus looked at Saul a long moment.

"Every nation under Roman rule has complied with that request. Why won't the Hebrews?"

"Well," Saul answered, "as it has been said of we Jews, 'I have seen this people, and behold, they are a stiff-necked people.'"

"Who said that?"

"Jehovah, the Hebrew God."

Titus was surprised at Saul's remark and laughed hard.

"Interesting thing for a god to say."

"Yes, especially since he's pretty much a stiff-necked God himself."

Titus laughed again, quite entertained by this backwater royal who had wanted to kill him only moments ago.

"Nero has made it a policy to leave the Jews to their own devices. Why should there be a groundswell of anti-Roman sentiment despite his benign neglect?"

Saul shook his head.

"I cannot say. I have never been to Judea. Perhaps it is just an empty puff of hope that will dissipate like so many times before."

"From your lips to god's ears."

"That's a Jewish saying."

"Works for me," Titus replied. "Who knows, King Saul? Maybe the fates will grant us the chance to meet in Jerusalem and see the great and holy Temple together."

Saul smiled, becoming more and more enchanted with Titus.

"From *your* lips to God's ears."

"Amen," Jesus spoke from behind the two men. "Amen."

— ⚜ —

Jesus, his son Saul, and his visitor Titus dined together in the manor house. Julius had ordered a lunch of cold roasted lamb, smoked venison, dried salted fish, boiled carrots and potatoes, breads and cheeses, oranges, apples, almonds and cashews, and a vintage local red wine put away several seasons past. Jesus ate sparingly, Saul ate heartily, and Titus ate and drank prodigiously. Their conversation roamed from what it was like to serve the empire as a general officer to what was the story of the wonderful wine.

Titus was a polite guest and a brilliant conversationalist. He was modest about his strength and prowess, though his reverence for his father, Vespasian, was so intense that he prickled defensively at any question regarding his father's relationship with Nero. For himself, he spoke respectfully about the emperor and comfortably about the assignments given him from Nero, including this one.

Jesus sipped at his wine and asked Titus to explain again why Nero should have any interest in meeting him.

"It's not like he follows minor religions," he told Titus.

"Ah, but that's where you're wrong. He is quite fascinated with the Jews' fanatical loyalty to their religion and has for years wondered what exactly has been fueling the growth of Christianity throughout the Roman world. He spent a lot of time during Paul's trial questioning him on its fundamental tenets.

"I sat in on some of those sessions. Imagine how surprised Nero was when Paul told him that you were still alive. He described your decision to remain on Earth as similar to the Bodhisattvas of the Buddha's religion in India, enlightened beings who choose to stay on Earth rather than be absorbed by the cosmos, becoming actively involved in the passions and deeds of men." Titus paused and studied Jesus' face. "Was he right?"

"I am familiar with Siddhartha's teachings. I am also aware of the diaspora of his enlightened disciples who are indeed designated Bodhisattvas, but I have not heard myself compared to them before. My first impression is that the similarity appears remarkably accurate."

Titus listened and then went on.

"Paul presented several scrolls to Nero concerning your life and times. He called them Gospels. He also provided at least a dozen copies of his own personal writings which he told Nero would serve as commentaries on those Gospels. To his credit, Nero read all of the documents in their original Greek, his favorite language by the way, and concluded two things. One, that you should be found and brought to his presence. Two, that every Christian anywhere should be hunted down and exterminated.

"He found Paul's religion oblivious of any respect for any authority except Jesus Christ, and his Father, Jehovah, the God of the Jews. He said that Christians were encouraged to be disobedient to Roman authority when and where it differed from their dogmas, even disobeying the commands of the emperor himself, if necessary. Such teachings led Nero to believe that such attitudes would surely and finally lead to non-payment of taxes, a refusal to serve in the military, and the fomenting of empire-wide civil disobedience.

"The emperor concluded that if their numbers were allowed to continue to grow as rapidly as they had since Jesus' ministry ended in Judea thirty years earlier, the day would surely come when they would overthrow the Roman gods, allow the empire itself to crash, and all would be lost. In short," Titus concluded, "Nero is now completely fearful of Christians. He will execute Paul and go from there to suppress their expansion."

"Is he going to arrest my father when you take him to Rome?" Saul asked, visibly worried by Titus' comments. The general shook his head.

"No. He regards Jesus as a Jew, not a Christian, and as such, his desire to meet him is limited to his curiosity about Jesus' life and teachings. He cannot understand how Christianity has managed to create a core of believers greater in their devotion to the crucified Christ than even the Jewish Zealots' exclusionary vision of a new heaven and a new Earth with no one in it but themselves."

"I think you overstate the position of the Jews," Saul told Titus.

"I long to be enlightened," Titus responded.

"The Jews wish only to have their land to themselves," Saul said.

"But don't they have that already?" Titus politely disagreed. "There isn't even a full legion stationed in Judea. There are only five thousand soldiers in Caesarea and fewer than that in Jerusalem. Jews have freedom of speech and freedom of movement. They are encouraged to pursue economic enterprises, allowed to accumulate wealth, and most importantly, every man, woman, and child worships the Hebrew god without restraint, interference, or fees.

"It is true that the empire levies an annual tax on all households, but Rome asks for no more than that. In return, Nero protects Judea from invasion, has created a network of the world's best roads, and does this all without one request for a thank you, or even a libation for himself and the divine Caesars who have given these blessings to Israel for a century."

"Jews want freedom," Saul responded. "A land with no foreign taxation and no foreign presence."

"But Judea is just a little bit of cheese on the international serving board," Titus responded. "If Rome should withdraw, every nation around that board will try to gobble it up."

Saul shrugged.

"It's a risk that Jews are willing to face," Saul answered.

Titus held up his silver wine goblet. One of the attending servants immediately filled it. Titus drank deeply, then he looked at Saul.

"Do you keep servants like your father does?"

"Yes. They are well-paid and appreciated."

"But they're not free."

"Yes, they are. Freemen all."

"With no land, no wealth, and no prospects. Jupiter spare me from that kind of freedom."

Jesus could see that Saul was not pleased with Titus' words, but to his son's credit he held his tongue.

"Now Jews, on the other hand, can own a farm, fish the seas, sell merchandise, be craftsmen, engage commissions as artisans, work as contractors, run import/export businesses—in short, they can do just about any damn thing they please. Seems to me they are a lot more free than the servants in your house."

"I cannot refute your logic," Saul replied somewhat frustrated, "though I think your characterization of Jewish freedom is nothing more than clever double-talk. Freedom is not just a legal term. It is a state of being."

"Then by your own logic," Titus answered back, "true freedom is not bound by an occupying power, economic poverty, or obligations to a family, a craft, or a particular town. Your father had true freedom, unafraid of being rejected, unafraid to face desertion of his followers, even unafraid of death on the cross. His life was forfeit, but his beliefs were never compromised. Now that's freedom, Saul. It seems to me that every believing Jew in love with Jehovah is already as free as Jesus ever was and as free as any Hebrew will ever be."

Silence descended over the table. Titus, Saul, and Jesus sat and waited to see who would speak up first. At last Titus did, looking at Jesus.

"I am sorry to press the reason for my presence here during this thoughtful exchange, but may I ask if you are willing to journey with me to Rome? I will conduct you there safely and arrange for your lodging while we wait for the emperor's return. I give you my word that you will in no way be humiliated or detained beyond the length of the stay required."

"How can you say that?" Saul challenged him.

"Because I have already obtained the emperor's word," Titus answered smoothly.

"Which is worth?"

"Worth every Roman life obliged to defend Nero's promises. If and when he breaks his word, the whole empire will reel and begin to crumble. The emperor is our father, and in that role we venerate and worship his holy name."

"You worship Nero as a god?" Saul asked.

Titus nodded.

"Yes, as a divinity who is part man and part god."

"Never heard of such a thing."

Titus smiled and looked towards Jesus.

"Many people throughout the world believe the very same is true of your father."

"How do you know so much about my father?"

"I read the Gospels Paul left with Nero. A very unusual kind of writing I have to say. Teachings, miracles, wisdom, conflict, and as Paul would say, all of it predicated on believing that the main character, your father, was crucified, dead, and buried, only to rise back to life on the third day.

"I've seen the wounds in your father's hands, and the *coup de grace* in his chest. I also see his face, as young as mine, his thick hair lush as palm fronds rising in the air, and his giant body, muscled and strong. I see immortality written on the body of Jesus of Nazareth.

"Allow me to clarify that I don't believe in his god, and I don't believe that he rose from the dead. I don't believe any of it. Yet there he sits, alive, healthy, back from the grave, the observable example of what I don't believe in. There is something of the divine in your father. May I add that I find him gracious, gentle, patriarchal, and a would-be kingdom builder which seems to fly in the face of his professed teachings.

"But then a dead man eating and drinking and conversing flies in the face of what I know, so maybe it's a wash. In another life, I myself might be subject to his persona and swayed by his philosophy which I believe can be summed up by a pair of words: Do good. His very words, I believe. And if I could be so bold, I perhaps could even shrink those two words down to one and sum up his complete philosophy in a single word: Sacrifice."

"You seem rather taken with his stories and words," Saul commented, not entirely kindly.

"I *am* taken with new ideas and the words that bring them to life," Titus answered. "There is more to being a man than taking a buck down in the forest at dawn. More to being a soldier than slaughtering an enemy in the heat of the day."

Saul didn't think there was anything better than taking a buck down at dawn, except maybe taking a man down in the heat of the day. He had found that killing Adheesh Sarvin, the Gypsy king, and strangling Vercingetorix with his bare hands, had far exceeded the power and pleasure of watching the life bleed out of a deer. That Titus had some intellectual depth and curiosity beyond bloodletting didn't impress Saul. And as for Titus' flattering view of his father, Jesus, he was still a Roman and could go fuck himself.

Jesus answered Titus.

"I will go with you to Rome."

"And so will I," Saul interjected.

"Bravo!" Titus exclaimed and raised his goblet. "Wine and conversation tonight, the trials and tribulations of the road tomorrow. Titus drank deeply of his wine.

Jesus raised his own silver chalice, a gift that Lazarus had given him for his last supper with his disciples, and drank from it. It had been cast with vines and grapes, an homage to one of Lazarus' favorite teachings of Jesus: I am the vine, and ye are the branches. He that abideth in me and I in him, the same bringeth forth much fruit. It was the only chalice Jesus had ever owned, used, and valued for its sentiment, hidden by his disciple John after the last supper and returned to him before he sailed for Gaul with Mary Magdalene.

Jesus studied Titus as the house servants brought more wine and dessert, sweet baked rolls filled with cheese and covered with honey.

"Do you think the emperor would consider a request from me to spare Paul's life?" Jesus asked.

"Oh, he'd be polite and listen, but it is likely that he made up his mind to execute Paul long ago. He believes that Paul is the leader of Christians everywhere, an impression Paul himself has willingly promoted. Nero wants to cut the head off the Christian snake, and he thinks that head is Paul."

Titus folded his arms as if he was done explaining. But he was not.

"So! Your plea would not result in clemency. And let me add, that if your veiled hope is to save him from crucifixion, you may spare your efforts. As a Roman citizen he will be beheaded. A quick, painless, even honorable death. Also, in conclusion, you needn't see Paul unless you wish. He is under house arrest continuing to lead the life of a scholar and missionary, undoubtedly generating his endless letters."

"May I think about it on our way, General?" Jesus asked. "At this point I can't imagine why I would spend any more time with him. His has twisted the meaning of my life to service a religion I did not teach and will not embrace."

"It's your decision," Titus said gracefully. "Deliver it when you're ready."

Jesus nodded. Once again he was impressed by the manners and upbringing of this high-ranking Roman.

"Did I tell you that I was a bachelor?" Titus said. "Are there any beautiful women here who would like to share my bed tonight?"

So much for manners and upbringing.

Saul frowned.

Jesus smiled.

Titus looked confused.

"What?" he asked. "What?"

CHAPTER THIRTEEN

Jesus, Saul, and Titus Flavius Vespasianus left La Valdieu early on a warm and lovely Gaul morning. Saul had blacksmiths at the castle shoe both his horse and the one he had selected for Jesus with iron horseshoes. Roman roads were paved in stone and there were more than five hundred imperial miles between La Valdieu and the city of Rome.

Titus estimated it would take three weeks to reach the capital judging by the time it had taken him to find Jesus. They would stop to feed and rest the horses at the end of each day on the road and take their own refreshment at inns Titus knew or knew of. He told Jesus that their accommodations would be superb, as innkeepers without exception were eager to serve and spoil a Roman general officer and his guests traveling on a mission for the emperor himself.

Jesus nodded as Titus spoke and watched the stable hands saddle the horses and strap on animal skins of wine and leather pouches full of dried apples, pecans, walnuts, and fresh bread. Jesus wore a light cotton robe expecting hot days as summer set in. Saul and Titus both wore steel breastplate, leather skirts, and their helmets. Their spears were fastened to their horse's harness, and their swords were sheathed and hung on leather belts around their waists.

They held the reigns with one hand and slung their leather-covered shields on their free arm. Saul tucked his sling in his belt and tied a small leather bag full of stones to it as well. Titus stuck a wooden club in his belt along with several throwing knives. Saul noted those and realized they were cousins of the metal-tipped darts Hebrew soldiers tossed to slow or stop the enemy at close range.

Roman roads or not, Titus was prepared to face brigands, bandits, gypsies, thugs, barbarians, mercenaries, and all other armed renegades. Saul, in fact, hoped for such encounters and wanted to be grossly outnumbered. It was one thing to defend oneself, but how much better to massacre a whole throng of troublemakers.

Goodbyes had been said, and with no particular ado Titus simply started off. The estate roads were laid in stone and well maintained. It wouldn't be until they reached Marseilles, however, that they could access the network of Roman-built roads. The morning passed uneventfully, Titus stopping every two or three miles to water his horse and drink some wine.

Jesus and Saul chatted while they watered their own horses and drank their fill. Their words were nothing more than small talk which belied the serious reason for this journey. But like all people everywhere, light conversation made the heaviness of the task easier to bear, even for such confident men as they.

At the end of the first day of travel, the sun was just beginning to set when they reached the outskirts of Marseilles. Titus led the troupe to an inn with the picture of a naked woman painted on a sign hanging over the door. Saul frowned. Jesus read the Latin printed over her head out loud, Cunnus Lingus. Titus dismounted and began to unpack his horse.

"Lingus?" Saul asked. "Isn't that the Celtic island off the western coast of Britannia?"

"No," Jesus replied. "That's Hibernia. Lingus is Latin for tongue."

"And Cunnus?"

"Cunnus means that we're not staying here tonight."

"What?" Titus asked, overhearing Jesus' conversation with Saul.

"We need food and rest," Jesus responded. "I suspect this inn caters to another kind of need."

"Bullseye," Titus affirmed, "and this place has exactly what I need."

"Across the street is an inn called The Slug and Lettuce," Jesus told him. "I believe it will service the kind of needs that Saul and I have, namely a hot dinner and a comfortable bed."

Saul gave his father a funny look, then realized exactly why Titus wanted to

stay at Cunnus Lingus. He chuckled and dismounted, leading his horse across the street toward Jesus' choice for supper and lodging. Jesus followed him and called back to Titus.

"See you at dawn outside your inn. Wash your mouth out before you join us."

"Ha!" Titus shouted back. "I always save the last of my wine for that very purpose."

— ⚜ —

The days on the road passed swiftly enough. The weather was hot, and the Roman roads were full of merchants with wagons, folks on horses and mules, and large formations of soldiers on the move. Titus said it was customary for half legions to move together, five thousand men followed by miles of supply wagons, though most often on this road they saw groups of a hundred soldiers led by a centurion.

Titus, Jesus, and Saul yielded the road each time any unit approached them on the road. They watched the legionnaires pass, noting that every soldier stared at Titus waiting at the side of the road, impressed by his blazing steel armor and his general's helmet with its gorgeous red plume. The officers turned in their saddles and snapped off sharp salutes to the unknown general. Titus saluted back stiffly and watched the troops move by.

On the twenty-first day of the trip, milestones began to mark the number of miles to Rome. One hundred seemed like the beginning of a long countdown, but the three men had already traveled more than four hundred miles toward their destination. These milestones were harbingers that the end of the trip was near and marked as well the first time any trouble occurred on the road.

It was late afternoon, the sun was still fairly high in the sky when the three men passed a tall, horse-drawn wagon with a canvas top stretched over a wooden frame. Two dark-faced men sat in front wearing colorful handkerchiefs on their heads. They slowed the wagon as the travelers passed, and then pulled onto the shoulder. Saul turned and looked back at the wagon in time to see the two men jump down with bows in hand.

"Archers in the rear!" he cried, sliding off his horse and holding his shield in front of him. He pulled his spear free of its harness and slapped the rump of his horse. It jumped and ran off. Titus moved just as fast as Saul, yanking his spear out of his horse's harness and slapping his mount on the side. He did the same to Jesus' horse and the animal shot off with Jesus holding on as best as he could.

Titus held his shield in front of him and stepped next to Saul. They took a dozen or more arrows in their leather-covered wooden shields before their attackers jumped back into their wagon. The driver pulled the horses back onto the road and whipped them into a panicked run. Without a word between them, Saul and Titus ran straight toward the approaching wagon. Despite the general's short stature and rotund figure, he easily outraced Saul, stepped to the side of the approaching horses and cut the leather traces that held them to the wagon. They bolted away and the wagon rolled to a halt.

The two riders jumped down to the ground and two more men hastened out of the back. All four were wearing long, colorful robes and patterned head wrappings to protect themselves from the heat.

Titus lifted his spear and with a mighty throw put it in the chest of one of them. He grabbed Saul's spear and shot it through the neck of another. The remaining two marauders had notched arrows to their bows. Titus and Saul held their shields up and ran toward the archers. The men's arrows hit the shields even as they dropped their bows and pulled out their swords to defend themselves.

Titus ran up to one of the men, jumped at least three feet high, and drove his sword down into the base of the man's neck. Saul's foe faced him squarely holding his sword in front of him. Saul slammed the sword with his own, spinning his opponent and causing him to drop his sword. But he came out of the spin with a dagger in his hand. Saul cut his forearm off. The man roared with pain and clutched the raw place where half of his arm had just been shorn away. He screamed as spurts of blood sprayed through his fingers.

Saul looked at the man's clothes. He was wearing a blue robe, the color of the tribe of Judah, and the dagger he had dropped was an assassin's knife carried by the Sicarii, the Jewish terrorists who murdered Roman soldiers and officials. Seeing Titus' helmet must have made him a target too enticing to resist.

Titus stepped up next to Saul and looked at the wounded man, who by now had fallen to his knees and closed his eyes.

"Finish him," Titus said.

Saul nodded, but hesitated. He had never killed a Jew before. Titus instantly discerned Saul's issue.

"For god's sake, Saul, this man and his kind betrayed your father. Get on with it."

Titus' words jolted Saul back to life. He kicked the wounded man and commanded him to open his eyes. He did. Saul put the point of his sword against his throat as the man stared in terror.

"When you see Judas again, tell him that Jesus' son says shalom."

With that Saul pushed his sword into the dying man's neck. Then swinging the sharp blade he beheaded the man with one stroke. The head fell and the torso dropped onto its side. Saul nudged the head away from the corpse with his foot. Both body parts gushed blood and bile. Titus went back to check on the other wounded men, beheading them with swift blows of his own sword.

"Nasty characters," he said. He knelt and wiped his sword clean on the robe of one of the dead men. "So where do these vermin go after death?"

"Into the dirt," Saul said.

"Jews don't believe in hell?"

"Not unless you count life under the Romans," Saul said and chuckled.

"Great body of Osiris," Titus swore. "I've never seen you laugh before."

"Yeah," Saul replied. "What was I thinking?"

"Is your father around anywhere?" Titus asked. He couldn't see Jesus or his horse on the highway.

"I'm sure he's fine. He hadn't ridden much before this trip, but these last weeks sharpened his skills."

"Watch for him while I check out the bad guys' wagon."

Titus climbed into the wagon and rummaged for valuables. Saul looked at the bled-out corpse of the man he had beheaded. Didn't matter after all that he was a Jew. Saul didn't feel anything. No remorse. No regret. Nothing. That was good. That was the way he wanted it. He wasn't his father whose sacred heart bemoaned the misfortune of any man who forfeited his life prematurely. He'd even told that repentant murderer on the cross next to him that he would be in paradise that very day. Too much kindness. A man should be more, more manly. Titus climbed back out of the wagon carrying a small olivewood chest inlaid with mother-of-pearl.

"Full of gold sesterces," he told Saul. "I reckon Jupiter provided these to pay for the thousands you still owe me." Titus grinned. "You lucky bastard. Not many men have two gods looking out for them."

With that Titus pulled his spear out of the dead man who was wearing it straight up like an erection. He wiped the big iron tip on the dead man's robe and hopped onto his horse. Without another word he trotted down the road following the direction Jesus' horse had gone. Saul fetched his own spear, cleaned it on the corpse it had created, then wiped both sides of his sword on his own calf admiring the streaks of blood it left behind. He got on his horse and rode after Titus. It had been a good day for someone else to die.

— ⚜ —

"I don't want to see Paul again," Titus said, bluntly. He was sitting in the main room of his spacious living quarters in the Praetorian Guard compound, drinking wine and sharing a midday meal with Jesus and Saul. A cohort of one thousand of the emperor's elite personal guard was with Nero in Olympia, standing by in case any Greeks decided to object to the innumerable first prizes the emperor had been awarded so far.

Titus' room was very large with several black-painted granite pedestals bearing the marble heads and robed torsos of Nero, Julius Caesar, Augustus, and his own father, Vespasian. Shuttled behind those prominent men stood a pedestal with the bust of an emperor who had been deposed and killed not so very long ago, Gaius Germanicus, better known by his childhood nickname, Caligula. Little Boots.

Caligula had made the mistake of thinking that the emperor's absolute power rested elsewhere other than with the wealthy people of Rome. Systematically he had ordered the assassinations of senators and confiscated their holdings until one cold January morning twenty years ago the upper class reminded Little Boots of their rights and needs by paying assassins to murder the twenty-nine-year-old Caesar.

Titus' father Vespasian had received this bust of Caligula from the wise and humble emperor who had succeeded him, Claudius. Someone had broken the nose off the sculpture. Claudius told

Vespasian to gaze at it periodically and remember that his own nose was just as vulnerable should he fail to please not only the rich, but the people of Rome as well.

Yeah, yeah, yeah, Titus thought, having heard this story from his father a dozen times. Whenever Vespasian traveled with Nero, he asked his son to keep it and watch over it. Titus wondered now and then if his father had his eyes on the throne as well as the sculpture.

There were several other rooms in Titus' apartment, all spacious, dotted with tall bronze stands bearing oil lamps and incense burners. Carpets from Turkmen lands covered the floors, each one supposedly taking slave girls ten years to weave. Silk banners of the legions he had served hung from poles stationed around the room, and in the middle sat a marble desk with several marble chairs clustered around it. There was a basket on one side of the desk for encyclicals from Nero and another on the other side for everything else, usually tossed without being unsealed or read.

In the rear of the apartment were sleeping quarters and a bath. Titus used both, but sparingly. He preferred inns and public baths in the center of the city that catered to military officers offering excellent food and exquisite women. Titus had been married twice, was widowed and divorced. The only use he had for women now could be dispensed within five minutes unless he was feeling lazy, or particularly liked the face or the body of the prostitute he had hired.

Now he helped himself to a lunch catered by the Praetorian kitchen. There was fresh bread, black olives, cold roast lamb, a dip of bitter herbs, another of honey and lemon, and fresh melon slices rolled in sugar. There were place settings on a round marble table for himself, Jesus, and Saul. Each setting had large and small silver plates and golden goblets of red wine. Two large silver vessels placed on the corner of the general's desk contained more wine and chilled water. The three men had arrived in Rome late in the morning and were now conversing about the day's schedule. Titus' remark of not wanting to see Paul resonated with both Jesus and his son.

"I don't want to see him again," Titus repeated. "He wears me out with his endless talk about the next life while I'm still trying to live this one."

"That very focus is responsible for much of the appeal of Christianity to the poor, the destitute, and the down and out," Saul commented. He and Jesus were dressed in light cotton robes and Titus was wearing a cream-colored Roman robe called a toga. It was so long and wide he had to lift and carry the excess material in the crook of his arm. Saul had seen wealthy Romans wearing them in Marseilles and thought such gowns the height of idiocy. They didn't seem any less ridiculous here in the heart of Rome itself.

"It's truly a religion focused on tomorrow," Titus agreed. "I want to think about today." He looked at Jesus. "I read in one of the Gospels that your last words were, 'Father, into your hands I commend my spirit.' Mine will be, 'Quick, I only have time for a woman and a glass of wine.'"

Jesus and Saul both laughed. Neither one of them had ever met a man like Titus, totally dedicated to the arts of war—an occupation that could get you killed every day of the year—yet also wholly dedicated to living life like a Sybarite: eating, drinking, and fornicating. It certainly wasn't the lifestyle of a typical Jew which usually dictated moderation in all things. A poor people, Hebrews felt blessed when they had *enough*, a word that was probably regarded as a bad word by most Romans. Titus' lifestyle was the product of a long line of rich, self-indulgent Latins. Jesus' and Saul's lifestyle harked back to the great patriarchs of Israel, who humbly gave thanks to God when there was bread on the table.

"I propose that only the wisest and the most patient man among us go and visit Paul," Titus suggested. "That person, it seems to me, is you, Jesus. As for Saul and me, we are young in age and lacking in maturity. Finding that our interest is discussing religion is equivalent to the time required to take a short piss, we will embark on improving our maturation levels with an afternoon of gladiatorial combat."

"I am not sure how fighting gladiators will improve your maturity," Jesus replied. "Might, in fact, set you back."

Titus grinned and began peeling an orange.

"I spent the finest years of my life learning how to fight. I look at a gladiator and I see a tutor-for-hire. Ready to help me keep those essential skills honed, don't you know?"

"No."

Titus shrugged and put a slice of orange in his mouth. "Not sure that it matters. At least not for me. Saul, on the other hand, has some ground to gain in terms of combat virtues."

"Hey!" Saul protested. "Can you back that up?"

Titus nodded.

"I remember like it was yesterday that you challenged a total stranger to combat who with one throw of his javelin knocked your ass right off your horse."

Now it was Saul's turn to nod. That *had* been immature. Now that he had come to know his attacker so much better, he realized gratefully that Titus had spared his life when it should have been forfeit.

"Well, I was standing up for myself then," Saul answered. "I have to say that it's been very mature of me since then not to challenge you to anything."

All three of the men laughed, then Jesus spoke.

"All right, I'll go and visit Paul. You two do whatever you like, just don't get hurt. Roman soldiers testing the blade of a general and his companion would be circumspect. But from what I've heard about professional gladiators, you both may come home in pieces."

Titus shook his head and ate the last of his orange.

"The best gladiators are brilliant fighters and rich as Croesus. Murdering roughnecks they are not. When they're not fighting, they're checking on their investments and bank balances. None of them is going to throw their luxurious retirements away by challenging me or Saul to anything more than sword slapping."

"Sword slapping?"

"Getting whacked by a sword instead of skewered by it."

"Still sounds dangerous."

"Not as dangerous as getting crucified, which would be the fate of any gladiator who injures me or my guest."

"Well, I pray that they are judicious in that case," Jesus said. "The injuries from a crucifixion are rarely reversible."

Titus arched an eyebrow.

"I said rarely."

"I heard you. I'm just surprised you can be humorous about that."

"Because in my case it *was* reversible. Makes me happier and happier every year."

Titus looked at Jesus.

"I am sorry that the religion about you, isn't about you. You are an amazing man."

"If I inspire you to do good, then I am proud."

"I didn't say I wanted to be like you," Titus said. "But for a man who doesn't fight, or drink, or whore, you are still a man's man." Titus' voice choked with emotion, something that surprised him and made him embarrassed. "There is still some hope however, that your son will turn out normal."

— ✣ —

Titus had a Praetorian escort Jesus on his mount to the small home where Paul was living under house arrest. On the way Jesus stared in awe at the colossal buildings that had been erected to honor heroic Romans, their heroic families, even their heroic pets. He was particularly impressed by the public baths constructed for use by the citizens. No one made any effort to restrict the fabulous baths for the rich, nor did they have to, actually. The poorer sons of the empire enjoyed the chariot races and gladiator shows at the circus a lot more than bathing.

Paul's adobe house with a red tile roof was guarded by a Praetorian wearing the special breastplate and helmet of his order. Paul was Nero's prisoner, and this was Nero's soldier. Paul handed him the stamped scroll that Titus had given him. The guard took it, recognized Titus' seal in the wax, then broke it and read Titus' request that Jesus be allowed to visit Paul. The guard handed the scroll back to Jesus and told him to wait. The Praetorian turned to the door and knocked. Then he opened it without waiting for a response and called inside to Paul that one Jesus, son of Joseph, had come to see him. Might he enter?

Paul came to the door and fell at Jesus' feet. Jesus grasped his shoulder and urged him to stand. Paul did, but he couldn't speak, so overwhelmed was he to behold Jesus again. The Christian missionary to the world hadn't changed much in the years since he had journeyed to Gaul to meet Jesus. The man was still shockingly handsome, his salt and pepper hair a concession to age, but his body was still slim and youthful. Paul was wearing a toga and a large signet ring covered with wax. Apparently he was still shipping out letters by the ton.

"Come in, come in," Paul said, and was bold enough to take one of Jesus' hands. He led him into his home. The house was modest, but it had a bedroom, kitchen, and a private bathroom with fresh running water to fill a sink, or the bath, and remove waste. The main room of the house had numerous wooden chairs with cushions, a wooden dining table, and a reclining couch that was covered with parchment scrolls and a few modern papyrus codices. Two small windows with bars faced the street. Paul offered Jesus a chair and sat down in one facing him. He shook his head and smiled happily.

"I can't tell you how much it means to me that you've come, my Lord."

"I am sorry for your circumstances, Paul."

"I'm not. My life is full because of you, and my eternal life assured."

"I've heard that you've been very busy."

"Very blessed, Lord. Very blessed. My preaching has been to both Jew and Gentile, and today Rome's own census numbers show that one in ten persons living in the empire has embraced your Christianity."

"It's not my Christianity, Paul."

"Yes, it is," Paul countered. "Our faith rests in the efficacy of your sacrifice and resurrection. You were sent to Earth as the Son of the Living God. You healed, you taught, you bore the sins of the world, and because of your obedience—even unto death on the cross—people everywhere are set free."

"Did Jehovah tell you that, because he sure didn't tell me."

"Of course he told you. He spoke through your mother Mary. He spoke through the praises and prayers of people who dropped everything to follow you. Didn't you hear the masses on Palm Sunday when they acknowledged that you were the messiah? God even spoke to you through Pontius Pilatus when he put the sign over your cross declaring that you were the King of the Jews. How could you not recognize all of those affirmations? As you yourself said on so many occasions, he who has ears, let him hear."

"Paul, kindly do not try to convert me to Christianity."

The flamboyant missionary fell silent for a moment, his countenance disappointed. Then he spoke from his heart.

"Lord, it is soul rending that you do not accept that you are the savior of the world. But that doesn't make it any less true. The forgiveness purchased by your sacrifice is the redemption of mankind even unto the end of the world. Does the dove know why it is sacrificed in Jerusalem? No, but that does not void the efficacy of the atonement his death brings. Is the lamb offered in the Temple aware that its blood sprinkled on the sinner washes away all his sins? Of course not, but that does not make its vicarious death any less meaningful and valuable. You do not see the reality. But God does. And Christians do. Therefore my dear Lord Jesus Christ, even though you stand in denial, salvation for the world is what makes your suffering, death, and resurrection matter."

Jesus sat and stared at Paul.

"If such is true, and you know that I deny the role that you give me, then why did you need to see me?"

Paul looked into Jesus' eyes.

"I am a dead man, soon to be executed by Emperor Nero himself. But I am ready to die.

I am ready to see my God. During your ministry, you often told penitents, 'Your sins are forgiven. Depart in peace.' I want you to promise me that you will be at my side when the moment of my execution comes. In that moment, I want to hear you say those exact words to me. 'Paul, your sins are forgiven. Depart in peace.'" Jesus sat and marveled at the faith of the little man sitting across from him. He looked at him for a long time. Then he nodded.

Titus and Saul were walking past old, neglected temples along the Tiber River erected in the days of the Roman Republic. There was garbage strewn on the temple steps mixed with feces and vomit.

Saul shook his head.

"What?" Titus asked.

"Such disrespect. Doesn't anyone care about these temples?"

"Not really, in case you couldn't tell. I don't think the gods care either. It's not like anybody gets a lightning bolt up their ass for being impolite." Saul barked out a sharp laugh. "Matter of fact," Titus went on, "most Romans would love to see someone get fried for ignoring protocols regarding the gods. Might prove that one of those characters actually exists."

"I believe that Jehovah the God of the Hebrews exists," Saul replied.

"Sure you so, but do you have any reason to do so besides other peoples' stories?"

"Jews have sacred writings which speak of God's blessings."

Titus frowned.

"I repeat, besides other people's stories?"

Saul didn't respond. He was being pressed in an area he'd never thought about.

Titus pressed his challenge.

"I personally refuse to believe in *any* god. I rely on myself. I rely on my friends. I do not rely on some deity I've never met."

Titus suddenly fell silent. He pointed at a small open area beneath the Marcellus Theater, the semi-circular marble venue on the Tiber with stadium-style seating and a large stage for plays, political rallies, and gladiatorial games. The marble theater was several stories high and blazed in the late afternoon sun.

Titus put a finger to his lips and walked silently to a metal gate that enclosed a small fighting arena under the theater. There was a dirt floor and stone columns supporting an iron superstructure above which tiers of wooden seats were constructed. Two men were working out on the floor and another was polishing his fighting gear and weapons.

Titus beckoned Saul back from the gate. He stopped a few yards away and spoke in a hushed voice.

"This is a practice area for gladiators. There are three men there right now. They are brothers who claim to be direct descendants of Lucius Junius Brutus who founded the Roman Republic more than five hundred years ago. Their family was almost destroyed during the civil wars of the last centuries, and their lands and titles were confiscated by none other than Julius Caesar.

"These brothers are brutes, murderers, and rapists, but Nero has a thing for them and their history. He protects them from the law *and* the aggrieved." Titus' eyes narrowed. "May I remind you that the emperor is away, and since it appears that there are *only* three Brutus brothers in the practice area, I propose we kill them."

Saul was stunned.

Titus ignored his reaction.

"Do you have your sling with you?"

Saul nodded.

"How many stones do you have?"

"A half dozen, maybe more."

"Enough to slow a man down?"

"One is enough to *take* a man down."

"Kill him?"

Saul nodded again.

"One of the brothers is wearing a solid steel mask with eyeholes the size of big coins. Are you good enough to put a stone through one of those holes?"

"Yes, if he looks at me more than two or three seconds."

"Good. That's very good." Titus rubbed his hands together. "The brother with that mask wields a short stabbing sword and a club with spikes. The brother that wears a mask with a metal mesh front and a steel back fights exclusively and exceedingly well with a net and a trident. The last brother can put a javelin down your throat while taking your head off with a curved Arabian sword. He wears a traditional legionnaire's helmet exposing his face, which doesn't matter because no one can get near him.

"I wish that I could claim that I could take on all three at once, but I cannot. Even armored as we are, they are too formidable. And, no disrespect intended, my friend, but any one of them could kill you before you say their ancestor's name. However, if you manage to take out the one with eyeholes in his mask before he knows what happened, that leaves the other two for me and I think those odds are acceptable. Let me add, however, anything you can do to hurt or disable either one or both of the remaining brothers while I am fighting them would be appreciated."

"Isn't that cheating?" Saul asked.

Titus raised his eyebrows.

"In a fight to the death, there is no cheating. Only living and dying." Titus grasped Saul's shoulder and looked him in the eye. "Are you with me?"

Saul reached for Titus' shoulder in turn and said, "I will fight alongside you as though you were my brother."

"Then there is no way we can lose. Put your helmet on and load your sling. When we enter the arena one or more of the brothers will taunt us. That's normal shit while everyone gets ready to fight. We, however, will attack immediately while the men are still gearing up. Move in as close and as quickly as you can. How fast can you use that sling?"

"I can get off a killing blow every two or three seconds."

"Jupiter's balls!" Titus exclaimed. "Fire away, brother."

Titus put on his helmet, carried his shield in one hand and his sword in the other.

Saul put on his helmet and carried his shield over his left forearm, carrying several stones in that hand as well. He held the loaded sling in his right hand. He and Titus walked up to the gate. Titus opened it and led Saul inside. The three gladiators glanced at the new arrivals. Titus and Saul started at a run.

The Brutus brothers frowned, not comprehending what was happening. One of them wore the mask with the cut-out eyeholes. At fifteen yard's distance, Saul stopped. He whipped his sling forward loosing the stone with such speed that it shot through the gladiator's mask eyehole, entered his eye socket, raced through his brain, and tore out the back of his skull. Blood, brains, and pieces of bone coursed down the dead man's back even as he crumbled to his knees and fell on his face.

The other two men stared at their fallen brother, at which point Titus attacked the one bearing a net and trident. The gladiator pulled on his helmet, the one with the metal mesh in front and steel in the back. He met Titus' sword with his trident and loosed his net at him. The general stepped back out of reach of the gladiator's trident.

The third Brutus brother watched, ignoring Saul who was at that very moment preparing to get off another stone with his sling. Saul shouted at him and the gladiator turned to face him. He took a stone to the forehead unprotected by his open-faced helmet. The rock entered his head at such a speed it literally caused the gladiator's head to explode. The big burly man fell over backwards like a great tree that has been felled.

Saul turned his attention to Titus defending himself from the aggressive trident work of the last remaining brother. He was following Titus around the ring waiting for another cast of his net and a kill with his deadly trident.

Saul cried out to the Roman.

"Son of Brutus, son of the Republic, your brothers are dead. Stop and hear our offer of clemency that you may live and carry on your line."

The gladiator stood and pulled his net and trident close to his armored chest.

"I am listening," he said in a strong, fearless voice.

"You and your brothers have acted with disdain towards the citizens of Rome. Two of you are now dead, shades waiting to ford the River Styx. If you throw down your arms and pledge to leave Rome you shall live. If not, we shall strike you down and carry away your head and the heads of your brothers as trophies." Saul paused, then said, "What say ye?"

"I say," the big man thundered, "who the fuck are you that you slay my brothers and threaten me?"

"We shall give you our names, but only after you show good faith and put down your weapons."

"Your names first, and *then* I shall choose what I shall do."

"I am Saul, Son of Jesus."

Titus spoke up.

"I am Titus Flavius Vespasianus, son of Titus Flavius Caesar Vespasianus Augustus."

"Titus, the son of Nero's henchman?" Brutus' descendent sneered.

"One and the same," Titus replied evenly.

"Not sure I can trust you," the gladiator said.

"What choice do you have?" Titus asked.

"I can choose to fight to the death and perhaps you puppets of the empire will be the ones who die."

"Or you can put down your weapons and forsake Rome before we come looking for you again," Saul added.

"What did I or my brothers ever do to you?" the gladiator cried, almost plaintively now.

Titus spoke.

"You and your brothers raped our sisters and wives and murdered our brothers and fathers. You made orphans wherever you have trod. I swear that in offending one of those little ones, you offended me and my brother."

The gladiator shook his head, then without a word dropped his net and trident, lifted the gargantuan helmet off of his shoulders, and held it in his hands. In a flash, Saul flung his sling and shot a stone that crushed the gladiator's nose and pushed the bone behind it into his brain. Without his mind registering what had just happened the man crumpled dead.

Titus stared at Saul.

"Bloody damn ghost of Caesar!" he exclaimed.

"You wanted him dead, right?" Saul replied. "Evidently that chap didn't know the rules. In a fight to the death there is no cheating. Only living and dying."

Titus walked over to Saul. He put down his shield and sword and offered his hand.

"You fight as well as any soldier I have ever seen."

Saul smiled and shook Titus' hand, honored by his words. Titus looked at the three fallen brothers. He looked back at Saul.

"The right to cut off their heads belongs to you."

"I decline," Saul answered. "If you wish to take trophies, the rite passes to you."

Titus lifted his sword as high as his shoulder and beheaded the first brother, then the other two. He nodded at Saul, wiped his blade on the plaited leather skirt of one of the corpses, then gathered all three of the heads by their hair and turned to leave. Saul joined Titus and asked a question.

"Am I mistaken or did you quote my father back there? You know, that part about whosoever offended one of those little ones?"

"I sure did. It's a heart tugging piece of your father's teaching and lent itself perfectly to this occasion."

Saul shook his head and Titus chortled. Then they both laughed loud and hard and walked out of the theater.

"I have to tell you," Titus added, "that it was your honeyed words that persuaded the last Brutus to put down his arms."

"Just talking shit," Saul said, brushing off Titus' compliment.

"Man, if I had your gift, I'd have every girl in Rome pulling up their dresses."

"Ha!" Saul said. "Speaking of talking shit."

"I mean it," Titus insisted.

"I suspect you are somehow trying to make me forget the great humanitarian thing you did just now, executing three men who mistreated women."

"You executed them. Not I. And for that I thank you."

Saul nodded and realized that in the last two days he had killed four men, all armed formidable opponents. However Jehovah had cast his fate, he knew in his heart that his future would play itself out with swords, and slings, and men dying.

Titus put his hand on Saul's shoulder as they entered the crowds on the street who stared at the heads dangling from Titus' hand. Without looking at Saul he spoke just loudly enough for him to hear.

"It is a privilege to know you, Saul, Son of Jesus. Jupiter spare me from ever facing you on the battlefield."

"From your lips to God's ears," Saul said.

"Which god?"

"Whichever one is listening."

CHAPTER FOURTEEN

A FORTNIGHT LATER, NERO RETURNED TO a triumphant march through the streets of Rome organized by the Senate in celebration of his Olympic victories. He had dominated the games, winning every event he entered. In an emotional thank you and cathartic farewell to Greece, he had proclaimed it a free state. Rome would no longer levy taxes on the nation. In an instant the young emperor was the hero of Athens. Rome's 3,036 contract tax collectors in Greece were not happy. But, all in all, they knew they were lucky to be alive. If Nero had increased taxes, they wouldn't be.

Nero sat in a military camp chair outside of the Senate building. Slaves held umbrellas over his head to protect him from the sun while others waved fans made of ostrich feathers to create a cooling breeze. He had been invited by the Senate to speak about the major events of his trip. Nero was flattered by the invitation, but he had mostly agreed to come because spies embedded in the senators' families reported that the Senate had made extravagant plans to fete him with buckets of money. Who could say no to that?

The emperor was a classically handsome young man, not yet thirty, with a perfect complexion and beautiful black curly hair. He was wearing a gold laurel wreath that he had won for poetry reading in the Olympics and a white toga with thick gold hems around the neck, the sleeves, and the bottom. Standing beside him was Vespasian, his most trusted aide and the commander of his legion of bodyguards, the Praetorians, who had accompanied him to Greece along with a thousand Praetorians. Next to the general stood his son Titus.

Vespasian was as dull as an unpolished bronze mirror, but he was intelligent and possessed an unerring ability to acquire and analyze details about any situation requiring a decision or an action by the emperor. Filtering such data through his own polished political instincts, he inerrantly proposed how Nero might wish to proceed on a given issue. The general was a stocky man, mostly bald, his lined and wary face stamped by his total commitment to his military career. He was strong, street smart, and ruthlessly confident.

While he and Nero had been in Greece, Vespasian had spoken with a hoard of paid informers, gathering both data and gossip concerning effective and ineffective Roman officials and loyal and disloyal Greeks. His secret network of spies extended well beyond Greece and provided insights into the royal, the rich, and the powers that ruled Parthia, Egypt, Punt, and the ever restless population of Judea, where he'd made every prostitute an operative and every merchant an informant.

A legation of fifteen Jews from Alexandria had come to Olympia to present grievances to Nero, but Vespasian's soldiers found a twisted Sicarii blade hidden on one of the men which was damning enough for Vespasian to jail them all. During the course of Nero's participation in the games, the general sent the Jewish legates on to Rome to be held for the emperor's disposition when he returned. Vespasian didn't like Jews and would recommend that the emperor crucify the assassins.

Nero looked at Vespasian and spoke.

"General, did your little spies find out how much gold the Senate is going to award me today?"

"Indeed, my Lord," Vespasian replied. "My folks spent a bit of quality time with most of the senators' house slaves. Are you sure though that you wouldn't rather wait and be surprised?"

"Ha! You speak treason, silly fool, and as my closest aide no less," Nero teased. "The only surprise I'm interested in at this stage of my life is how many times I can achieve orgasm in one night."

"Alone, Sire, or in the company of others?" asked Vespasian.

"Both!" Nero exclaimed.

"Then I'm sure it would be yet another victorious evening, Majesty."

"Twice over, Bacchus as my witness," Nero declared. "A wreath for solo achievement and another for team effort!"

Vespasian guffawed loudly, and Nero grinned naughtily. Titus laughed as well, delighted that the emperor not only loved sex, but loved to talk about it, too.

"So speak up and redeem my confidence in you, fop in armor," Nero commanded.

"The senators have raised a gift of fifty million sesterces, Lord."

"Well, by Diana's bullocks, that will go a long way toward balancing out the loss of tax revenues from Greece."

"Indeed. And though the money is intended for your private benefit, you may hear a patriotic voice or two asking you to consider donating the Senate's gift directly to the empire's assets."

Nero looked pensive.

"Do the senators like me?"

"As much as it benefits them and their estates."

"So, that means they don't," Nero concluded, "yet they funded a gift for me of fifty million sesterces. To pacify me, do you suppose? Redirecting the money to the state treasury would only take the edge off that fear and likely result in far less generosity next time. I think for the sake of keeping the senators anxious and afraid, I'll keep their gift." Nero smiled a thin smile. "A win-win situation if ever there was one."

Titus shook his head in admiration. The man would have his cake and eat it too. Such unbridled greed for gold had made Nero appear unstable to many in the patrician class, and guarding their wealth from the rapacious emperor offered the best reason for them to fear him. They ponied up gold to keep his acquisitiveness at bay, and Nero, knowing this, would accept their bribes and leave them alone. Indeed, a win-win.

"Titus," the emperor addressed Vespasian's son. "To enrich this already wonderful day, I want you to take the Jewish prisoners you sent from Athens and crucify them on the Appian Way. Crucify Paul of Tarsus as well."

"Your Majesty, Paul of Tarsus is actually a Roman citizen. The law requires that we employ a quick and painless means of execution for him."

"What the fuck!" Nero hissed. "Are you sure?"

"Governor Felix in Caesarea could not have sent him for you to hear his case if he were not a Roman citizen."

Nero scowled.

"Well, hell."

Vespasian spoke up.

"Behead him. It's humiliating and the drama titillates the crowd."

"May I say," Titus answered, "rendering all respect to my esteemed father, that Paul is regarded as the premiere messenger and missionary for Christianity. I suggest that he be executed without announcement or acknowledgment, void of any spectacle. Let his followers wonder what happened to him. Behead him privately and bury his headless remains on the spot, unknown, unvisited, and unimportant."

"Perfect," Nero said, accepting Titus' advice. "Do it and be sure that the dead man knows that his uncelebrated end was your idea. Then return here and describe your success. Also, Titus?" Titus looked at the emperor. "Be quick. I'm not sure how much longer I can tolerate your father's bad counsel."

Titus bowed his head.

"So shall it be done, Emperor. Enjoy the obsequiousness of the Senate, and may I humbly recommend that you retain my father's services long enough to have him carry all the gold the senators are going to give you today?"

Nero chortled, entertained.

"Bless you, son," he said. "For your sake, I will savor the humility of the senators today *and* enjoy watching your father stagger back to the palace weighed down by all the booty!"

Titus shook hands with his father and bowed his head again to the emperor. He crossed the forum returning to his rooms at the Praetorian compound. He'd arrange transport of the materials necessary for the crucifixions and assign a handful of Praetorians to perform them. He'd send another small detail of Praetorians to fetch the Jewish prisoners and take them to the lowest reaches of the Appian Way exactly where travelers got their first view of Rome. No one could misinterpret the point of the executions and their strategic placement. Fuck with Caesar and this will be your fate.

He'd ask Saul if he wanted to accompany him to the executions. He knew Jesus' son was no friend of the Sicarii whose member Judas had betrayed his father. He'd wondered if he should ask Jesus if he wanted to be at Paul's execution, perhaps to say a prayer for him, or the other victims, all of them his countrymen. That stuck in his thoughts for a moment. Pray for the victims? Titus closed his eyes and shook his head. You're getting soft, Titus Flavius Vespasianus, and that will never do. He decided to invite Saul, as that man was all about blood, but not Jesus. His presence could invite all kinds of touchy, feely moments he'd prefer to avoid. Yes on Saul. Nix on Jesus.

"Where's Jesus?" Paul asked.

Titus and Saul stood at his front door.

"He will not be privy to your demise," Titus answered coldly.

"But he promised he would come," Paul insisted. "Have you forbidden him? Why would his presence matter to you in the least?"

"Your *execution* doesn't matter to me in the least. I could not care less who sees you die."

"Then I beg you to allow him to come. Saul could fetch him if you'd allow it."

Titus glanced at Saul.

Saul nodded.

"Fine," Titus told Paul, "but only because you're a Roman citizen. You're being executed for crimes against the religion of your fellow Jews. Shame that has to fall on a citizen, but my duty has been commanded by Nero himself."

"Thank you, General. I am not afraid to die, but my desire is to have my savior at my side."

Titus looked at Saul again.

"Please ask your father to join us if he is willing. I will precede with Paul to Milestone 12 approaching Rome via the Appian Way. The other prisoners will be crucified promptly, but I will wait on Paul's execution."

"What other prisoners?" Paul asked.

"Some Alexandrine Jews. Just as irritating as you. Glad to get rid of all of you."

"Are they Christians?"

"Jupiter forbid. Plain Jews are bad enough. Go now, Saul. We'll expect you with or without Jesus no more than ninety minutes from now."

Saul left and Titus had two Praetorian guards put Paul in hand and foot irons.

"I can't walk in these," he protested.

"Fine. I'll have you dragged to the beheading stone."

Paul didn't speak. It was the first time he had heard any mention of the method of his execution.

"Will I be buried?" he asked quietly.

"Of course. Right where your head falls."

Paul pictured that and felt fear course through his veins for the first time. He prayed to the Father, not asking to be spared, but pleading to see Jesus before his death. Two Praetorians walked beside the wagon carrying Paul. Titus led the small procession on horseback out of the city and down the Via Appia.

When they arrived at their destination, Titus left the soldiers to guard Paul and rode on to where three additional wagons held the Alexandrine Jews and their crosses. He ordered the squad of Praetorians to strip the men and nail them to the crosses. The naked men were forced to lie prone on the wooden beams, have their hands and feet nailed, and their arms secured with ropes. The men screamed without end as their crosses were hoisted and dropped into holes dug into the hard soil facing the road.

Paul could hear the nails being pounded, the cries of agony being shouted by the men being crucified. He could hear the thump of the crosses falling into their holes, and more agonized cries from the men now hanging on their crosses.

A face appeared over the top of the wagon and peered down at Paul. It was Jesus, looking sad, yet comforting. Saul lowered the back of the wagon and stepped in to help Paul. He slid his feet down onto a grassy knoll wearing his leg and wrist irons. He could see a tall flat stone protruding from the ground and Titus waiting beside it. Saul went to Titus and asked that Paul's cuffs be removed. Titus gestured to a soldier who unlocked Paul's irons and released him.

Paul thanked Saul and knelt at Jesus' feet.

"Dear Jesus, bless me before I die. I know that you are God's only begotten Son, holder of the keys of death and life. Blessed Savior, grant me the forgiveness of my sins. I have lived to teach your love and grace, but now the time of my departure is at hand. I am ready to enter into the kingdom that you have prepared for me."

Jesus gently laid both of his hands on Paul's thick salt-and-pepper hair.

"Paul, God forgives your sins. Be of good cheer, for your trust in him has made you whole."

Paul stood up and embraced Jesus.

"Thank you, Lord Jesus," he said, quietly. "I long for the day when I shall behold you seated at the right hand of God."

Paul turned away and walked to the stone. He looked at Titus.

"Do your duty, General. I am ready to leave this place."

Paul knelt down and Jesus appeared at his side. He knelt next to him and put his arm around Paul's shoulders. Titus gripped the pummel of his sword with both hands, raised the blade, and with one swift blow, cut through Paul's neck. A great gush of blood shot out as his head fell to the ground. Jesus continued to hold Paul's body close while the Praetorians dug a grave for the dead man.

Saul picked up Paul's head and closed its eyes. He was stunned to realize only in this moment of Paul's death that this little Jew had had all the zeal and energy of Titus, but had used it to do good right up to the very end. He watched Titus wipe Paul's blood from his sword with a cloth. The wrong man just died, Saul thought, feeling the sting of that truth to the very core of his being.

Jesus stood and lifted Paul's body by himself. He carried it to the grave. Saul stepped inside and helped lay Paul's body to rest, placing his head above where it had been severed from his neck. Jesus asked Saul to fold Paul's hands over his chest, then began to sing an old prayer sung by Hebrew children before bed, one he himself had chanted with his mother Mary every night as a child.

> Now I lay me down to sleep,
> I pray the Lord my soul to keep.
> If I should die before I wake,
> I pray the Lord my soul to take.
>
> Amen.

Jesus looked down at Paul's face one last time. Then he turned and walked away. Saul could tell that Jesus wanted to be by himself. So be it. He watched as his father stepped onto the Appian Way and headed back to Rome.

Then Saul's eyes were drawn to the rows of crosses erected on either side of the stone highway. The men writhed in agony, moaning and crying, shitting and pissing on their naked bodies. He looked back at Titus. The general was dismissing the Praetorians. The wagons departed, and they followed after.

Titus walked over to Saul. He gazed at the dirt mound over Paul's grave.

"The man died like a Roman. Courageous. Confident of his place in the next life.

Bravo for him."

"I hope that someday I am able to leave as bravely as he did."

"Not for a long time, if you please," Titus replied. "You have much to live for."

Saul gazed at the men hanging on the crosses by the highway.

"What happens to them?"

"They die. Some take longer than others, but in the end there will be fifteen corpses."

"And they'll just hang there until the crows pluck off their flesh?"

"You'd be surprised what the wild dogs can do."

"The biggest tragedy for those men is not having a burial and a grave."

"More tragic than being nailed to a cross?"

"Jews don't mind dying. They are brave and most of them believe they will rise someday to see Jehovah."

"But he won't show up in time to bury them, eh?" Titus teased, rudely.

Saul looked at Titus.

"Would you allow me to end their suffering now?"

Titus thought about that for a moment. He was not compassionate, but he honored that trait in Saul.

"I grant you the right to do so," he said.

"Show me how to administer the same deathblow that my father received on the cross."

"I will," Titus answered, but shook his head. "I warn you though, it's a bloody mess. The blow kills the offender, but drenches you in blood. After fifteen of them, you might as well throw your clothes away and walk home naked."

Saul just stared at Titus.

Titus grinned.

Saul followed him to the first cross. The crucified men were planted on alternating sides of the Via Appia facing travelers on the highway. Saul looked up at the man on the cross, elevated only slightly higher than him. The man was white-haired and old. His body was flaccid and the ropes tied around his arms kept his hands from ripping free. He was in great pain and clearly embarrassed that he was naked. Above his head a small piece of wood had been nailed to the cross and Latin words had been painted on it detailing the man's name and his crime. It read, "Aaron, son of Josiah, traitor to Rome."

Titus placed the tip of his sword at the bottom of the man's sternum and looked at Saul. The crucified man's eyes went wide with surprise. "First, push your sword in about two inches deep which gets it in behind the ribs. Then shove it straight up. It will pierce the lungs and split the heart, killing him before you can pull your sword out. Do this one while I watch."

Saul nodded, shed his robe, untied his sandals, and placed his clothes away from the man on the cross.

"Nice farmer's tan," Titus commented. Saul looked at him, puzzled. "Your arms and legs are tan, but the rest of you is scary white."

Saul shook his head, then looked at Aaron and spoke to him in Hebrew.

"Bless me, Aaron, son of Josiah, for I am about to send you to your fathers. May we meet in paradise."

Tears formed in the man's eyes.

"Bless you, my son," he responded. "There is no blood guilt in this act. I thank you for your deed of kindness."

"Close your eyes," Saul told him. The moment that Aaron did Saul pushed the tip of his sword into Aaron's flesh and up into his body. The act was so swift that Aaron did not even cry out. He exhaled his last breath and his corpse sank down, held to the cross by the ropes and nails. His eyes opened slowly and Saul reached out and closed them again. He stepped back from the cross and pulled his sword out. Blood shot out of the corpse, but not much and not long.

Titus nodded and walked away.

One of the younger men hanging on a cross close to Aaron's began to sing the Hebrew Prayer for the Dead. Voice by voice, the rest of the victims joined in, still proud, still strong, still Jews, brothers in the faith of Abraham, Isaac, and Jacob. It didn't matter that Rome had humiliated them, they were righteous before Jehovah, and dying with dignity far from their families in faraway Egypt.

Saul crossed the highway and walked up to the next victim. Young, with black curly hair and a muscular body, it was the same man who had begun singing the Kaddish for the first dead man. He sang even as he watched Saul approach, offering up words celebrating the passing of the first victim and praising the release coming for them all.

> O, God, full of compassion, who dwells on high, grant true ascent of the dead on wings of the seraphim, into the exalted spheres of the holy and pure, where shines the Lord's resplendence on the souls who have come to their eternal home, may their place of rest last forever.
>
> Amen.

Saul stopped in front of his cross. The crucified man stopped singing and greeted him with a nod and a blessing, *Shalom*. Peace. Saul read the crucified's name printed on the plaque above his head. He spoke to him.

"Bless me, Caiaphas, son of Amos, for I am about to send you to your fathers. May we meet in paradise."

The crucified man looked into Saul's eyes as the others continued to sing.

"Bless you, my brother," he said. "May your father and kin esteem you for the lovingkindness you show to me."

Saul administered the coup de grace. Caiaphas moaned once and died, his blood gushing down Saul's arm. And so it went for almost an hour. Saul killed the crucified men, one by one, while the remaining victims sang the Kaddish for the mounting number of dead. When Saul reached the last man, there was no one left to sing for him. Saul told him, Daniel, son of Matthew, that he himself would sing the Kaddish after he was gone. And he did. Daniel's blood flowed, his body sagged, and Saul dropped his sword to the ground, closed his eyes, and lifted his arms in prayer one last time.

Saul washed his face and his hands in the bucket of water left behind for him, then cleansed his chest and abdomen, his legs and feet. He washed the blood off of his sword and dried it. Then he put on his robe and sandals and walked back to Rome.

End of Part IV

CHAPTER FIFTEEN

Lazarus had left Judea for good and had been welcomed this morning by Jesus. He had been stunned to see that Lazarus' back was so completely bent that his old friend's face was pointing directly towards the floor. He craned his neck to lift his head and behold Jesus.

"Sweet Lazarus," Jesus replied, putting a hand on his friend's stooped shoulder. "You're not standing very straight these days."

"Agreed," Lazarus replied, in a chipper voice, "but I have to tell you, I've seen some great floors."

Jesus smiled.

"Let me help you, dear friend," Jesus said, and grasped Lazarus' upper arms with both of his hands. He slowly helped Lazarus stand up, straightening him up until he could look at Jesus face-to-face. Tears of gratitude came into his eyes and he embraced Jesus.

"Feels like you tweaked a few other things when you were fixing my posture," he said.

"A little bit here and there."

"A little bit? I feel as young as you look!"

"And why not? Age is but a number."

"Well, you obviously subtracted a few numbers off of my total just now. It's almost like being resurrected all over again." He suddenly knelt before his oldest and dearest friend. "Thank you, Lord Jesus. Praise be your holy name."

"Lazarus. Please stand up."

"Would you bless me first?"

Jesus placed his right hand on the top of Lazarus' head.

"May God, the Father of us all and the King of the Universe, bless you and keep you."

"Amen."

Lazarus rose, and gazed at Jesus.

"I have seen with my own eyes the beginning of the end of Judea. Our countrymen have risen up and murdered every Roman soldier, every foreign merchant, and every pagan family. I fled, flying out the door with only the money I had in the house. I left everything else behind. Judea is lost."

"You are sure of this?" Jesus questioned. "The conflict has only just begun."

"I learned this morning when our ship arrived in Marseilles that the emperor has already sent down the Syrian Legion from Damascus and is preparing to dispatch another five legions from Rome commanded by General Vespasian. His son General Titus is second in command.

Jesus stared at Lazarus. He could think of nothing to say.

Now Lazarus, Saul, and Jesus sat together in the manor house study, talking late into the night. The room was lit by the small flames of countless oil lamps. All three men reclined on comfortable overstuffed couches drinking mead, a honeyed wine that Saul's senior knight, Keir, had imported in abundant quantities from his Norse homeland for the kingdom's wine cellars. Lazarus was recounting the events in Judea that led up to the revolt and forced his decision to flee.

"As you will recall, the first widespread stirrings of revolt happened during Caligula's reign, when the emperor demanded that his statue be set up in every temple in the empire. The Jews refused. Caligula was furious and threatened to tear down the Jerusalem Temple. Jews all over the nation protested in the first real unified disobedience against Roman rule since General Pompey had conquered Judea eighty years before. The Kanahim, the Zealots, who for decades called for the overthrow of the Roman oppressors, suddenly found themselves leading a nationwide movement. Though Caligula died and his orders were withdrawn, the Hebrew fervor did not abate, but rather continued to build.

"Then early this year, the Roman governor Procurator Gessius Florus secretly raided the treasure of the Temple. It is likely that he would have gotten away with it but for the network of spies amid the Temple's servants and the governor's slaves. Florus' servants witnessed the plunder, leaked the truth to servants in Jewish households, and the fireworks began. The governor fled to the Roman capital, Caesarea, and Zealots overran the garrison of Roman soldiers in Jerusalem and slaughtered them all.

"Violence spread like wildfire throughout the city, and everyone took to the streets killing Roman citizens, their families, and every foreigner in Jerusalem. I myself witnessed a screaming gang of men and boys attack my Greek neighbors in Bethany. The master of the house, his wife, and their children were dragged out of their house into the street. The man and his two young sons were cut down by swords, and his wife and girls were stoned." Lazarus shook his head at the memory of the cold-blooded murders.

"Is that when you decided to leave?" Saul asked.

"Yes. I was sure that Roman reprisals would be swift and even more terrible than the Jewish-wrought blood and gore. I mounted my horse and rode to Joppa that very night. The rural countryside beyond Jerusalem was calm, and most families were asleep. But by the time I reached Joppa the next afternoon, the whole seaport was a madhouse, people running shop to shop, house to house, crying that Jerusalem had been purged of all of its Roman soldiers and citizens.

"I secured passage aboard a Phoenician vessel bound for Marseilles, and the captain told me that word from ships arriving from Damascus brought news that the Roman legion posted in Syria had been deployed to Judea by its governor, Cestius Gallus. Ten thousand legionnaires were marching to destroy the Zealots who occupied Jerusalem.

"By the time I landed in Marseilles after a week at sea, the population of the city was in a state of utter shock having received news that the Zealot army had taken to the field and had not only advanced on the approaching legionnaires from Syria, but had engaged them and killed every single soldier. No one could believe it."

"And what do you imagine will happen now?" Saul asked.

"It doesn't take much imagination," Lazarus replied. "Nero will send an overwhelming number of soldiers to kill everyone in Judea."

"Surely you exaggerate," Saul remarked.

"Well, maybe not everyone, but Nero doesn't want to face a new revolt every time the Jews get pissed off, so he will likely destroy their ability to ever rebel again. His legionnaires will execute anyone who carries a sword and then kill as many more Jews as it takes to put true fear into the hearts of the survivors about challenging Rome in the future."

No one spoke. What could be said? None of the three men could even begin to comprehend the tidal wave of destruction that would rise to engulf the land of the Hebrews. The lush farmlands of Galilee would be plowed under and salted. The cities and towns of Judea would be leveled and their inhabitants slaughtered.

Roman legions would surround Jerusalem, systematically breech its walls, and massacre the men, women, and children who had sought refuge in the city. The Temple would be looted and burned and its sacred walls turned to rubble.

After a long silence, Saul spoke.

"I am leaving at dawn to make my way to Jerusalem."

"But Saul," Lazarus pleaded, "you will surely die."

"I deem that as likely, dear friend. But with the sulfur and brimstone of Jehovah in my veins, I will wreak havoc on Rome's sons until I am slain."

Lazarus just shook his head.

Jesus spoke.

"It is his will, Lazarus, and I daresay his fate. Someday the empire's mighty legions will be dust and its emperors nothing more than characters in books or letters chiseled into marble ruins. What Saul does by joining the rebels is to hasten that fall by some few hours, or days, maybe even weeks or months. And though he die, his sacrifice will not be in vain."

"So be it then," Lazarus agreed, reluctantly. He looked Saul squarely in the face. "I will tell your son and daughters of your beauty and bravery, of your willingness to defend your homeland as your last gift to your people and their sacred land. And I will tell them how we wept and mourned when we heard your decision, but blessed the Lord and thanked him for your courage."

Jesus stood up. Saul stood and walked over to his son. They embraced. Lazarus joined them, weeping. Both Jesus and Saul began to cry as well. The Lord giveth, and the Lord taketh away. Blessed be the name of the Lord.

— ⚜ —

At dawn, Jesus stood in the courtyard with his son Saul and his daughter-in-law RoxAnna. Her son Prince David stood between RoxAnna and his father Saul. Keir, captain of the knights, was present as a witness. Everyone was dressed in plain blue wool robes, warm in the cool morning air. Even RoxAnna had forgone her usual elegant attire for a robe and a shawl to cover her shoulders.

Saul reached his hand out and put his hand on David's head. The boy was not yet ten, but his entire life was about to change.

"With the power invested in me as king of this realm, La Valdieu, I abdicate my throne and my powers to you, David, son of Saul, son of Jesus, investing in you the title of king and granting you and your descendants all rights to this land." He then reached out and touched David's cheek with his fingers. Saul then looked at his wife and his father.

"I also bestow upon you my father Jesus and my wife RoxAnna, the roles of joint stewards to King David until such time as they shall mutually deem him capable of ruling without mentor or advisor."

He kissed his wife on the lips. Then he embraced Jesus one last time and whispered in his ear, "Remember your promise."

"Neither heaven nor earth will keep me from seeing you again, my son," Jesus responded. He kissed Saul on both cheeks.

Saul left the courtyard. His traveling clothes, armor, and weapons were in the stable with his saddled horse. Jesus, RoxAnna, and Keir watched him ride off. No one spoke. What words could describe what they were feeling? Saul's choice to join the rebels reminded Jesus of his own past blindness when he had given up his family, his friends, and even his own life because he believed that it pleased God. He and Saul had both chosen catastrophic, suicidal paths to walk that were, more likely than not, in vain.

Father like son.

Jesus was gathering tomatoes from the plants he personally tended on the side of the manor house where the sun shone strongest in the summer. He was wearing a loincloth and a loose cotton shirt. He had on a cotton keffiyeh, a flowing headdress woven in a red-and-black Arabic pattern worn by desert dwellers to keep the sun off their heads.

Jesus' grandson David was picking the ripe tomatoes. The boy had black curly hair and olive skin like his father Saul and he had inherited his fiery intense personality as well, the evidence of which was not pleasant to watch when he got it in his head to be angry about something he was not happy with. He was also like his mother RoxAnna, elegant and charming, when he was in the mood. He seems eerily like Emperor Caligula, Lazarus confided to Jesus one recent afternoon after David had had a meltdown over not being given a key to the castle's huge iron doors.

"I am a royal prince," he screamed at his mother. "Why can't I have a key?"

RoxAnna looked at him and replied evenly, "Because you'll lose it. End of discussion."

The expression on young David's face could have fixed Medusa herself, but RoxAnna was immune to it and left David on his own to settle down again.

Today he was as sunny as the day itself, enjoying being in the garden with his grandfather, picking tomatoes and dropping them into a tin cup he carried. Lazarus was reading the latest of a long string of letters that had been sent by Saul, now absent from Gaul more than three years. He had joined up with the Hebrews fighting to overthrow Roman rule. He had made his way to Galilee, north of Jerusalem, and fought under Josef, son of Matityahu, general of two Jewish legions. A ferocious fighter and born leader of men, Saul had rapidly risen through the officer ranks to become the number two ranking officer behind Josef himself.

Hebrew battle fatalities had been devastating in the Galilean theater of war, the troops overwhelmingly outnumbered by the four Roman legions led by General Vespasian. Not only did the Latin commander beat down and slaughter the rebel soldiers, he leveled all the towns and villages in Galilee, killing the women, children, and the elderly, seizing produce and livestock and burning crops as he pushed the Zealot army south toward Jerusalem.

The Jewish legions fought like madmen, but were soundly defeated again and again. Losses for both sides were staggering.

Some twenty thousand Rome soldiers had been killed and more than a hundred thousand Jewish soldiers and civilians. The loss of Galilee forced the remaining rebel soldiers and the remaining inhabitants to flee to Jerusalem. The back of the revolt was broken, but the harsh reality of this did not really sink in for Saul until General Yeshua deserted the battlefield and surrendered to Vespasian.

The Hebrews retreated to Jerusalem while the Romans regrouped. Vespasian prepared his army for a long siege of the great Jewish city. Jesus had received two letters from Saul this very morning couriered by different messengers. Jesus had handed them to Lazarus and asked him to read them first, previewing the news and warning Jesus of the contents. Was Jesus afraid of what Saul might reveal? Absolutely.

Lazarus read the first letter out loud. His voice was strong, but it wavered at the end as he read Saul's final salutation.

Dear Father,

May this letter find you and all my family happy and blessed.

Sadly, I cannot say that the same is true here. I have brought the remainder of the Galilean army inside the relative safety of the great walls of Jerusalem. The city is packed with families from all over Judea. The spirit has gone out of the vast majority of people here. The Zealots control the city, hunting down and murdering any Jews who speaks surrender.

The Roman army will arrive here in days. Jerusalem has three concentric walls, the outer one so tall and thick that it will require the Romans to build ramps to take it, then hauling their siege engines over it to attack the inner walls. How long will that take, one wall and then the rest? Who can know?

Estimates show three to five years of grain stored in the city which will keep everyone fed for a long time. Will God intervene in the meanwhile? Will the Romans tire of the endless warfare and the growing numbers of legionnaires killed by rebel sorties day and night? Never and never would be my guesses.

Kiss my wife and children for me. I do not believe that I will see them again, but I count on the day when I embrace you whatever the circumstances are that bring you to me.

Respect and honor from your son,
Saul

Jesus had listened to Lazarus read while he hoed and weeded. He understood the dire situation that faced Saul and the Hebrew refugees. There was no escape, save death, a fate the Romans were anxious to grant every Jew in Jerusalem.

"Well, lads," Lazarus called out interrupting Jesus' thoughts. "How about a drink of cold water?"

Jesus walked over. Lazarus handed him a goatskin filled with cool water. Jesus thanked him and drank. David ran up and had a big drink. Water dribbled down his bare chest. He wiped it off and dropped his cup of tomatoes. They scattered all over the ground.

He looked at Jesus. Jesus looked at him.

"I command you to pick those up, Grandpa," David said, putting his hands on his hips.

Jesus shook his head.

"I command you to pick those up, Uncle Lazarus," David tried.

Lazarus grinned and said, "Not me."

"I command you to pick these up, Prince David," he said.

Jesus clapped, Lazarus grinned, and David laughed with delight. Then he picked up the tomatoes one by one and put them back in his tin cup. Jesus wasn't sure that his grandson had truly grasped the concept of servanthood, but he was very pleased that the smart little boy had figured out how to save face and still get the job done. It was a lesson not many princes learned.

"Back to work, royalty!" Lazarus joked. "And while you toil, I have another missive from our beloved Saul to read to you." Jesus and David returned to the tomato patch and Lazarus broke the seal on the scroll that had been delivered in a tied parchment wrap. He unrolled the scroll and scanned it silently. Then he read it out loud.

Dear Father,
    May you, Lazarus, RoxAnna, and my children be blessed!
    A Roman legionnaire approached the Jaffa Gate under a flag of truce tonight and handed over a scroll impressed with the wax seal of General Titus. Of course, I know him and I recognize his mark. I was surprised to receive the scroll and amazed as well that no one had opened it on its journey to me. The gate guard who received it from the Roman messenger is one of my officers, which likely explains its unmolested journey to my hand. The Zealots and their spies are everywhere, trying to make sure that all one million men, women, and children trapped inside Jerusalem stay put.
    The message from Titus contained friendly greetings as though I was some long lost friend. He wrote that Nero was driven from his throne and committed suicide rather than face death at his enemies' hands. All of the Roman officials and commanders of the army legions in Asian Minor have acclaimed Titus' father Vespasian as the new emperor. He has put Titus in command of the entire Roman military presence in Judea and swore by Jupiter's throne that he will send two more fresh legions to his aid. He is leaving for Rome to claim the emperor's title and secure the Senate's approval.
    Titus knows that I am the de facto commander of the remaining rebel forces after the desertion of Yosef, son of Matityahu, whom the Latins call Josephus. He is personally serving Titus now and revealed my presence in Jerusalem. Titus asked me to find a way out of the city to meet him and discuss a surrender sparing the lives of Hebrew non-combatants. He also

offered his promise to do all in his power to save the Temple from destruction.

I am going to make the effort to find a way out of the city tonight. The revolt is done. There is no reason to see a million Jews slaughtered and the Temple destroyed. I am sending this letter so that you may understand the mission I am undertaking. May the God of Abraham, Isaac, and Jacob find it in his heart to spare me until we meet again.

My love to all.
Saul

— ✢ —

The sky was black when Saul met the night watch at the Jaffa Gate. They allowed him to leave through a small iron door in the wall that opened into a tunnel. It continued sixty feet through the mighty wall then descended beneath it continuing another mile beneath Golgotha where it opened into a cave. He asked the men to watch for his return in the early hours before dawn.

When Saul exited the cave, he could see the fires of the Roman lines in the distance, protected by barricades of short wooden walls, ditches, and spears thrust into the ground facing attackers. He made his way across an empty stretch of land where the vegetation had been cut down and the ground scorched. As he approached the Roman camp, soldiers behind the final wall spotted him and challenged his right to approach.

Saul held his arms up high and called out, "Bearing a letter with permission to enter signed and sealed by General Titus."

The Roman guards allowed him to enter by a gate, keeping their javelins trained on him despite the fact that he wore no armor and had no weapons. He spoke Latin with the guards while their captain read the letter from Titus and examined his signature and the wax impression from his ring.

"Did you learn to throw your javelin in Gaul?" Saul asked one of the guards, a thin, dark-skinned handsome man.

The legionnaire looked surprised.

"Yes. I come from Gaul and joined the army there."

"I thought I could tell by how you held it at the ready," Saul explained. "My family farms in the kingdom of La Valdieu."

The guard's face brightened.

"I know that kingdom. I grew up near Marseilles."

It turned out that the entire watch contingent was from Gaul. They had no issues with Jews. It was just their job to hold the line against the rebels, and when the day came, kill them. Good soldiers all, Saul thought. Just following orders. The captain asked Saul to come with him, and they walked through the huge Roman camp. There were tens of thousands of tents with campfires burning as far as the eye could see. Saul walked with the captain of the guard for at least a mile before they entered a group of larger and more elegant tents.

The captain stopped at the one that was clearly the largest of all, a composite of several tents cobbled together like the ones used by the Bedouin nomads of the Sinai. The captain spoke with the centurion commanding the guards surrounding Titus' command headquarters. The officer and his men were dressed in full battle armor—steel helmets, breastplates, plaited leather skirts, iron greaves to protect their shins, sandals that strapped up to their knees, and a sword and a spear.

The centurion entered General Titus' tent. Moments later, Titus himself stepped out and looked at Saul. He walked up, put his hand on his shoulder, and greeted him respectfully.

"Welcome, Saul. I must begin our meeting by telling you that even after all of this time in Judea I have encountered no finer warrior than you." Titus shook his head and looked sad. "What a tragedy that we are on opposite sides."

Saul stared at Titus. The general looked as handsome as Saul remembered, with his blonde, curly hair, and angelic face. He was wearing a white cotton shirt and a plain blue cotton skirt. He was bathed and perfumed and his fingernails were manicured and perfect. The blood of hundreds of thousands of murdered Jews appeared not to have left any stain on his fair skin.

"Will you come in?" Titus asked.

"Yes," Saul answered. "Your offer to speak about sparing Jewish lives and saving the Temple is more than gracious considering that the last of the Jews are penned up like sheep and ready for slaughter."

"Thank you for your realistic appraisal of their plight," Titus replied gravely. "Let's see what can be done."

Saul followed Titus into his quarters. The tent was black, sewn from dyed goat skins. The ground beneath it had been leveled and covered with multiple layers of thick woolen Oriental carpets woven with scenes of gods and men, naked women and satyrs, land animals and sea creatures, and every mythical beast sung about by minstrels. Great cedar pillars held up the multiple tops of the long tent, which was lavishly furnished with a mahogany dining table and twelve chairs, couches and chairs draped with quilts and filled with pillows, a rosewood desk and wooden camp chair, and several marble pedestals bearing Flavian family busts.

The surface of Titus' desk was covered with topographical maps and designs for ramps and siege engines for the storming of Jerusalem's walls. There were several other chairs around the desk, and occupying one of them was Josephus, son of Matityahu, the former commander of the Zealot army of Galilee. He was no longer a patriot, but a turncoat, a traitor, and an informer. Titus ignored Josephus and invited Saul to sit with him at the dining table, ordering one of his stewards to provide a light meal for him and his guests—bread, roast lamb, olives, pecans, boiled potatoes and carrots, fresh orange slices dipped in carob sugar, and wine.

Titus sat down and pointed at the chair next to him. Saul sat there. Titus waved Josephus over to join them. An African servant came to the table and set a bowl of clean water in front of Saul.

The man was dark brown with a shaven head and dressed only in a loincloth. He was a young man with muscles that waxed and waned when he moved. Saul washed his hands and accepted a towel from him. Then the servant took the basin, knelt, undid Saul's sandals, and washed his feet. He dried them, bowed, and left.

Saul stared at Yeshua, son of Matityahu. His old commander stared back. It was he who had decided to call himself by the Latin version of his name now, Josephus, and pronounced his father's name in the Roman way as well, Mathias. Saul had fought as second-in-command to Josephus until they had been separated during the fearful battle over the strongholds of Jodapatha. The Romans had prevailed and opened an uncontested road for their legions from Galilee to Jerusalem. Saul had led the retreat of the Jewish army, only later hearing that its leader had fled the scene of battle and surrendered to Rome.

Titus watched Saul and Josephus staring at each other.

"Well, no introductions are needed here," he said jovially. "It's clear that you two despise each other already."

Josephus smiled. Saul did not.

"What happened to you?" Saul asked accusingly.

"Meaning what?" Josephus replied.

"After the defeat in Galilee, one of your officers told me a story about a cave where you and a few dozen soldiers found refuge. You ordered your men to kill themselves rather than be captured. But when they had, you retreated from the cave and surrendered."

Josephus nodded calmly, showing no emotion.

"All of what you say is true. The only part you are missing is the prayer I made to Jehovah, blade at my wrist, and the answer that he gave." Saul narrowed his eyes, but listened. Josephus went on. "God said, 'Put down the knife from your hand and help my people survive.'"

Saul was flabbergasted.

"Do you swear?" he challenged Josephus.

"I offer my oath, though it is by Jupiter that I now swear."

"You turned you back on Jehovah?" Saul cried, offended.

"Never. But I realized that it was a different god speaking to me than the one I expected."

"Because?"

"Because he was speaking Latin."

Saul's face turned sour and he stopped talking.

"Yet was not the god's word revelatory?" Josephus challenged. "General Vespasian spared my life, and his son General Titus appointed me his translator."

"Gentlemen, gentlemen," Titus stepped in. "There is formal business at hand, and I must ask that we attend to it. Eat, drink, and let us begin." The general swept his hand towards the meal that his servants had placed on the table. Titus picked up a silver flagon and poured wine into three silver chalices. He handed one to Josephus, one to Saul, and kept the last. He offered no toasts. His father had taught him that toasts were for sentimental buffoons. Real men liked gold, promotions, and praise from the emperor. Toasts and accolades were pseudo-honors for the runners up, not for the winners.

As his guests served themselves, Titus addressed Saul.

"So, how bleak are the circumstances inside Jerusalem, if I may enquire?" His tone was, if anything, concerned. Saul wasn't sure that Titus had a sympathetic bone in his body. He answered only out of his own concern for the survival of the Jews trapped in Jerusalem, knowing that only Titus had the power to save them.

"The city is tense, but it is not for lack of food, nor for the lack of fighting men with arms. There are likely two hundred thousand men who could be forged into an army capable of marching out of Jerusalem and challenging your legionnaires."

"Are you the man who could make that happen?" the general asked, his voice on edge.

"No," Saul answered. "No man can make it happen. Every religious party makes war on the others, and the biggest faction, the Zealots, murders anyone who advocates surrender or even negotiation with the Romans."

"You are describing a fearful situation," Titus responded, more sympathetic now.

"I am."

Titus looked at Josephus who had not touched his meal. He was drinking wine and his face looked weary. Saul did not know it, and Titus did not mention it, but Josephus' father, a Sadducee and priest, his mother, a descendant of the Maccabees, and Josephus' own wife were all in Jerusalem, detained by the Zealots. He drank and did not speak. Titus looked back at Saul.

"Do you have conditions?" Titus asked. "There are not many that I would consider granting."

"You mentioned in your letter that you would be willing to spare non-combatants, and, if possible, the Temple."

"That I did," Titus replied and drank his wine. "But only if Hebrew combatants are surrendered for execution."

"That would mean the slaughter of a quarter million men!" Saul protested.

Titus' eyes narrowed and he spoke through clenched teeth.

"No one who actively fought against Rome may live."

"But if a surrender is not arranged, thousands, even tens of thousands more of *your* soldiers will die taking Jerusalem."

"Those noble lives will be invested in the glory of the empire, their hearts and souls sacrificed for Rome's eternal greatness."

Saul stared at Titus. His empty rhetoric revealed that he and the Roman general had placed entirely different valuations on the lives of the young men fighting in this war. Whereas he had huge interest in saving the Jewish men holed up inside Jerusalem, Titus regarded his legionnaires as fuel to be fed to the roaring fire he would build to consume the rebels.

Saul shook his head slowly.

"What?" Titus bellowed suddenly furious. "I am offering an escape for your women and children, *and* giving my promise to leave your holiest shrine intact. Isn't that worth accepting?

Roman justice will be meted out only to those who killed sons of Rome."

"I killed sons of Rome," Saul said, and stood up. "What would your plan be for me?"

Titus scowled and threw his chalice on the table.

"You would be my friend, my brother. Be as Jewish as you wish, only accept a place in the Roman world as Josephus has done."

Saul spit on the carpet at his feet.

"I would rather die."

"Then do so!" Titus cried. He reached for swords he'd left on a chair by the table judging that this very moment might come. He picked up a Roman short sword and tossed it to Saul. Saul caught it and watched Titus lift another sword and face him with it extended in his hand.

Titus literally jumped across the space separating him from Saul and stabbed straight at his abdomen. Saul parried the thrust, looped his blade over his head, and swung straight down towards Titus' head. The general quickly stepped aside and Saul's sword dug into the table. Titus stood back and waited for Saul to pull it free. Then he leapt onto the table and slashed his sword at Saul. Saul slapped it away with his own sword and stepped back to prepare for Titus' next stroke. The two men faced each other, swords extended, waiting to see who would make the next move.

"You've become considerably more competent with a blade," Titus commented.

"I've killed a lot of Romans since you saw me last."

"Remember when we fought the Brutus brothers?"

"Of course. I actually thought very highly of you then. My mistake."

"I want you to think highly of me again, brother. I have never met anyone like you, Saul, son of Jesus. I am putting my sword down and asking you to once again consider how we can save your people."

Titus put his sword on the table and stood with his arms at his side. Saul stared at him, but before he could respond, the twisted blade of a Sicarii knife was thrust into his back, driving deep between his ribs and into his lung.

"No!" cried Titus as Saul collapsed on the floor. Pain shot through Saul's chest. His breaths became labored and shallow. He began to lose consciousness. The last image he beheld was the face of Josephus looking down at him, the assassin's knife in his hand. A betrayer to the last.

CHAPTER SIXTEEN

It had been almost two months since Jesus had received Saul's message about Titus' invitation to meet his son face-to-face. He had not slept well during that time, and nightmares of Saul's death filled his sleeping hours. He was at breakfast one summer morning when the confirmation of his fears arrived.

He, Lazarus, and RoxAnna sat at an outside table on the stone patio behind the manor house. Julius supervised the breakfast settings and servings and managed the servants who brought fruits, juices, cheeses, nuts, honey, and freshly baked breads. Saul's wife looked drawn and worried. She had spent three years fretting about Saul's doom, and the last two months with no news from him after writing about his intention to meet with Titus had been the worst.

RoxAnna wore a scarlet gown, gold slippers, and a thin gold circle rested on her head. She was every inch the queen mother, still elegant and beautiful in her early forties. If Saul was dead, Jesus thought it unlikely that she would ever marry again, considering that she had her hands full being a doting mother to her young daughters, Adair and Rowena, ages nine and six, and a royal steward to her son,

King David, who was quite famously living up to the knights of the kingdom's nickname for him, the Wild Man of Gaul.

Jesus was wearing a blue cotton robe suitable for the hot summer day ahead. Lazarus wore a light wool robe, though the morning was already warm. In his sixties, he often complained that he never seemed to get warm enough. Jesus told him to take a bride.

"I will when you do," Lazarus countered.

"You're the one who's always cold," Jesus answered, "and you never married. Don't you think it's about time?"

Lazarus just smiled and shook his head.

"Saul is dead I just know it," RoxAnna spoke. Her tone was sad and listless.

Jesus looked at her.

"I hope you don't say that around your children," he said.

"They hardly even remember him," she replied. "I can't believe we didn't get a mosaic done of our family."

"Don't be giving up just quite yet, dear," Lazarus said. "Saul has always been a winner."

"It's been two months since his last letter, Lazarus, time enough for a dozen letters to have reached us if he was all right. Plus, how many Jews do you suppose survive a meeting with Titus Flavius Vespasianus?"

"Saul did," Jesus replied. "Remember when Titus came here and knocked him off his horse with one cast of his spear?"

RoxAnna nodded. Saul's breastplate needed to be restored after Titus' blow had crushed in one whole side, and Saul had rubbed his breastbone for weeks complaining of soreness. The only way she could get his attention off the pain was to encourage him to rub *her* breastbone. That had been years ago. Her body had grown used to his absence now, and her womanly attention had been completely directed to raising her three beautiful children.

Rowena, with her thin graceful figure, was approaching her now. She was a serious girl with freckles and strawberry blonde hair. She wore it in cornrows, imitating her grandfather's white locks. She stopped in front of RoxAnna and curtsied.

"Mother, I am a messenger sent by your son, the king, David. He has Adair captive and is demanding ten Roman sesterces to release her."

RoxAnna drew her daughter close and embraced her.

"Is this a new game?" she asked. "Did your brother really send you to demand a ransom?"

Rowena stepped back from her mother and explained.

"David says it's a smart way to get you to give him some money."

"Where is your sister?"

"On her bed, tied up."

RoxAnna rolled her eyes. David acted more and more like a royal despot, enchanted by wealth and manipulating everyone into helping him acquire it. She rose from her chair.

"I'll be back," she said.

"We'll send ransom if you're not," Lazarus called after her.

"That kid is going to rule the world," Jesus said admiringly.

Lazarus nodded, entertained. "I suspect his bocce's are already bigger than mine."

Jesus frowned.

"What?"

"Bocce balls. A game where you try to toss your lead ball next to your opponents' balls and knock them out of the ring."

"Never heard of it."

"It's a Roman game."

"Figures."

"Can you imagine David and his father Saul playing against each other?"

"Ha!" Jesus barked and choked on his bite of strawberry. He paused to recover and his face grew wistful. "I'd give the rest of my life to see that, my friend."

Both men ate silently for a while.

"And who would win?" Lazarus finally asked winking at Jesus.

"Assuming such a contest wouldn't take place until David is fully grown, yet before Saul is snared by his dotage?"

"I think it would be a hard contest to call," Lazarus mused. "Two hotter heads I have never encountered."

"Are you forgetting Simon Peter?"

"Oy," Lazarus groaned. "He was hot-headed *and* stupid. Remember when you teased him about his tendency to cower by nicknaming him the Rock?" Jesus chuckled. "After you left, he told everyone that you meant that he was the rock on which you founded the Christian church."

"I thought Paul claimed that honor."

"He did not, though I think he could have."

"You won't get any argument from me."

"You can acknowledge what he accomplished," Lazarus responded, "and you're not even a Christian."

"Height of irony, eh?" Jesus remarked without rancor, despite the fact that Paul had used the story of Jesus' life and death to forge a new religion that the entire Roman world was embracing. Not the Jews, however, and not Jesus either.

"I say that David would win the contest with his father," Lazarus said, returning to the earlier topic. "His temper far outstrips Saul's. Saul is violent to the core, but is mindful in his everyday dealings with others. David erupts all the time and his temper consumes him no matter who he's with. Where does that come from?"

"*My* Father," Jesus said.

Lazarus pointed towards the heavens above.

"That one?"

"That one."

"Yet you don't have a temper."

"Maybe it skips a generation."

"Nope. Saul is David's father, remember?"

Jesus just shrugged his shoulders. He'd never met his own father. He had no idea whether Jehovah even *was* his father except, perhaps, weighing the evidence of his resurrection and apparent longevity. As for himself, he continued to believe that he had served God in the way he thought best, teaching, living, and dying at the Father's will.

RoxAnna returned to the table.

"All's well," she said. "The prince has graciously released his hostage."

"And what did it cost?" Lazarus asked.

"Nothing. I told him he'd be sent to bed without meals for the rest of the day."

"Harsh," Jesus commented.

"I don't give a rat's ass," RoxAnna snapped. "It worked."

Lazarus and Jesus looked at each other, and then laughed hysterically.

"Maybe David's temper has a more female origin," Lazarus suggested.

Both he and Jesus laughed so hard again that RoxAnna turned her chair away from them and ate her breakfast alone. Men.

Keir, the captain of the castle guard, approached the diners, accompanied by Miquel. They stopped at the table where Jesus was sitting and knelt. He motioned them to stand.

"I am sorry to interrupt you, Lord Jesus," Miguel spoke, "but Keir has just received an urgent letter for you."

Jesus felt himself begin to tremble. He glanced at RoxAnna and Lazarus. They were staring at him. Lazarus appeared fearful. RoxAnna looked like she was ready to burst into tears.

"Is it from Saul?" Jesus asked.

"No, Lord. It is a sealed parchment bearing the wax impression of Titus Flavius Vespasianus."

Jesus' heart sank. Word had already reached him that Titus and his legions had won the war against the Jews. In light of that, a letter from the conquering general could not contain good news. Titus and his legionnaires had broken through the walls of Jerusalem, had massacred all of the refugees, and razed the Temple to the ground.

Jesus took the scroll handed to him by Keir. He looked at Titus' seal, then broke it and unwrapped the scroll. As a gesture of courtesy to RoxAnna and Lazarus who were as desperate as he for news of Saul, he read it out loud.

To: Jesus, Son of Joseph
From: Titus Flavius Vespasianus, Son of the Emperor

Greetings, Jesus, son of Joseph,

I write this to inform you that the Jews of Judea were unable to repent of their rebellion and have consequently been conquered and their nation reoccupied.

Many Roman soldiers were killed suppressing the revolt, and upwards of half of the entire population of Judea is dead or enslaved. Such was the price paid for the murder of the soldiers and citizens of Rome.

Your son Saul joined the revolt and served as a general, leading rebel forces in Galilee before being defeated and forced to retreat with the remnant of his men to Jerusalem. Prior to its destruction, I invited Saul to visit me granting him papers of safe passage in order to see if there was a way we could bring about a surrender of the masses in Jerusalem and end the war.

While visiting me, Saul's anger led him to challenge me to fight one-on-one. He was injured, but not by my hand. Another person with us defended me and wounded Saul. Regretfully, he has been imprisoned since that fateful night.

He has expressed an urgent desire for you to come. He wishes to share with you his thoughts and hopes for his family. Saul will not surrender even now, or I would gladly spare his life. Without that, I must with deep regret, inform you that I have issued orders for his crucifixion one month from now.

RoxAnna cried out and buried her face in her hands. She sobbed and wailed as though her life was over. Despite the last three years on her own, the loss of her protective and loving husband would change her life forever. Any hope of a reunion had just ended, and her aloneness was confirmed and sealed forever.

Lazarus got up and put his arm around RoxAnna's shoulders. She turned and put her face against his chest, lamenting Saul as though he were already dead. Jesus had, in fact, believed that Saul was already dead. Now he had to force himself to accept that his son was alive and sentenced to hang on the cross. Jesus raised his eyes to the sky. Why Father? You've had Roman and Jewish blood in fearful quantities. Must you have my son as well?

Jesus looked back at Titus' missive and silently read the rest.

Saul has asked that you be present at his crucifixion. I have granted his request because of the respect I have for you and the affection I still bear for Saul.

Please take your earliest opportunity to travel to Judea. You may sail safely to Joppa, as the port has been pacified.

Send me word, and make haste.

Honoring you and your son, Signed by my own hand and sealed with my personal mark,

Titus

No one talked for a very long time.

Then Jesus spoke to RoxAnna.

"Dearest girl. I promise that I will do everything in my power to find some way for your husband to survive. Saul is a hard man and hard of heart when dealing with the Romans. Titus is also a hard man, and a stubborn one, but he may see his way to pardon Saul when the moment comes to condemn him or spare him."

"Please, Lord Jesus," RoxAnna whispered. "Save him for me and his children."

Jesus understood RoxAnna's agony. There was no one in life to compare to a loving spouse. Any time he let down his guard, he ached to have Mary back. She had cared for him, teased him, slept with her arms around him. He missed her voice, her laugh, and the look that she gave him in private, letting him know that it was him, and him alone, whom she adored.

Jesus rose and offered his hand to RoxAnna.

"Come with me, if you would. I'd like to play with the children and hear their happy laughter before I leave."

RoxAnna rose, teary-eyed, and took Jesus' hand. He looked at Lazarus.

"My friend, would you please ask Keir to pick a half-dozen knights to accompany me to Jerusalem? Have Julius pack food and water for the first day of our journey. And tell Miguel that I want a saddle bag filled with gold coins. One can never know exactly what Titus will need to make the right decision concerning Saul's life."

Lazarus nodded and watched Jesus and RoxAnna walk slowly away from the manor house and begin the walk up the stone road that led to the cliffs above and the castle of the king, *the substitute king*, elevated by his warrior father who'd been the scourge of the Romans for three years. Alas, not any more. Unless some great miracle occurred, Saul would soon have the crossbeam of his cross tied to his outstretched arms and led to the place of the skull, the bald stone pate of Golgotha, and be crucified.

Dead man waiting.

Jesus could see the white clouds of smoke rising over Jerusalem long before he and his knights reached the top of the hills surrounding the city. From there, they beheld the ruins of Judea's capital. No one spoke. That smoke was the epitaph for the Jews who had been killed when Titus' legionnaires took the city. They had, however, made the

Romans pay a fearful price for their victory. Jewish soldiers in the city mounted hundreds of suicidal attacks on the legionnaires as the triple walls were being attacked.

The first such attacks were initiated when Roman engineers were constructing the Roman camp across the Kidron Valley outside the walls of Jerusalem. The foray was sudden and unexpected, launched when most of the construction workers were without swords or armor. The Romans beat back the attack, only to be surprised by a second and equally ferocious attack.

Hundreds of Roman soldiers were slaughtered in the chaos, and only a rally led by General Titus himself forced the Zealots to retreat. From then on, fully armed work crews finished the camp and began construction of three earthen ramps needed to drag battering ramps up to the great outer wall of Jerusalem. Thousands of Hebrew soldiers poured out of the city day after day killing hundreds of legionnaires. Despite the barrage of continuing attacks, however, the Romans finished the ramps in fifteen days, dragged their battering rams up to the wall, and broke through.

Inside the city, the Roman soldiers faced fanatical resistance as they brought their battering rams to bear on the second wall. Zealots killed hundreds of legionnaires, yet Titus' siege weapons breeched the second wall in five days. The opening was wide and despite ferocious hand-to-hand fighting with the Jewish defenders, Roman troops were able to enter and pacify the area, ready to focus on the third and final wall. Earthen ramps were again built. It took almost three weeks for the dirt and stone ramps to be constructed and the battering rams pulled into position, only to have the ramps collapse and the siege engines fall into great holes the Jewish defenders had dug underneath them.

Frustrated and amazed, Titus ordered the siege ramps to be rebuilt. It took three weeks with Zealots taking down legionnaires every hour with cascades of arrows. When battering rams finally broke through the last wall, the Romans faced yet another stone wall built by the Jewish defenders. That wall was quickly breeched and General Titus led a strike force of a thousand legionnaires into the heart of the city.

The Zealots fought ferociously, but were cut down by Titus' endless reinforcements until the last rebels retreated into the walled Temple complex. It took several days of unrelenting combat for Titus' troops to clear it and attack the final Jewish contingent holed up in the Temple itself. They were exterminated in hand-to-hand combat and the Temple burned. Then the legionnaires swept through the city, killing anyone who was left alive. The slaughtered bodies were left where they fell.

Armies of eagles, hawks, and vultures filled the skies. Bears, cougars, and coyotes scoured the city gorging themselves. Behind them came the rats and the maggots feasting on endless rotting bodies. The smell of the corpses became overpowering, but it did not drive the Romans out of Jerusalem. Titus' triumphant legions—even though reduced by thousands of fatalities—still numbered more than fifty thousand men, and they systematically looted the city. They stole tools, household goods, precious materials, metals of all kinds, and dug up every basement floor in every home and public building, hunting for treasures hidden away before the end.

After Jerusalem fell, Titus separated out five hundred of his most elite soldiers and directed the recovery of the gold and silver that had decorated the front of the Temple and its interior walls. The great cedar roof had burned and fallen, but the limestone walls of the temple building still stood covered with the precious metals. The soldiers salvaged thousands of pounds of precious metals from the ruined Temple, and under Titus' personal supervision carried away all of the Hebrew holy objects from the Holy of Holies, including the Ark of the Covenant and the giant gold and silver Temple menorah. Then he ordered his combat legionnaires to bring the battering rams onto the Temple platform, smash the pillared courtyard halls, and knock apart the Temple building itself so that not a single stone remained stacked upon another. His soldiers leveled everything, turning Herod's Temple into a quarry for used stone.

Jesus, Keir, and his knights rode down the mountain heading for the remnants of the outer city wall where the Jaffa Gate had stood. They crossed over the infamous bald expanse of Golgotha, its stone crown exposed like the top of a buried skull, a pate as large as a city square, gleaming white even in the shroud of smoke covering the city.

Called Calvary by the Latins, a translation of its Jewish name, Golgotha, the skull, generations of Jews had been crucified there by Roman soldiers. Jesus stopped and looked at its vast height and width. He had hung here on a cross himself, abandoned by friends and rejected by God. Now, his own son Saul would be crucified here if Jesus could not dissuade Titus from executing him.

Jesus turned and looked back at the mountain they had just descended. Once heavily forested, it was now a barren place of tree stumps and scab rock. Beneath the devastation, burrowed into its limestone depths, were the tombs of Jerusalem's richest families. A wealthy follower named Nicodemus had offered his for Jesus' body, and it had been purchased decades later by another wealthy follower, Lazarus, for Jesus and his family. He would have to go and look at it later, for that sad place was now very likely the place where he would bury his son, Saul.

Jesus rode into Jerusalem, city of God, city of death. He remembered a story in the Scriptures where Jehovah had levied a fearsome punishment on his chosen people for some transgression, only to lament his actions afterwards, saying he had longed to take them to his bosom, like a hen gathers her chicks. Truth was though, he hadn't. He had destroyed them with fire and blood. Looking at the charnel house that used to be the City of David, Jesus recognized it for what it had become, the destructive work of God. Jehovah's actions always spoke louder than his words. He looked at the devastation, then overcome with grief, Jesus wept.

— ⚜ —

Jesus and his group were intercepted by a Roman patrol whose officer read Jesus' scroll, signed and sealed by General Titus. They were escorted to the general's tent which was pitched several miles south of Jerusalem alongside the Kidron River where the water was fresh and the trees tall and full.

Titus' aides welcomed Jesus respectfully and had servants arrange baths, meals, and lodging for him and his knights. Jesus had his own private quarters with a bath and bed chamber. He was provided with a fresh robe while his own robe was washed and dried. He was escorted to Titus' dining table where he was seated and told that the general would be joining him shortly. Titus' military tent was as grandly furnished as Jesus' manor house in Gaul.

Servants brought food and wine to the table. There was roast lamb cooked in garlic, fresh fish from the Mediterranean, boiled beans and potatoes, fresh baked bread, and a citrus fruit salad. There was no food in Judea. Everything at this meal, as well as all of the food stuffs necessary to feed Titus' army, was brought in by thousands of carts from Joppa's seaport, fifty miles away, provisioned by the Senate of Rome itself.

Titus entered the room and raised his hand to salute Jesus. He was dressed in a cream-colored toga, his hair damp from a recent bath, and his arms and legs glistening from the residue of his oil massage. He was only twenty-eight, but the son of Vespasian, who had been invested by the Roman Senate to rule as emperor, looked tired and worn. His forehead was lined and patches on his cheeks and hands were raw from sunburn and endless scratching. His eyes were hooded and his mood was morose. He sat down and drank from his wine. His boyish energy and charm were absent.

"I am wearied by death," he said. "I wonder if that makes me less of a Roman."

Jesus studied Titus' face. The general drank again from his goblet of wine.

"Or perhaps more of a man?" Jesus asked.

Titus put his cup down and gazed at Jesus.

"The highest calling for a man is to fight and defeat another man. The highest calling for a nation of men is to fight and defeat another nation of men. That is what we have done here. Man's work."

"Yes," Jesus replied looking into Titus' eyes, "and as a bonus, you and your men were able to murder hundreds of thousands of old men, women, and children."

"Not a bonus," Titus corrected, without appearing offended by Jesus' words, "a necessity. Every living Jew, man or woman, young or old, who remains in Jerusalem, or inhabits any of the remaining towns and villages in Judea, will at some point in their lives try to kill a Roman. Therefore, the only Jews I don't have to worry about are the ones rotting in Jerusalem's ruins."

Titus glanced at Jesus' troubled face.

"I know you don't agree. That's fine. You're Jewish no matter how many years you've lived in Gaul. You know exactly what I mean. Jews don't quit, and they can bear a grudge forever. Even as we speak, hundreds of diehard rebels have taken refuge in an old cliff-side castle Herod the Great built in the desert. Insane. There is no way anyone will get out of Masada alive." Titus shook his head in frustration and drank his wine.

"I didn't know you hated Jews so much," Jesus responded.

General Titus was exhausted, frustrated, and bored.

"I don't hate Jews, or at least I didn't. They are the only people I have ever warred against, though, that didn't know when they were defeated. Stupid."

"Or patriotic."

"Occupied nations don't get to be patriotic. Just occupied."

Titus chuckled at his own remark.

"Tell that to the Jews."

"We did. They didn't get it, so I had to kill them all."

"How is my son?"

"He suffers from his wound."

"But it's been weeks since he was hurt."

"The wound became infected, even though he was treated by my own personal physician."

"When may I see him?"

"Now. He is imprisoned with other Zealots in the rear of the camp. I'll have him brought after we sup." Titus looked at Jesus' untouched plate of food. "Have we supped?"

"I apologize for not partaking. I came when I got your warning that Saul was going to be crucified. I cannot focus on anything else."

Titus nodded.

"Perfectly natural for a good father. You must understand that I am extending a clemency of sorts to Saul. He excelled on the battlefield and hundreds of my men went to their graves because of his prowess with sword and sling. I should take him back to Rome in chains with Zealot leaders like Simonn son of Giora, a warrior almost as great as your son. He and the rest of the Zealots will be executed in front of the masses of Rome, tied and strangled like beasts. As horrendous as it must be for you to contemplate crucifixion for Saul, it is by far a less heinous end for your son than his cohorts."

Jesus looked at Titus. The general's cold blue eyes returned his gaze. There was nothing he had to say to the victorious Roman. Judea had been judged, slaughtered, and silenced. To be fair, Titus had only brought to an end what the Jews had begun. He had served the will of Jehovah, knowing it or not, for Almighty God had decided for whatever reasons to bless Rome and condemn Judea.

Despite occasional moments when Jesus had believed that God had some bit of love left in his heart for the Jews, the Hebrew deity had managed to demonstrate yet again that in the
so-called Holy Land, violence, not mercy, utterly ruled him. The old Scripture verse Jesus had repeated all of his life almost had it right. The Lord giveth, and the Lord taketh away. Only the ending needed to be modified. And the Lord taketh away again, and again, and again.

Jesus spoke to Titus.

"I thank you from my heart for sparing Saul the humiliation of being executed in Rome. May I request your permission to be present at his crucifixion?"

"Granted. I have assigned a centurion to do several crucifixions at first light tomorrow morning. Now that you've come, I will add Saul to the list of the condemned. Show the centurion the pass I sent to you, and he will allow you to witness Saul's execution. I will be there also. It is my way of honoring you, Jesus, son of Jehovah, and your son. I deeply admire both of you.

"Saul is the true reflection of your God: heroic, violent, willingly embracing death. You, on the other hand, are the best man I have ever met. Entirely without evil, yet somehow able to accept Saul and me despite our violence and gore, and find it in your heart to forgive your god for making us who we are."

Jesus stared at Titus. He had no counter argument. God had left him to die on the cross at Golgotha. Now, despite Saul's sacrifices for Jehovah's besieged people, the Almighty had turned his back on Saul as well. But Saul would not be alone, not for one moment. Jesus would be there. And ironically, Titus, his executioner would be as well.

"May I see Saul now?" Jesus asked.

"Yes," Titus replied. "I'll occupy myself elsewhere while you have your private time together." Titus rose, filled his golden wine goblet, took food on a silver plate, then left and gave orders for Saul to be brought to the tent.

Saul was escorted by four legionnaires. They were dressed in full armor including helmets and they carried swords in their hands. Saul was naked and locked in leg irons. His wrists were cuffed in irons as well, connected by a chain. No chances were being taken with this prisoner, once the greatest soldier among the Zealot champions.

Saul saw Jesus and a grateful smile came to his face. The guards removed Saul's irons and withdrew outside of Titus' tent. Jesus stepped forward and put his arms around Saul. He held him tight. His son smelled of blood, dirt, and his own waste. Saul's cheek was fiercely hot. Jesus pulled back and looked at his son's face. It was red and soaking with perspiration.

Jesus touched his face, and then moved around behind Saul and looked at his back. Half of its surface was swollen and feverish. Saul was not healing, he was dying of an infection engendered by the wound in his back, covered over by cloth bandages. Jesus held Saul close again and placed his hands over his wound. At the very least, his son would go to his death whole and strong.

In a moment, Saul's fever vanished. He stood straight and looked at his father. Jesus dipped a hand towel in a bowl of water on the table and wiped Saul's face. Then he turned him around and removed the bandage from his back. His wound was healed, the flesh whole and sound. Jesus washed it with water, then looked at his son again. Saul's face was triumphant and brave. He quickly washed himself and put on the fresh white robe Titus' servants had left for him.

"Thank you, Father." he said. "Your strength has flowed into me."

Jesus nodded and looked into Saul's eyes.

"I have missed you so much, dear boy. I bring news of your wife and your children, and I want to hear your dark tales of war. No matter how long or short our time together may be tonight, I will be with you tomorrow when you go to be with our fathers."

Saul grinned.

"You mean die?"

"Yes," Jesus smiled sheepishly. "Sorry to be melodramatic. You will be crucified on the same ground where I died more than thirty years ago."

"I am honored that you will be near," Saul said, serious now.

Jesus nodded and tried not to tear up.

"How did you get that wound in your back?" he asked.

"Compliments of the Jewish traitor, Josephus."

"He stabbed you in the back?"

"I made the mistake of fighting Titus, though he provoked it and provided the sword. Josephus used his knife to make sure that the great general lived to kill more Jews."

"Which he has become quite practiced at. Jerusalem is in ruins, and the Temple has been pulled apart block by block. Nothing remains but rubble."

"It doesn't matter," Saul said. "Titus didn't kill all the Jews, and as long as Hebrews exist they will survive and endure. God may bathe his promises of fidelity with Jewish blood, but if he is nothing else, he is constant. As long as Jehovah endures, so will the Jews. And as long as they survive, this city will not be abandoned."

"How do you know this to be true?"

"Call it the instincts of a man shaped in the image of God."

"That's good enough for me," Jesus said earnestly. He looked over at the uneaten food on Titus' table. "Come, son, let us sit, and share a meal together. We'll talk of your dear mother Mary, your loving wife RoxAnna, and your beautiful children. We'll sing the Kaddish one more time for your brother David, for your uncle Alejandro, for his son Arduous, and for you, my son."

Both men stood silently for a few moments, then Jesus offered Saul a chair at the table. He sat in one beside him and ate while Saul did as well. And they did indeed speak, all through the night in fact, when at last four new soldiers came for Saul.

Jesus embraced him for a long time, then looked into his eyes.

"I believe in my heart that I will see you in paradise, Saul, where you and all the heroes from ancient times will be waiting for me. Please pray that my own death may be honorable and meaningful, when in that moment I pray one final time for my own Father to be with me at last."

Saul nodded and laid his head in the crook of Jesus' neck.

"I have always loved you, Father."

"And I have loved you, my son, from the moment you left your mother's womb."

"Looking for a sword," Saul said.

He and Jesus laughed, amazed that any humor could exist in these anguished circumstances. Saul was taken away, and Jesus watched from the tent until he and the soldiers were gone. He saw that the sun was rising over the broken walls of Jerusalem as it had for a thousand years. As it had the day of his crucifixion. As maybe as it would over and over far into the future. With all his heart, with all his soul, and with all his mind, Jesus clung to Saul's words that as long as Jews existed, the city of David would stand and welcome the sun of another day.

CHAPTER SEVENTEEN

JESUS HEARD THE CRUCIFIXION DETAIL on the move before he saw it. He stepped outside Titus' tent and watched the centurion in the lead. He was tall and thick-bodied, blonde and fair, a splendid piece of Nordic timber lumbered by the Romans to help them kill their enemies. Behind him marched fifty legionnaires, all of them dressed in armor. There had been enough surprise attacks by Jewish rebels even after their defeat that Titus' standing order for any activity outside the Roman camp required helmets, breastplates, leather skirts, and swords.

After the first twenty-five soldiers had passed came the Jews who were sentenced to die. There was about a dozen men, some young Zealots, others middle-aged, Sadducees and Pharisees. The condemned had been stripped naked and each man was carrying the cross beam he would be nailed to. Some men groaned in agony as they walked to Calvary, and each one who did received a soldier's lash on his back or legs, its leather thongs embedded with bits of metal opening rivers of blood every time it landed.

The last of the condemned was Saul. His cross beam was being carried by two soldiers, and he was allowed the dignity of wearing his robe and sandals. Titus walked next to Saul, and behind him followed the remaining twenty-five legionnaires, the last ones leading donkeys with carts packed with food and drink, nails, ropes, and mallets. It would be a lazy comfortable day for the crucifixion detail. It would a day beyond horror for the crucified.

The centurion's soldiers would let the crucified men hang until sunset. Anyone still alive then would have their legs broken forcing them to dangle from their arms. Blood and bone would spew from their legs and hanging taut their lungs would be crushed. In minutes the suffocating victims would bleed to death. One or two of the Zealots might be accorded a coup de grace. Jesus hoped that his son would be offered that merciful last blow.

Titus and Saul saw Jesus. The general held out his arm in a salute which was immediately imitated by the centurion. Saul caught his father's eye, thankful beyond all reckoning that he had come. Saul walked on whispering the prayer that Jesus had taught him. He had prayed it every morning of his adult life, his first act of each new day, reminding both himself and God that they had a relationship that would be honored until the end of Saul's life. This was the last day he would offer it to Jehovah.

Our Father, which art in heaven,
Hallowed be thy name,

Thy kingdom come, Thy will be done
in earth as it is in heaven.

Give us this day our daily bread.
And forgive us our trespasses,
As we forgive those who trespass
against us.

And lead us not into temptation,
But deliver us from evil,

For thine is the kingdom, and the power,
And the glory, forever. Amen.

The column of soldiers and prisoners wound its way through the desolate streets of Jerusalem to Calvary. The centurion delegated the crucifixion work to his lieutenants and their crews. He and his own detail of two soldiers took responsibility for crucifying Saul. Titus and Jesus stood aside and watched. Saul's cross bar was bolted to the main upright while he was stripped and the irons removed from his hands. He was made to lie down on the cross, his hands and feet were nailed. His arms and legs were bound with ropes, and his cross was raised.

Saul did not cry out. He would not give his Roman executioners that pleasure. He watched as Jesus walked up to his cross. It lifted him only just above Jesus' natural stature. His father stood close and looked into Saul's eyes.

"What can I say or do?" Jesus asked quietly.

"Thank your Father," Saul answered in a strong voice, "that he brought you to me in the hour of my death."

Jesus tried not to cry, but tears formed in his eyes.

"Please, Abba," Saul went on. "Help me die proud."

Saul had used a term of endearment that children used for their fathers, Daddy.

Jesus wiped his eyes.

"And so you shall, pride of my heart. So you shall," he promised.

The morning passed in silence. Jesus stood next to Saul, his curled fingers resting against Saul's cheek. At noon, Jesus asked Titus if all of the crucified men could be given a drink of water. Titus sat in a portable camp chair and nodded. He ordered it to be done and handed his own wooden bowl of water for Jesus to carry to Saul.

Jesus took it to his son and lifted it to his parched lips. Saul drank greedily. Jesus held the bowl for him until he had finished it all.

"Father," Saul whispered. "It's going take days for me to die."

"I think Titus intends to finish at sunset. He told me that he had granted Keir's request to bring a donkey and a cart with shrouds and spices for your burial. We will bear you to the tomb, and there Keir and I will anoint your body and sing the Kaddish for you."

"Exceedingly kind of Keir, I must say," Saul said slowly, "but all things considered I'd rather be in Gaul with RoxAnna and my children." Saul tried to smile, but he could not.

"Of course," Jesus said.

"But I gave them up, didn't I, Father?" Saul said, in true misery. "I left the ones I loved so I could kill the ones I hated. I would have you tell them that whatever actions they choose in this life, I pray that they will choose wisely and carefully. Tell them that I chose unwisely, regretting my decisions in the final moments of my life and grieving for my mistakes."

Saul dropped his head and began to cry, and Jesus did as well. Jesus moaned in his grief even as his son wept for the family he would never see again. After a while both men grew quiet. Jesus put his curled fingers against Saul's cheek again.

Saul spoke.

"Father, when the time comes, I want you to ask Titus if he will allow you to administer the coup de grace for me."

Jesus shook his head, over and over.

"I cannot, my son. Ask me anything but that."

"I don't want anyone to send my soul to God but you. I want to die as a Jew, honored in that final moment that the greatest Jew who ever lived will be the one releasing me."

Jesus shook his head, but remained silent.

Throughout the afternoon, Jesus led Saul in a recitation of the Scriptural verses he had taught him throughout his boyhood, and as the sun finished its journey across the Judean sky, Jesus led Saul in one last verse that had been his son's favorite ever since he had heard it the first time as a little boy.

The Lord is my shepherd, I shall not want.

He maketh me to lie down in green pastures, he leadeth me beside the still waters.

He restoreth my soul, he leadeth me in the paths of righteousness for his name's sake.

Yea, though I walk through the valley of the shadow of death, I will fear no evil, for thou art with me.

Thou preparest a table before me in the presence of mine enemies, thou anointest my head with oil, my cup runneth over.

Surely goodness and mercy shall follow me all the days of my life, and I will dwell in the house of the Lord forever.

Dusk's shadows began to crawl across the face of Calvary. The older and weaker men had already died on their crosses. The younger ones had survived the day and now steeled themselves for the brutal extinguishing of their lives. At Titus' orders, the soldiers began to break the bones in the lower legs of the surviving victims. Swinging fire-hardened wooden clubs, the legionnaires smashed shin bones into fragments that erupted through the flesh of the crucified men. The victims screamed in agony, experiencing pain they could not have ever anticipated.

Saul spoke.

"Father, you know that I have loved that Psalm of David all of my life." He paused to take a breath, pushing his feet against the block nailed below to take pressure off his lungs and gasp for air. "But only today have I learned that the Lord referred to in those verses is you."

Jesus put his face against Saul's.

"I will love you until the day I die," Jesus whispered.

"And I will see you then, Abba."

Titus watched as Jesus stood close to his dying son. He approached. Jesus turned and looked at the general.

Titus spoke to Saul.

"Hail and farewell, my friend. I offer you the stroke that will set you free."

"My father will do it."

Titus was stunned. He looked at Jesus as if to say, can that possibly be true?

Jesus looked at Titus. Then back at Saul. Saul held his eyes. Could he kill his own son? Could he deliver him from this rock that had claimed both of their lives?

He spoke to Titus without looking away from his son.

"I will do it."

Saul began to cry, tears of joy flowing freely.

Titus handed his sword to Jesus.

"Do you know how to do this?" he asked.

"Yes. You may recall I had it done to me."

Suddenly, Jesus grabbed the top of Titus' breastplate with his left hand, and put the tip of the sword at Titus' throat. "Pity you have not had it done to you." Titus looked into Jesus' eyes and did not move. Jesus gazed at him and was suddenly filled with the same violent hatred that Saul bore for all Romans. He held the sword at Titus' neck for a long moment, wanting nothing more than to kill him, but finally lowered the sword, and turned to the man he did not want to kill, but would.

He kissed his son on both cheeks, then raised the sword and pressed the tip to Saul's naked chest, just below his sternum. He stared into his son's eyes.

"I will see you in paradise, son," he said.

"Be quick, Father," Saul responded, and braced himself.

Jesus leaned in towards his son and with one lightning stroke thrust the tip of the blade into the flesh behind Saul's ribcage, up through his lungs and into his heart. Saul did not utter so much as a moan, but expelled his last breath with a peaceful sigh. Jesus withdrew the sword. Saul's blood gushed out onto his hand and drenched his robe. Jesus closed his son's eyes and handed Titus his sword. The general sheathed it without wiping it and stared at Jesus.

"For what it's worth," he said, "you made the right choice."

Titus and Jesus locked eyes, knowing what could have happened if Jesus had slaughtered Titus. Saul would have died, he would have died, and nothing about Rome and its genocidal dealings with the Jews would have changed an iota. He had spared Titus, the killer born to the Roman emperor. And he had killed the son born of his own flesh. What was done, was done forever. Titus lived. Saul died.

The general turned away without a word. Jesus watched him leave Calvary in the last light of day, then turned and wrapped his arms around his dead boy. Saul was warm and his flesh was soft. His spirit had flown, but Saul's body—the body that Jesus had treasured since the day of his birth—hung without life on the cross.

Jesus closed his eyes and began to weep again. He wanted to believe that Saul had gone to God, but all he really knew was that he was holding his dead son's body. It made everything he ever desired or believed seem specious and spent. He put his face against Saul's cheek and held him while he mourned. He clung to Saul as the sky grew black. He was not taking his arms off of his boy until he had to.

Jesus turned eighty. His body did not. Everything else had changed though. RoxAnna's daughters had grown into beautiful young women, and she had married them off to crown princes in kingdoms bordering La Valdieu. She believed that in time all of the various kingdoms would someday be united and ruled by her son David and his descendants.

RoxAnna, now in her early fifties, had begun to look older. She had her hair dyed and chose gowns that hid her aging figure. She envied Jesus' youthful appearance, yet loved her father-in-law with such admiration that she even tolerated the fact that he was alive and her Saul was dead. She still remembered her husband's face, his urgent touch, his violent persona. Their son David, who was twenty-one now, was the most driven boy she had ever known. He hunted, ran, wrestled, and fought with every knight in the kingdom. She was glad. Only such a monarch could look north to expand his Frankish kingdom with treaties or wars.

For her part, she believed that God's blood ran through David's veins and that his distant progeny would continue to rise in power and strength until her family dominated Europe and destroyed Rome. Thus, planning the destruction and death of the Roman Empire, she spent her days content to hold the reigns of La Valdieu while she dreamed of the holocaust of fire and destruction that would extinguish the hated Romans.

Jesus knew RoxAnna's heart. Over the years, he had watched her transform from a beautiful and delightfully funny girl into a middle-aged woman whose heart was filled with hatred and revenge. They rarely spoke, and then usually only at some state function. But Pepin, her chief advisor, confided black secrets about RoxAnna to his old friend Miguel, the spritely perfectionist who for decades had managed the estates of the castle and Jesus' lands as well. His hair was white and he had grown portly. But he was intensely loyal to Jesus and always helpful, not to mention so efficient that no one could imagine anyone else doing his job.

He repeated Pepin's stories to Jesus. RoxAnna's daily rants against the Romans stirred David's fury to the point that he would take his sword in hand and cut his mother's furniture to pieces. She made him swear every day to avenge his father. She made him promise that every one of his children would be raised to long for the day that Rome's emperor would be slain and his flesh fed to the dogs.

Pepin and Miguel were convinced that RoxAnna had gone mad. Jesus didn't comment, but he feared that they were right.

And so the streak of fury and violence had passed from Saul to his son David. Who knew how terrible his future progeny would be? Jesus shook his head. How could such a line of violent killers have been spawned by his loins? Whose seed had set the fire that raged in his kin?

During Jesus' earthly ministry, gossips had circulated rumors that his mother Mary had been a child prostitute. When Joseph found that out in the course of her confession that she was pregnant, he resolved to break off their courtship. He changed his mind only when he dreamed that the son of her body had been blessed by Jehovah himself.

But Joseph's night fantasy was scant validation that Jesus was the son of God. Maybe Jehovah was not his father. Maybe he *was* the child of some violent and deranged Jew who'd shot his destructive seed into Mary's womb. Jesus made himself put such thoughts aside. No mortal man had given him eternal life, Jehovah had. And if the streak of violence Jesus beheld in his offspring came from anyone, it very likely came from God himself. So be it. It still made him afraid to think what his house might be like a thousand years from now. Then it occurred to him that he might be around to see it. He shivered at the thought.

Jesus still thought all these years later of Saul's crucifixion. He remembered him being nailed to the cross, recalled the last hours they spent together, and shrank in despair living yet again the moment in which he had ended his son's life with his own hands.

Keir and the knights who had accompanied him helped take Saul's body down from the cross and transport it to the tomb. He and Keir washed Saul's body and wrapped it in fine linen, winding the linen cloths around his body in the Egyptian style, packing myrrh and other spices to cover the smell of decomposition when

Saul's flesh melted from his bones. After they were finished, the great stone outside of the tomb was rolled down its channel to block the entrance. Keir used a Roman substance called cement to permanently affix the rock to the tomb. Titus had given him a bag of the stuff in powder form with instructions on how to mix it with water and make a stiff paste to seal the door and fill the channel locking Saul in his tomb forever.

That was fifteen years ago. Saul was not the only dear one gone from his life. In the years since Saul's death, his daughters had moved to marry men in distant kingdoms. Keir had died of a stroke during a skirmish with Germanic nomads. Lazarus had died of old age, claiming happily to the very end that fading away slowly was so much more pleasant than his first fever-driven dive into the grave.

Jesus had sat and wept for hours after Lazarus passed, keening next to his dead body before he allowed it to be removed and prepared for burial. No man had been a better friend to him than Lazarus of Bethany. Supportive follower, loyal friend, and generous benefactor, Lazarus was, in fact, responsible for the safety, the land, and the wealth that Jesus and his offspring enjoyed. Jesus had him interred with his wife Mary in La Valdieu family tomb.

With his friend's death, Jesus felt very alone. And almost on that very day, he received for the third time in his life a hand-delivered, sealed parchment from Titus Flavius Vespasianus.

— ✣ —

The general's life had been full and imminently successful in worldly terms since Jesus had last seen him. Titus returned to Rome from Judea and took command of his father's elite bodyguard, the legion of Praetorians, who only served the emperors of Rome. He oversaw the dismantling of Nero's huge palace, the so-called Golden House, and supervised the hundred thousand Jewish slaves who built the grandest showplace ever raised to host Roman games.

Emperor Vespasian, Titus' father, named it the Flavian Amphitheater. When finished, it was the largest structure of its kind in the Roman world. It quickly got a nickname from the crowds that filled it to cheer circuses, gladiators, wild animals, and public executions. They called it the Colosseum, the Big Place. After a strong and popular reign, Vespasian died, and Titus had been selected by the Senate to succeed his father.

A Praetorian detail consisting of a general and six legionnaires arrived at the castle asking for Jesus. Miguel had immediately fetched him from the manor house telling him that the Roman soldiers had brought a message for him from Emperor Titus. Jesus could not imagine any reason why the man who had crushed Israel and killed his son would have any further interest or use for him.

Jesus walked up to the castle, was greeted with a bow from RoxAnna, then followed Miguel to meet the Praetorian general who was waiting in the throne room. The officer knelt down when Jesus entered. Jesus saw a large gold cross affixed to the general's breastplate. Keeping his face lowered, the man spoke.

"Bless me, Lord. I defend Rome, but my heart and soul belong to you."

Jesus looked down at the middle-aged soldier. He was all muscle, hair still black, armor spotless.

"Rise, General."

The Praetorian did. He was of average height, his face lined and tanned, and his eyes glistening black and hard.

"Where are you from, my son? What is your name?"

"I was born in Spain, my Lord, and my name is Alejandro, son of Antonio."

"I once had a wonderful friend named Alejandro. Perhaps when you finish your soldier's contract, you might return here again and visit me."

"It would be my greatest dream, Lord Jesus. Thank you."

Jesus extended his hand and put it on Alejandro's head.

"May God bless you, and keep you, and give you his peace."

"Amen," the soldier said, gratefully.

"Serve your Master, Alejandro, son of Antonio. There is good in him."

The general stood and handed Jesus the parchment he had carried from Titus. It was rolled and sealed with the impression of the emperor's insignia, captured in the hot wax and saved intact until the recipient broke it and opened the scroll. Jesus cracked the seal and unrolled the parchment.

To: Jesus, Son of Joseph,
From: Titus Flavius Vespasianus, Augustus Caesar, Emperor Of Rome

Greetings.

Peace be to your family, Jesus, son of Joseph, and prayers to the gods for your happiness and prosperity in faraway Gaul.

I remember you with respect and admiration. I remember your son Saul with veneration and sadness. Never have I met such a warrior. We should have been brothers. I grieve his absence, as I am sure you and his kin do as well.

I have spent the last decade overseeing the rehabilitation of Judea on my father's behalf, Emperor Vespasian. It may take a century for the land and people to recover, but the Jews are a strong-willed nation and willing to do whatever it takes to restore the land of their fathers.

With my own father's passing and my elevation to rule in his stead, I will not have the time to continue supervising the Hebrews. Another procurator will doubtless govern them as poorly as the idiots who preceded him and will likely drive the Jews to distraction by his efforts to line his own pockets instead of seeing to their success and prosperity.

Therefore, I am going to propose to the Senate that it appoint a client king to rule Judea, one able to govern with wisdom and justice, yet aware of, and in line with, Roman desires, much the way Herod the Great did at the time of your birth.

I would like that ruler to be you, Jesus. There is no more admired Jew than you in the empire, and I, myself, know the talents and capabilities that you have.

If you accept, I would like you to establish a new capital and rule from a different seat of power than Jerusalem. Too many memories. Too much blood.

Jericho escaped the wages of revolt. May I ask you to consider that city? It is a luxurious oasis today, spread along the beautiful Jordan River. Its twenty thousand date palms are protected by Rome itself. That vast agricultural abundance and its income would be my personal gift to you and your heirs. Cleopatra lusted after them and Mark Antony forced Herod to cede them to her. But those two star-crossed lovers are gone, and you're not. So they're yours. (I hope that made you smile just a little.)

Think and pray on my request. If amenable, advise me of your acceptance, and make preparations to journey to Rome when you have settled your affairs in Gaul. Grant me time while you are here to help prepare for your new role. Titles are important, and I think the right one for you is *Jesus of Nazareth, King of the Jews.*

May my deified father bless your decision. Or maybe Jupiter. Or Jehovah. Take your pick!

Truly your servant, Signed by my own hand and sealed with my personal mark,
Titus

Images of Jesus' life exploded in his mind like Roman candles. His mother's teasing blue eyes and red pouty lips looking at him as a baby.

Sweet old Rabbi Jacob complaining that he and Jesus disagreed on just about every Scripture they ever studied. Mary snapping at him to act godly because someday he would be the messiah. Touching his witty and fun-loving father's tattoo of a green-and-gold mermaid and wanting one just like it. Discovering that he was taller than any other boy in Sabbath school. Then taller than anybody, anywhere. Seeing the vast blue Sea of Galilee the day he began his ministry. Gathering his disciples. Noticing Mary Magdalene. Performing healings of the blind and the deaf and the lame, as close an affirmation as he ever got from Jehovah that he was indeed the messiah. Anger rose when he recalled his persecution by the Pharisees and Sadducees, hearing them repeat lies about his teachings capped by their appeal to the Roman governor for his crucifixion and death. Surprised by life, he had risen from the dead, fleeing to a new life in Gaul with Mary Magdalene. Jesus pressed his hands to his temples and shook his head.

He looked up. RoxAnna, Miguel, and General Alejandro were all watching him silently. He looked at them. Then he lifted his eyes and beheld the great castle walls out the window, built to keep his family safe. The walls hadn't worked for them any more than they had worked for the Jews. Pain and death had lived inside this place. His wife was dead, his sons were dead, his closest friends were dead. Only Miguel remained, and hate-filled RoxAnna ruling for David, her royal pawn.

Was that all there was to show for his fifty years in Gaul? And now today, like a lightning bolt from heaven, he had received a royal invitation from Emperor Titus to return to Judea and rule the very people who had rejected him. Back to Judea, the land of betrayal, torture, and execution.

Judea was a crushed nation. The surviving Jews would be suspicious of him. And no matter what Titus promised, the Senate would be scrimping and frugal, resisting the allocation of funds that he would need to rebuild the towns and restore the countryside. Yet he could not deny that Titus was offering him the opportunity to once again try and build a profoundly different Promised Land.

What choice should he make? What choice did *God* want him to make? He knew that the irony of the title that Titus had chosen for him was obvious to the emperor. He had surely asked for the Roman records of Jesus' execution and understood both Pontius Pilatus' intended praise for Jesus, as well as his simultaneous insult to the Hebrew leaders, when he had the board nailed to Jesus' cross proclaiming *Jesus of Nazareth, King of the Jews.*

Jesus sat down in the closest chair. He sat there for a very long time.

The End of Volume 1

Acknowledgements

Michael Baigent, Richard Leigh, and Henry Lincoln, the authors of *Holy Blood, Holy Grail* who decades ago got me thinking about about the legends and the possibilities of a life of Jesus beyond the Gospels;

Mark Meyer and Jerry Sexton, master copy editors; Vincent Chong, who brilliantly interpreted a Medieval school of art and created a whole new vision of the Pensive Christ; and Lionel Blanchard, my loyal publisher and loving friend.

www.ingramcontent.com/pod-product-compliance
Lightning Source LLC
Chambersburg PA
CBHW070536010526
44118CB00012B/1145